SEARCH
FOR
MEANING
AT THE
BROKEN PLACES

By Harvey Shrum, Ed.D

Bless you prison. Bless you for being in my life.
For there lying on the rotting prison straw, I came
To realize that the object of life is not prosperity as
We are made to believe, but the maturing of the soul.

- Aleksandr Solzhenitsyn

Search For Meaning At The Broken Places

Copyright ©2011 by Harvey Shrum

Rhodes-Fulbright Library

ISBN: 1-55605-429-7   978-1-55605-429-7

Library of Congress Control Number: 2011922171

WYNDHAM HALL PRESS
5050 Kerr Rd
Lima, Ohio 45806
www.wyndhamhallpress.com

Printed in The United States of America

Acknowledgment

I wish to acknowledge my gratitude to several who were instrumental in the birth and growth of this book: Dr. Ira Progoff whose Intensive Journal was instrumental in changing the lives of men incarcerated at Folsom State Prison and California State Prison - Sacramento; Dr. Viktor Frankl for his wisdom expressed in *Man's Search for Meaning* and referring me to Dr. Joseph Fabry; Dr. Fabry for his roundtable discussions on Logotherapy at Folsom State Prison and his reading, editing of and recommendation that I pursue publication of this manuscript; Marcella Hardt, Intensive Journal consultant/leader and friend; the men incarcerated at Folsom State Prison who, I hope learned as much from me as I learned from them; and to my grandparents, parents, wife, children, and grandchildren who continue to give my life meaning.

TABLE of CONTENTS

*"Ultimately, man should not ask what the meaning of his life
is, but rather he must recognize that it is he who is asked."*
– Viktor Frankl

*"A major part of the meaning of life is contained
in the very process of discovering it.
It is an ongoing experience of growth that involves
a deepening of contact with reality."*

– Ira Progoff

*"The world breaks everyone, and afterward,
some are strong at the broken places..."*
- Ernest Hemingway

Please note that this journey on which you are about to travel requires
a notebook or audio tape for responses to the feedback questions, and
writing exercises. You may wish to use colored pencils and highlighters
in some exercises.   Ultimately, these exercises represent lifelong
exercises.

I.
The Journey Begins

The journey begins with a paraphrase of a quote by Viktor Frankl: *The pursuit of pleasure, power and prosperity that dull existential pain is inversely related to the pursuit of meaning. The irony is that the more persistently pleasure, power and prosperity are made the focus of our energies, the less likely that meaning or purpose in life is achieved and so the more likely that pleasure, power and prosperity continue to be sought when meaning fails to be achieved. The spreading existential frustration lies at the root of this phenomenon. Sadly, the pursuit of pleasure, power and prosperity often results in addictions, aggressions, depression, bankruptcy, divorce, incarceration, underemployment, and occasionally the morgue precipitated by anti-social thoughts, behaviors and low self-esteem. The gift is that thoughts, attitudes and behaviors can be changed in meaningful ways when experiential, creative and attitudinal values are embraced.*[21]

In the words of Winston Churchill, writing this book has been an *adventure*. It began as an *amusement*, writing notes alongside senseless doodling on scraps of paper in my car, at the movies, or in the middle of the night, waking from a dream with hidden meaning. But then it began to take shape and a life of its own, requiring on-going spiritual nourishment as it shed words and phrases, making way for clearer words and concise phrases. It started to vaguely resemble a *mistress*, then a *master*, and eventually a *tyrant* and *monster*. And just as I was about to be *reconciled to my servitude* with rewrites upon rewrites, spurred on by innumerable life-altering and meaningful experiences, I *killed the monster, and flung it out to the public*. It is the same with artists, musicians and orators who feel that they can improve upon their best ad infinitum. Good, better, best; they never let it rest until their good is better, and their better is…well, better. Intuition does not provide the answer. It takes practice to know when to let go, whether it is a manuscript, a painting, a musical score, a stage play, or a speech.

Every human being is unique with unique needs. Thus, no individual therapy in the field of psychology is a panacea for what ails humanity. For over twenty-five years I have been sharing an evolving synthesis of Logotherapy (Viktor Frankl's existential or height psychology), the Intensive Journal (Ira Progoff's depth psychology), and the stages of grief (Elisabeth Kubler-Ross) with individuals and groups in prisons, with veteran groups, with college students, with church congregations, and with family, friends and strangers alike. The bond that many of these individuals and groups share is what Viktor Frankl calls "the existential vacuum" or "existential frustration," an inner emptiness shared especially among human beings broken by physical and mental abuse, illness and disease, among wartime veterans, Holocaust and genocide survivors, and the incarcerated. Many share the symptoms of Post-Traumatic-Stress-Disorder (PTSD) which will be discussed later in Chapter IV.

Viktor Frankl says that existential frustration refers to a general sense of meaninglessness or emptiness, as evidenced by a state of boredom. It was a widespread phenomenon of the 20th Century, states Frankl, and continues into the 21st Century as a result of the rapid rise of industrialization, the loss of traditional values and dehumanization of individuals. Frankl states that people may experience existential frustration without developing existential neurosis. He goes on to say that many feel that life has no purpose, no challenge, and no obligation to pursue the former. Often, says Frankl, individuals attempt to void their existential frustration with the "will to power" or "will to pleasure."[20]

Individuals driven by the "will to pleasure" or "will to prosperity" may respond to their existential frustration by pursuing mental or physical objects that produce varying levels of neuromodulator dopamine in a desperate attempt to anesthetize their existential pain. Dopamine is a neurochemical responsible for fixing attention, increasing the effectiveness of attention (i.e. increases synaptic interconnections and speed of neural activity), and also bestows an appetitive value on behaviour that is often perceived as pleasurable. It activates or modulates global states of the brain depending on the unpredicted sensory attributes of the chosen mental or physical objects

– pornography, gambling, video games depicting violence, compulsions, or food.[34]

Those driven by the "will to power" may pursue power to overcome feelings of inadequacy, or fill their days with meaningless and repetitive busy work.[20] For young males who feel locked out of the social and economic mainstream, or who experience the emotional or physical absence of a loving father, running with a gang or joining the military can be forms of social achievement, as can engaging in violence perpetrating by gangs or nations. Staying calm under threat of apprehension, fast talking his way out of dangerous or life-threatening situations, or garnering the respect of peers and affection of young, impressionable women is a heady way to live. Young males yearn for the comradeship gang or nation wars provide, but that is not true friendship.

Warfare can become an addiction; it is its own subculture. In a firestorm, when danger is omnipresent, there is no past, no future; only the present in a way that is like a drug. Everything that was once familiar – civilian family life, parent-teacher meetings, your children's school and sporting events, home maintenance – becomes stressful and strange prior to war has become familiar. It perverts, corrupts and dehumanizes the young person, ultimately inviting him to his own demise. Wars are heady, intoxicating and addictive, and can lead to unprovoked thrill killing of innocent civilians, and occasionally fellow soldiers.

Experiential, creative, and attitudinal values are surface manifestations of what Viktor Frankl calls supra-meaning or transcendence. Supra-meaning is the idea that there is, in fact, ultimate meaning in life, meaning that is not dependent on others, on our projects, or even on our dignity. It is a reference to God and spiritual meaning. Logotherapy puts therapy in a spiritual context. It literally means therapy or health through meaning. The primary premise of Logotherapy is that the search for meaning in life is identified as the primary motivational force in human beings. However, many find life utterly meaningless.

This sets Frankl's existentialism apart from the existentialism of someone like Jean Paul Sartre and other atheistic existentialists who suggest that life is ultimately meaningless, and we must find the courage to face that meaninglessness. Sartre says we must learn to endure ultimate meaninglessness; Frankl instead says that we need to learn to endure our inability to fully comprehend ultimate meaningfulness, for "Logos is deeper than logic."

Frankl's existentialism understands the human to be challenged by the reality of temporary existence, and the view that life has no inherent meaning; meaning must be constructed; it must be discovered. Authentic human beings are those who can face existential futility and yet still go on to construct a meaningful life.

Existentialism entails living a life that is honest, insightful and morally correct. Authenticity is about living genuinely with one's fears or anxieties and achieving meaning despite the temporary nature of one's existence. In other words, life has no meaning unless you create or discover it. Friedrich Nietzsche says the only logical response to this void and meaninglessness is to rise above it.

For life to have meaning, says Viktor Frankl, it must offer the opportunity and experience of transcendence. Frankl notes that the word *geistig* (the spirit) refers to the capacity for self-transcendence, which is basic to human nature. The most meaningful experiences in life are those that transcend the individual and offer caring moments with others. Frankl says that the human spirit can also be experienced in the form of suffering. He says that meaning can be found in suffering by transcending the moment to understand the fullest impact of the experience. He points out that "life can be made meaningful (1) by what we give to the world in terms of our creation; (2) by what we take from the world in terms of our experience; and (3) by the stand we take toward the world, that is to say, by the attitude we choose toward suffering."[22]

We are all responsible for our choices, Frankl says, but even honest choices won't always be good ones. We still feel guilty over failing to fulfill all the possibilities in our life. Existential guilt, or existential anxiety or angst is inescapable.

Rollo May says if we lose our commitment to a set of values we will feel lonely and empty. Life will appear to be meaningless. Ultimately we need therefore to take responsibility for ourselves and find meaning in our lives.

Viktor Frankl (1905-1997) spent from 1942-1945 in several Nazi concentration camps. The Frankl family was initially deported to the Nazi concentration camp, Theresienstadt in July 1942. Frankl's father died in Theresienstadt of starvation, in 1943. In 1944, Frankl and his wife Tilly, and shortly thereafter his 65 year old mother, were transported to the extinction camp Auschwitz. His mother was immediately murdered in the gas chamber. Viktor's pregnant wife, Tilly was moved to Bergen-Belsen, where she died at the age of 24 after being forced to have an abortion. His younger brother died in a branch camp of Auschwitz while working in a mine. Following a brief incarceration at Auschwitz, Viktor Frankl was transported in cattle cars, via Vienna, to Kaufering and Türkheim (subsidiary camps of Dachau). Only Viktor and his sister survived the camps with the latter immigrating to Australia.

In 1945, in the last camp Frankl came down with typhoid fever. To avoid fatal collapse during the nights he kept himself awake by writing on slips of paper stolen from the camp office. On April 27, 1945 the camp was liberated by American troops. In August Frankl returned to Vienna, where he learned, within a span of a few days, about the death of his wife, his mother and his brother. These tragic discoveries would have broken many men.

During his time in the camps, Frankl observed people who survived horrific circumstances but were able to resist despair. He felt that those who were able to do so were people who found some spiritual meaning in their lives. Frankl concludes from these examples that the prime motive of human behavior is the "will-to-meaning". Frankl says that in order to find a meaning in our troubled existence we need to discover meaning through values and we have a moral duty to discover those values. Frankl suggests that we discover our values through work, through love for others and through confrontation with our own suffering.

Frankl devised a treatment to help people find the meaning in their lives. It is called Logotherapy from the word *logos*, Greek for meaning. Logotherapy views psychological problems as symptomatic of the person having lost meaning in life. Once meaning is rediscovered, the problems tend to resolve naturally. This is done by confronting patients with their responsibility for their existence and by assisting them in choosing values that lead to the discovery of meaning.

Following World War II, Frankl published his book, *The Doctor and the Soul*, which led to an appointment at the University of Vienna Medical School. He wrote another book in less than ten days, *Man's Search for Meaning*, for which he is best known in America. Viktor Frankl founded Logotherapy (from Greek logos, "word or meaning") and Existential Analysis, the Third Viennese School of Psychotherapy. A young student of Sigmund Freud, he was familiar with the First Viennese School, Psychoanalysis. He was also familiar with the Second Viennese School, Alfred Adler's Individual Psychology. He knew Freud and Adler personally and published several articles in their journals.

The focus of this book, *Search for Meaning at the Broken Places*, is to address the needs of those in difficult transition periods – newly unemployed due to recession or similar financial crises deciding to look for another job and to pursue entrepreneurial skills; men and women enthused about or doubting their love and commitments; widows and widowers pondering life without their friend and partner; parents' grief over the loss of a child or grandchild; and those devastated by cancer, loss of mobility due to amputation or paralysis, or loss of sensory perception. As mankind continues to evolve during difficult transitions and unavoidable pain and suffering, so too will the field of psychotherapy. Viktor Frankl acknowledges that Logotherapy is just one of many tools, demonstrating how complex and multidimensional human beings are.

Search for Meaning at the Broken Places is dedicated to helping individuals live more creatively by embracing the *gift* of unavoidable pain, suffering and brokenness in all of its forms. It is dedicated to helping them avoid the temptation to drug, divert or bury their physical, emotional, mental and spiritual pain; to help them view all experiences as related parts of a larger whole, parts inextricably blended with one another, like brushstrokes upon a canvas within the process of spiritual growth and creativity. It does not provide ultimate answers, only guidance in discovering the "meanings of the moments," meanings which must be discovered in response to life's demands.[17] So, by remaining aware of the life of God within and around us, they can affirm their lives by creatively embracing, accepting and living through unavoidable pain, suffering and brokenness in order to become what they are not – a *masterpiece*, a creation of God.

Search for Meaning Exercise: An autobiographical sketch often begins with a list of short chapter headings that map one's life from the beginning to the present. In this exercise jot down eight to twelve significant emotional, life-changing events, referred to in the Intensive Journal ® process as *Steppingstones*. [The Intensive Journal will be described in detail in Chapter X.] These events are the ups and downs, the main events that shape an individual's life. The list usually begins with the event of one's birth. This may be followed by objective markers in one's life – fights between one's mother and father; suffering a traumatic accident; first day in school separated from family; dropping out of school to run the streets; graduating from high school or college; changes in family cohesiveness or residences; birth or death of a loved one or life-long friend; major financial changes such as bankruptcy; marriage, separation or divorce; job promotion, demotion or being fired; long-term incarceration or hospitalization; devastating or life-threatening illness or disease. Positive and negative events are often viewed subjectively. However, they are unique life experiences that will not be repeated. They cannot be denied or removed. Steppingstones are often *spiritual* gifts, meaningful gifts that occasionally are realized only with the passage of time and deep contemplation. List them as they come to mind, disregarding when they occurred. These events made you who you are today, but not who you will be in the next moment, hour, day, month, year or decade. When you have completed the list, go back over the list and number them sequentially as to when they took place. You will refer back to this list in later exercises.

II.
In the Beginning was "Logos" (The Word)

Birth and death are not two different states, but they are different aspects of the same state. There is as little reason to deplore the one as there is to be pleased over the other.

\- Mahatma Gandhi

Ernest Hemingway is alleged to have written this short story: "For sale: baby shoes, never worn. " Naturally there are lots of ways to interpret that story. Did the person ever have a baby? Did the baby die? Were the shoes found in an attic brand new? It's all open to each individual's view and takes on the world, which is why the shortest of the short are often so wonderful and meaningful. They give us only a glimpse of the whole picture, allowing us to fill in the missing parts. Of course, the story is only legend. Hemingway was a gifted writer who was against wars. If he were asked to write a six-word short story about wars, I can't help but believe that it would have been: "*Army boots, worn once, in battle.*"

"Life is to be celebrated unconditionally," Jimmy's parents often reminded him in different ways. When Jimmy experienced defeat, disaster or depression they implied, without being specific, "What was the *gift* here? What lesson did you learn?" Both his parents and grandparents taught him to celebrate the life of a loved one, a friend or pet, not its death. They taught him that he is in charge of his life span to the degree that he makes both conscious and unconscious choices. Jimmy's grandparents lived until their eighties, despite the vices, the chewing of tobacco that would eventually take their lives. They began chewing tobacco during their youth while picking tobacco and cotton during the Depression to stave off chronic hunger pangs. Such choices would end the life of millions more years and decades earlier, but they drew strength from their *positive attitudes* and healing from their *spiritual dimension*. Life often ends far sooner, sometimes through no fault of our own – acts of war, a drive-by shooting, an airplane crash, a viral epidemic, or an object falling from the sky. Everybody will die, but as Jimmy's parents and grandparents taught him, not everyone truly lives.

The River

It is a warm summer day, 1954. School is out. Billie and Danny had just reached the top of the hill overlooking the river. Danny turns and yells down at Jimmy, "You're not going to believe this. There are four naked girls down by the river. Hurry, Jimmy!"

Jimmy sprints to the top of the hill. Out of breath, standing next to his friends he looks in the direction Billie and Danny point and there, grazing near the river, he sees four young fillies…three brunettes and a blonde. Four beautiful mares, that is, grazing near the river!

"Gotcha," laughs Billie. He and Danny turn toward the river and begin running through the tall grass, fresh growth following an early summer rainfall. Jimmy follows, stopping near the river bank. There, they tare off their clothes, and jump off the river bank. Jimmy wades past the young willow saplings poking out of the water. He swims out a bit further and begins to float on his back, watching the clouds overhead and enjoying the cool waters on a hot summer day.

Swirling around in the near frigid waters, Jimmy notices an object floating downstream…debris…the norm after the spring thaw of snow packs at higher elevations. But this is strangely different…a pink baby bracelet on an outstretched tiny arm protruding from a gunnysack…a brief encounter…with many questions and few answers for a ten year old boy. Samuel von Pufendorf said it best in 1673, "More inhumanity has been done by man himself than any other of nature's causes."

"It's… it's a baby girl." Many random questions quickly run through his head. "From where did she come?" "Will her mother and father miss her?" "Does she have a brother or sister?" "Will they miss her, too?" "What is her name?" "Did she misbehave?" "Did nobody love her?" The questions continue with no response.

Jimmy continues to stare at the floating, lifeless baby girl, with numb body and mind, unable to move, unaware of the life that continues to take place around him, unable to comprehend the apparently unfeeling hands that tossed the baby into his weekend playground. He stares fixated as the gunnysack slowly floats downstream toward a bend in the river. Then slowly, Jimmy's senses return one at a time…blackbirds chirping in the distance…leaves dancing among the branches…fish and sand crabs nibbling at his feet…horses racing through the fields. The world begins to come alive again with sights, sounds…and the smell of death.

Death is foreign to this innocent 10-year-old child. It has no meaning. Alone, Jimmy briefly ponders the meaning with Mother Nature, but lacks the life experiences, the wisdom and maturity to comprehend, or the words to inquire. Death rarely confronts a child except with a brief statement from the news media or in Saturday cartoons or cowboy movies. It definitely never happens in Abbott and Costello movies, except with animated mummies or Bella Lugosi or Frankenstein's monster. But when it does the dead magically resurrects again and again the following Saturday morning.

Jimmy slowly swims away into deeper waters, a child just beginning to see an unfamiliar and unkind world. It is a world very different from the security of loving parents ready to wipe a snotty nose, to give a warm, fuzzy hug or to kiss the tears and hurts away. The formation of neighborhood gangs is just beginning to materialize and he has learned the art of surviving attacks by groups of his peers.

From the center of the river Jimmy continues to glance back as the gunnysack-wrapped bundle continues to slowly round the bend in the river and float out of view, but never out of his subconscious. That short cerebral video clip will forever be present.

Suddenly, Billie breaks the silence yelling, "Let's go bareback riding!"

Jimmy swims to the edge of the river bank and walks over to where his childhood friends wait, not saying a word about what he had seen. They turn and hurry over to the grazing mares. Jimmy helps the other two climb upon the mares before he too hops onto a third mare. Together they ride off bareback along the river, enjoying the warm sunshine on their back and imagine flying over the open fields atop Pegasus.

The vision of that baby girl would continue to haunt Jimmy with unanswered questions. But this was a time to simply let go, to simply store this story away, and enjoy the summer. It would not be the last time that he would witness this river carrying lifeless infants and others, in the summer of 1954, to unknown parts downriver. It would not be the last time he would witness the inhumanity of others. It would not be the last time he would witness man's fixation on wars – wars on illiteracy, disease, crime and drugs, and terrorism, and yes, wars to end wars – wars that paradoxically more often than not make things worse.

Ernest Hemingway experienced war firsthand, wrote dispatches from innumerable frontlines, and used war as a backdrop for many of his most memorable works, such as *Farewell to Arms*.[30] Commenting on his war experiences years later in *Men at War*, Hemingway wrote: "When you go to war as a boy you have a great illusion of immortality. Other people get killed; not you.

Then when you are badly wounded the first time you lose that illusion and you know it can happen to you. After being severely wounded two weeks before my nineteenth birthday I had a bad time until I figured out that nothing could happen to me that had not happened to all men before me. Whatever I had to do men had always done. If they had done it then I could do it too and the best thing was not to worry about it."

In later years, while swimming in frigid waters or stirring his toes on a river bottom the memories occasionally come back to Jimmy. In those peaceful moments, the world temporarily goes silent again as in a silent movie as the childhood images come back to him.
Jimmy can still feel the warmth of the four-hoofed body gliding beneath him. He can still see the arm of the lifeless baby protruding from the gunnysack-wrapped bundle floating past him. The vision of the pink bracelet never leaves him. It is part of his psyche, an individual thread, a simple brushstroke on the canvas of his life stories. It was a brief

encounter between two human beings existing in one state, but two realities.

In later years, Jimmy would experience the gift of grief, pain and wonderment again and again, not only as a sibling who lost a brother, but also as a father and grandfather who lost a child and grandchild, and many friends along the path of life.

For Sale – Baby Shoes – Never Worn: A Brief Novel

"Jimmy, wake up! My water broke and I'm having contractions." Jimmy's wife is expecting their first child. The bed is wet but, thankfully there is no sign of blood. Jimmy hurries to dress while his wife puts on her robe. He then grabs the overnight bag and guides his wife to the car. It is a short drive to the hospital, but it seems an eternity driving on a highway freshly cleared of eight feet of snow fallen over the last two days.

Twenty minutes later they arrive at the hospital. After entering the hospital and registering, Jimmy is told to go to the visitor's lounge. He is told that a father is not yet allowed in the delivery room to assist his expectant wife. He waits, listening for the first sounds from his newborn baby.

Thirty minutes later the doctor comes to deliver the news. The doctor moves his lips, but no audible words come out. Then, he hears them resound off the hospital walls: "Your baby did not survive. We did everything possible. I'm sorry." Jimmy shakes his head, "What did you say?" The doctor repeats, "You have a beautiful son! Your wife is doing well." The earlier message he heard was from three years previous.

Jimmy's first child dies in the winter of 1970 before it can take its first breath of air, before it can take nourishment from its mother, and before it can take its first step toward its meaning potential. It would take many years for him to discover the meaning and gift of that moment.

The death of a child is the most devastating event any parent can experience. The agony runs deep within one's spirit. It may take years to accept it and many more years to comprehend the meaning. Grieving and discovering the meaning take time. Its pathos comes in unrelenting ways on all members of the family – the parents, grandparents, and intimate friends alike.

The laceration resulting from the death of one's child, at birth or at any time prior to reaching adulthood, can be so deep that many marriages are not able to survive it. Irreplaceable dreams are crushed and disintegrated. The devastation cannot be understated.

Healing seldom takes place in silence or isolation. Those who are the best healers tend to be those who have been broken and wounded themselves and have come through their suffering scarred, but not destroyed. A tragedy has happened. The only response is, "How will I respond and can meaning ever be restored?"

Traumatic experiences can break a person, destroying his trust in his faith and the world, or it can provide a spiritual opening to a deeper sense of life's meaning. Survivors of the genocide wars in Somalia and Rwanda tell horrific stories about rebels entering their village, burning the whole village and its crops; killing loved one who are thrown in village wells; daughters, wives and mothers raped and shot in front of them; a suckling baby pulled from its mother and thrown into the fire. For some individuals suffering is often traumatic suffering that may be followed by years of post-traumatic-stress-disorder. For others trauma may lead to a spiritual awakening and growth.

St. Francis Assisi was a man of privilege whose war experience turned him toward a life of poverty and service. Max Cleland's war experience turned him toward a life of service to his country.[10] Nelson Mandela's years of imprisonment and separation from family became a forge for spiritual growth, strength and political commitment.[50]

The Tasks of Grief

As a person faces mortality either in his or her own death or that of a loved one, the first thing he or she experiences is the story of the person. Each person's story reflects both who she or he is and what she or he has done. A funeral eulogy is a time to tell the story of the deceased. The spiritual nature of the event is inescapable. It can be a time for celebration of the deceased's life or a time for grieving.

The task of grief, according to Frankl, tends to be twofold: The first aspect is to find meaning in the story. What is it about the story of this person that offers meaning to the person articulating the eulogy? Meaning is often found by asking the question, "What is it about this story that would be important enough to you to want to share with someone else?"…"This leads to the paradox that man's past is his true future. The living man has both a future and a past; the dying man has no future in the usual sense (except in those who follow him), but only a past."[26]

In the hearts and minds of family and friends, the stories of the person's life reflect shared meaning. In this way there is a future, even after the death of the loved one. Paradoxically, the real hurt in grief is the fact that stories have endings. Yet when the story is understood in meanings, there are no ends, only meanings that can be passed on from generation to generation, cherished as they are told and retold.

The second task of grief is to understand the responsibility that is called for by the loss of a loved one. This is particularly true in incidents such as a car crash or in war where one person lives and the other dies. Frankl suggests that to honor the life of the deceased is to move beyond survivor guilt, which often accompanies this type of situation. Frankl suggests that there should be no such thing as survivor guilt, but only *survivor responsibility*, to honor the story of the deceased. Each person has responsibility to transcend the circumstances of the incident and cherish the memory of the deceased; a responsibility to celebrate the story of another's life, not the end of the story. Death need not be the final chapter of growth.

We have all lost a loved one – a grandparent, a parent, a brother or sister, a child, or a close friend; perhaps a pet. Life often does not seem fair. Sometimes an elder or spiritual leader has words of wisdom that helps us through these difficult chapters in our life. Viktor Frankl says that "life has meaning under all conditions, until the last moment of our lives." This is also true for elements of the "tragic triad" – unavoidable death, guilt and suffering. What counts is not the length of life. "Either life is meaningful," says Frankl, "or then there is no sense extending it infinitely. Even when we find ourselves in an inescapable situation of suffering, by the attitude we adopt in the face of an unchangeable fate we can invest meaning in the very last days of our lives."

In suffering, what matters, says Frankl is the attitude we take toward situations where the suffering has become unavoidable.[20] Tolstoy's short novel, *The Death of Ivan Ilyich*, tells the story of a man who, at the age of 60, learns that he has only a short time to live. He suddenly starts to revaluate his life. Acknowledging that he is about to die, he sees everything with different eyes. He views his whole life as being wasted. He has experienced periods of infatuation, but not really loved. His life does not have a real content. He is ashamed of himself and sincerely repents and regrets.

Only a great artist like Tolstoy is capable of recounting such a change. Tolstoy shows how this man, in confrontation of his former self, for the first time in his life, begins to grow, to go beyond himself, to fulfill his deepest meaning. He experiences his life including its failures. By acknowledging his failures, he transcends them, he goes beyond them. Literally to man's last breath, neither suffering, nor imminent death, nor guilt can do away with the potential of discovering the infinite meaningfulness of life, regardless of its demise.

Some who witness death handle it well, combining their natural grieving with a sense of celebration for a long, fruitful life. Others become paralyzed with grief and experience the loss as a terrible tragedy. A child's life cut short either by disease or accident may appear to be a greater loss than an elder dying from an expected and natural cause. Some survivors completely shut down, unable to function because they could not accept the fact that death is definitely part of the process of life. For them, perhaps there is no closure to issues left unresolved, and thus no blessing on their part given to the deceased loved one. The connection between life and death must come from the family. It must come from survivors who have experienced death, but become spiritually stronger.

If life is truly a gift, so too are all experiences. Then, "in all things" we can and must "give thanks," particularly for events, circumstances, pain and suffering over which we have no control. All that we experience and all whom we encounter grace and benefit us in some way – birth and death; physical, emotional and spiritual growth and deterioration; friendships and hardships; love and hate; guilt and suffering; marriage, separation and divorce; work and play; financial gain and loss; war and peace; health and illness; periods of ecstasy and bouts of depression. The meaning of life is to discover its gifts and ultimately the lessons uniquely intended for individuals who experience them. Our purpose is to pass on the wisdom and values; to give them away; to make the youth our disciples.

Death – The Last Stage of Growth[40]

The dying, states Elisabeth Kubler-Ross teaches us to accept ourselves in our true complexity. Without judgment, we gradually learn to accept our warts and craziness of mind, and to accept them without mistaking them for who we really are. We learn to never mistake self-talk for reality which tends to be negative most of the time.

The dying teaches us that happiness comes from learning to let go of the things that tend to cause suffering. Though survivors may lose much, they find something much deeper that is of even greater importance that can never be taken away, a lifetime of family memories forever stored in our minds and hearts, in photographs and videos, and in diaries and journals.

The dying teaches us that it is possible to let go of wanting, that our true sources of satisfaction lie in what we already have, and have always had – simple awareness.

The dying teaches us that the real tragedy is not the loss of possessions, not even the loss of loved ones. The real tragedy is losing our connection with our humanness, with compassion, with kindness, and with forgiveness – for ourselves and those about us. Seemingly safe, secure people, those who avoid pain at all cost, have merely saved up their suffering; put off their pain; maintaining their defenses.

Viktor Frankl concludes that the meaning of life is found in every moment of living.[20] Life never ceases to have meaning, even in suffering and death. In a group therapy session during a mass fast inflicted on the camp's inmates trying to protect an anonymous fellow inmate from fatal retribution by authorities, Frankl offers the thought that for everyone in a dire condition there is someone looking down, a friend, family member, or even God, who expects not to be disappointed.

Frankl concludes from his experience that a prisoner's psychological reactions are not solely the result of the conditions of his life, but also from the freedom of choice he always has even in severe suffering. The inner hold a prisoner has on his spiritual self relies on having a faith in the future and that once a prisoner loses that faith, he is doomed. Frankl often quotes the words of Nietzsche, "He who has a why to live can bear with almost any how."[20]

The Beginning of a Masterpiece

A child is a masterpiece in the process of becoming. We have all witnessed a masterpiece in the making when a child is born. Seeing the seductive smile of a newborn, we cannot help but wonder what she is thinking. In every birth, we know we're witnessing a one-of-a-kind, unique experience. A newborn makes us forget the artist, God. Instead, we direct our attention to the artist's work. We wonder how this beautiful work of art was created, but for the time being we are transposed, so deeply brought into this creation that our consciousness is actually expanded. No one walks away unaffected. We remain mystified before this great work of art – ten fingers; ten toes; the wonderful smell unique to babies.

We have seen countless masterpieces in museums around the world - the *Mona Lisa*; the statue of *David*; other masterpieces by such artists as Picasso, Matisse, Giotto, Diego Velazquez, Botticelli, Leonardo de Vinci, van Gogh and Salvadore Dali. Is there any doubt that a newborn is the greatest of all masterpieces?

A newborn instills in us a sense of the infinite, the feeling that anything is possible. She is perfect in the same way a rose is perfect. We can add nothing nor do anything to improve it except to pass on a millennium of cultural values, or, in the words of Viktor Frankl, "experiential, creative and attitudinal values." We idealize the work of art that the master managed to create, the genius we would like to believe exists inside all of us. And because the imagination knows no limits, art offers the mortals a chance to become immortal.

From the moment a child is born and throughout her life, experiential brushstrokes continue to be added to the original three-dimensional canvas that uniquely describes a newborn's life as an *unfinished masterpiece*. Each of the infinitely many experiential brushstrokes is unique and meaningful. Each person is unique in what

she experiences, who she encounters, what work she creates or deed she does, and by the attitude she takes toward unavoidable suffering.
Human Dimensions

Frankl says that human beings are three dimensional – somatic (physical), psychic (mental), and noetic (spiritual). The physical dimension (soma) of a child lets her know when something is wrong – a fever or headache, a stomachache or neck pain, a lacerated finger or broken bone. From early childhood, however she observes countless television commercials that emphasize magic pills, powders and potions to camouflage her pain.

The psychological dimension (psyche) is often driven by the ego which sometimes results in addictions to alcohol, drugs, sex, food, gambling and even work. Sigmund Freud infers that man is driven by the 'will to pleasure,' an ontological stage of life unique to young children.

It is Alfred Adler's position, however that man is driven, not by 'the will to pleasure,' but by the 'will to power,' attempting to overcome low self-esteem and feelings of inadequacy and inferiority. Driven to extremes it may result in the addictive powers of anger and aggression with the release of adrenaline in the bloodstream. However, both Freud's and Adler's inferences about human drives are historical products of their times.

The noetic or spiritual dimension is the third human dimension. When we fail to have meaning in our life, it often leads to the neurotic triad of depression, addiction and aggression.[20] Over forty percent of Americans, says Frankl suffer from a lack of meaning and thus, an existential frustration. If meaning is what we desire, then meaninglessness is a "vacuum" or emptiness in our lives. Whenever we have a vacuum, of course, things rush in to fill it.

Frankl suggests that one of the most conspicuous signs of existential vacuum in our society is boredom.[20] He points out how often people, when they finally have the time to do what they want, don't seem to want to do anything. People sometimes go into a tailspin when they retire. That was the scenario when Jimmy's father retired the first time. Students suffering from meaninglessness may get drunk every weekend. Others may submerge themselves in passive entertainment every evening. The "Sunday neurosis," Frankl calls it.

So mankind attempts to fill its existential vacuum with pleasure, power or prosperity, stuff that, because it provides some satisfaction. Our hope is that they will provide ultimate satisfaction as well. We fill our lives with pleasure, eating beyond all necessity, having promiscuous sex, living the high life, or surrounding ourselves with powerful and important people. We seek power, especially the power represented by monetary or tangible things such as mega-mansions to demonstrate our success. We fill our lives with work that fills our lives eighteen to twenty hours a day, six and seven day a week. We may fill the vacuum with intangibles such as anger and hatred and spend our days attempting to destroy what or whom we think is hurting us. We may also fill our lives with a neurotic obsession with germs and cleanliness, or a fear-driven obsession with a phobic object.

The defining quality of these vicious cycles is that, whatever we do, it is never enough. For extreme examples, we may direct our attention to the two million men and women currently in prison, countless youth who are or have been incarcerated and over five million previously incarcerated in America who suffer from this malady of meaninglessness, often pursuing a course of action resembling pseudo 'religious' practices to be discussed later.

In the psyche we are driven, by emotions, instinct, and needs. In the spirit, says Joseph Fabry we are the driver.[16] We make decisions about what to do with our motivations, with the gifts and handicaps of our body, and with the circumstances in which we find ourselves. The spirit is the area of human freedom, but also of human responsibility. To lead a fulfilled life, we must be aware that we have this spiritual treasure chest within us, and we must make use of its contents.[13]

Joseph Fabry states human beings have a unique spiritual dimension. It is a specifically human dimension with abilities that "other creatures *do not have*. Every human is spiritual; in fact, spirit is the essence of being human. You have a body that may become ill; you have a psyche that may become disturbed. But the spirit is what you are. It is your healthy core... It is the medicine chest. *"*[16; 17]

Fabry also suggests that one acquires meaning by involving oneself in "Socratic dialogues" within. Five guideposts, says Fabry, where meaning is most likely to be found are "self-discovery, choice, uniqueness, responsibility, and self-transcendence.[16] Meaning does not spontaneously appear. It often appears as eureka discoveries through listening to dreams, conscience, or a series of seemingly unrelated experiences.

These five guideposts described by Fabry in *Guideposts to Meaning* (p. 10) are:

- Self-discovery. The more you find out about your real self behind all the masks you put on for self protection, the more meaning you will discover.
- Choice. The more choices you see in your situation, the more meaning will become available.
- Uniqueness. You will be most likely to find meaning in situations where you are not easily replaced by someone else.
- Responsibility. Your life will be meaningful if you learn to take responsibility where you have freedom of choice, and if you learn not to feel responsible where you face an unalterable fate.
- Self-transcendence. Meaning comes to you when you reach beyond your egocentricity towards others.

Self-Discovery

Jimmy is midway through the sixth grade at Taylor Street Elementary School. It is a school located in the Heights, an area populated by low-income minorities. In school, Jimmy is in his sixth year of being grouped with the lower-achieving students. It is a grouping that he has embraced without question in a community where often abusive teachers are never challenged.

On Tuesday afternoon a meeting takes place between Jimmy's parents and his teacher. The teacher welcomes Jimmy's parents and invites them to take a seat near her desk. "I have the progress report for your son here before me," says the teacher. "He is turning in most of his assignments, he is well behaved in class, but he is not performing up to sixth-grade level. Currently, he is reading at the second-grade level. His math level is at the fourth-grade level. I am concerned because it has been my experience that he will probably continue to perform below grade level throughout his education."

Upon returning home, Jimmy's parents have a discussion about their son's low achievement. The next evening Jimmy's father sits down with him and begins to introduce the "joy and magic of learning." These exercises appear to instill in Jimmy a strong desire to increase his knowledge and skills in all academic areas and then on the strength of that knowledge, to learn even more. He is uncertain how or why it began, but he continues to expand his knowledge and to accelerate his recreational reading skills every evening while listening to classical music; not the usual music listened to by the typical twelve-year-old in the 1950s. He continues this routine for the balance of the academic year.

At the beginning of the seventh grade, Jimmy is retested. His reading and math levels increased to above twelfth-grade level, a metamorphosis that took place over a course of only six months thanks to caring parents who believed in each of their children's unlimited potential. Jimmy would never again lose his desire to discover the meaning of his early childhood experiences or his love for learning.

Uniqueness

Uniqueness is the story of every human being. For example, if I take ten pennies and mark them, number 1 on penny one, number 2 on penny two, and right down to 10, and I randomly put them in my pocket, the chances of pulling out penny number 1, the first time, are one in 10. Each round of pulling pennies from my pocket is followed by a return of them to my pocket. The chances of pulling out numbers 1 and 2 in that order during the second round are one in 100. The chances of pulling out numbers 1, 2 and 3 in that order during the third round are one in 1,000. But the chances of pulling out numbers 1 to 10 in order are one in 10 billion. Now, consider the fact that each human being is born with approximately 100 trillion cells. The chances of her being born with a unique meaning potential are one in 10 to the 100 trillionth powers!

Furthermore, each one of those cells contains chromosomes and genes. In every cell there are about 50,000 genes. Every gene has between 100 and 1,000 pieces of information. So, in every cell – and there are a hundred trillion in the body – there are more facts than in *The Encyclopedia Britannica.*

Everyone has her own specific vocation or mission in life to carry out a meaning potential, which demands fulfillment. Therein she cannot be replaced, nor can her life be repeated. Thus everyone's task is as unique as her own specific opportunity to implement.

Uniqueness does not happen by chance. If an individual puts the parts of a complex wind-up watch in a hat, shake them around and toss them out until she gets a neatly assembled watch, she will be busy until doomsday. It will never happen.

An explosion in a print shop does not create *Webster's Dictionary.* All the monkeys in the world pecking away at a computer console cannot write *Hamlet.* All the letters of the alphabet without Shakespeare cannot come up with *As You Like It.*

It matters not what an individual expects from life, but rather what life expects from her. Individuals only need to stop asking about the meaning of life, and instead to think of themselves as those who are being questioned by life – moment by moment – to act responsibly. Life ultimately means taking the responsibility to discover meaningful answers to problems that confront them moment to moment and to fulfill the tasks perpetually set before them.[20]

The Seed of Potential

The seed of meaning potential begins with the first brushstroke upon the canvas of one's life. It may begin when two loving individuals make a commitment to one another; it may begin with conception as the sperm and egg of two loving and responsible human beings unite.

The ancient ritual of planting the seed of the Chinese bamboo tree provides an excellent analogy. Planted, watered, fertilized and cultivated year after year for four years the 'seed' shows no detectable growth resembling the tree it was meant to be. Then, in the fifth year the seed explodes into a 90-foot tree over the course of six weeks. It has been growing a broad root system, a foundation to anchor it when it evolves into a 90-foot tree. Human values are the foundation that provides us a basis for meaningful growth.

Each person is a human being, a whole person in the same sense that a tree is a whole tree. A tree grows as a whole integral being, even in the midst of garbage or desolation, gradually unfolding the many possibilities that are present in the original seed. Any one of us can count the seeds in a fruit, but nobody can count the number of fruit lying within each seed. By comparison, the life growth of a person moves toward the unfolding of what it is to be human with its infinite possibilities. Sometimes, an infant is born in abject poverty. But poverty does not an evil person make. Even an acorn can grow strong in a junkyard. The unfolding life of an infant is not always uniform, nor without pain, grief and suffering. Even under ideal conditions for growth she may experience stress and distress.

The pressures of living in 'modern' civilization have the effect of fragmenting the lives of single and married individuals. People's lives become compartmentalized, so that they live as partial beings driven by the desire for pleasure, power and prosperity rather than as whole beings. They live in terms of their physical, intellectual or emotional selves or in terms of a particular set of values and expectations to which society or peers have conditioned them. They live their lives seeking to fulfill the external expectations rather than the inner needs of development that would fulfill their meaning potential. In the process, brokenness happens.

Brokenness as a Rite of Passage

"If you do not initiate the youth, they will burn down the village" is an African proverb that emphasizes one of the most important transitions in the life cycle, the passage from childhood to manhood. Ceremonies marking this event were common in pre-industrial societies and are still practiced in a number of non-Western cultures. The coming-of-age or initiation rituals are a universal key part of every traditional culture. However, modern culture in the 21st Century lacks anything resembling meaningful rites of passage.

The purpose of rites of passage is to provide a vehicle for children to transcend their youth in the process of becoming adults. Through rites of passage, the youth are provided an opportunity to discover their gifts, their vision for their role in the community, and their own personal "medicine" or wisdom for dealing with the challenges that lay in front of them. Elders facilitate these discoveries, and support young, initiated adults in the integration of their visions, roles, and paths into the fabric of the community. The rites of passage support the transformation of the child mentality into the adult mentality, shifting from self-centeredness to a sense of community connectedness. It is the belief of indigenous cultures that one can not possibly function as an adult without the rites of passage experience. Clouds must be broken to give rain. Soil must be broken so that plants may grow. Wheat cornels must be broken to make wheat flour. And bread must be broken to give strength. "We are helped not through our brilliant logic or persuasive speech, but through the sharing of our struggles, failures, disappointments, and losses and how we have overcome tragedy and trauma."[7] Those that have been broken physically or emotionally have an opportunity to not only become strong at the broken places but to also mentor others through their brokenness. Brokenness is part of life; it is what separates humanity ethnically and culturally.

A key element of every indigenous society's culture is its traditional rite of passage. It transforms a boy into a 'man,' not in physical way, but in a psychological and spiritual way. Through rite of passage, youth discover their gifts, their vision of their role in society, and their own personal wisdom for dealing with the challenges that lay in front of them. Elders facilitate the discovery process and support the integration of visions, roles and paths into the fabric of the community. Rite of passage supports the transformation from the child mentality to the adult mentality, recognizing the difficulty with the transition without the rites. Rite of passage is not without dangers; some youth experience trauma, even death. There are some common elements that all rites of passage share:

- Rite of passage is typically experienced only once.
- Those participating in rite of passage exercises do not know where they are.
- Boys and elders must accept an unknown outcome.
- Boys feel exposed, vulnerable, naked and completely unprotected.
- Boys are not given a choice about turning back.

- Rite of passage generally involves the youth' body and senses.
- Rite of passage facilitates the discovery of meaning and purpose.
- Rite of passage guides youth in shifting from self-centeredness to a sense of community connectedness.

Most rites of passage fall into three main phases: separation, transition, and incorporation. In the separation phase, the participant is taken away from his/her familiar environment and former role and enters a very different and sometimes foreign routine that they are forced to adjust to and become familiar with. A rite that would fall into this category would be birth. The infant leaves a very safe and secure environment in their mother's womb to an extremely different one in the real world. Death can also be a separation rite, depending on a person's belief about what happens after someone dies. Societies have devised ways to mark these separations and aid in the transitions that will take place. For instance, the naming of babies marks the significant event of birth. Funerals and the many different funeral customs mark the separation that takes place when a death occurs. Funerals can also help those left behind to make the necessary changes needed to adjust to being separated from loved ones.

During the first phase of a typical rite of passage the youth are prepared by the elders of their community with the teachings and cosmology needed for the journey. Next, the youth are separated from their normal surroundings. Often, they are brought to a remote area outside of the community, a location known only to the elders. The youth often spend long periods of time alone, forgoing normal comforts and securities. This phase is usually an awe-inspiring experience, involving a degree of actual danger and challenges to the youth, physically, emotionally and spiritually.

The transition phase is the time that the participant learns the appropriate behavior for the new stage they are entering. This phase can include the time when a person becomes engaged to be married. At this time, they are learning about the new stage of life they will soon enter — marriage. They are also adjusting and preparing for it, or making a transition. The transition phase may also include the time that children enter adolescence and leave their childhood behind. This is the time when people learn and grow and prepare to be an independent adult in the real world.

The last phase, incorporation, takes place when the participant is formally admitted into the new role in their community and helped to integrate their experience. Marriage is a good example of a rite that would take place in the incorporation phase. After people are married, they have taken on a very new and different role, having prepared for it in earlier transition and separation rites. They are given support to apply what they have learned and to further develop their vision.

Rite of passage is the story of life. It is the story of brokenness and growing stronger at the broken places. It is about transcendence followed by re-integration into one's community. When a plant or animal encounters an event that brings damage to the organism, it inherently attempts to repair the damage or develop strengths in other areas. When a human being loses one of its senses, it typically develops strengths in its other senses or becomes stronger in the broken places. *Strong at the Broken Places,* a DVD based on a book by Max Cleland, is about four individuals – Arn Chorn Pond, Michael MacDonald, Marcia Gordon and Max Cleland - who become strong at the broken places by transforming their lives creatively, socially, spiritually or existentially.

Arn Chorn Pond is a survivor of the Killing Fields of Cambodia where he was forced to fight as a child soldier. Arn transforms his life, directing his energies to helping youthful gang members escape their tragic lives.

Michael MacDonald grew up on South Boston, losing brothers to gang shootings and criminal activities. He eventually forms a nonprofit organization that purchases guns from gang members, thus reducing gang violence and death in Boston.

Marcia Gordon is a sexual-molest survivor who counsels others who have been sexually abused.

Max Cleland lost both legs and an arm in the Vietnam War. Cleland summarizes the essence of the book, stating that "in the service of love, only broken hearts will do. Others want to hear of your weakness and how you made it back..."[10] The basic foundation of Cleland's book comes from a quote by Ernest Hemingway in *A Farewell to Arms*.[30]

Nelson Mandela was imprisoned for 27 years on Robben Island off the coast of South Africa, beginning on Saturday, June 3, 1964. During the first 14 years he did not have a bed in his cell; he had to sleep on the floor in a prison cell that was smaller in length than his height. He missed out on the joys of watching his children grow up and on being with his wife who also was imprisoned. But in the end, he still had a choice, regardless of hardships in his attitude toward an apparently inescapable, unavoidable situation.[50]

Viktor Frankl states that "whenever one is confronted with an inescapable, unavoidable situation, whenever one has to face a fate which cannot be changed, e.g., an incurable disease, such as an inoperable cancer, just then one is given a last chance to actualize the highest value, to fulfill the deepest meaning, the meaning of suffering. For what matters above all is the attitude we take toward suffering, the attitude in which we take our suffering upon ourselves."[20]

Suffering is Inevitable; Misery is an Option.

Jimmy's first child dies in 1970. His wife, Carla is mentally ill, addicted to prescription drugs, homicidal, and secretly having extramarital affairs. The facts are inescapable, yet psychic release and meaning are still possible. Jimmy always has a choice. He can remain a victim or he can choose to be a survivor. He can choose to escape the lessons, to let go of the gifts or to discover the meaning of his story, to transcend and grow strong at the broken places. However, as Ernest Hemingway states, not all become strong at the broken places.

Jimmy is both mommy and daddy to his children. The reverse sexist attitude of society and therapists persuades him to remain in an emotionally abusive marriage. There are early signs of what was to come: threats of suicide; accusations of extramarital affairs, drug use, and incest; repeated escapes or unauthorized releases from mental hospitals that lead to bankruptcy; and threats that could lead to the loss of his job and community trust.

Uncertain of the kind of psychological abuse he would return home to, Jimmy constantly edits his statements. Occasionally, his wife leaves the house for several days without notice, leaving Jimmy to scramble for a baby sitter while he goes to work. Jimmy instinctively knows that there are problems, but knows not where to turn. He is blamed for everything that goes wrong in the marriage and in general, even if it has no basis in reality.

Carla criticizes nearly everything Jimmy does and nothing is ever good enough. No matter how hard he tries, there is no pleasing her. Carla seeks her love and support through others. She is not only manipulative in the marriage, but with her physicians and therapists as well. One moment she is kind and loving. The next she is throwing objects, screaming, threatening, breaking objects, or curled in a fetal position on the kitchen floor before being transported to a mental hospital. Jimmy never knows whether he will be returning home to Jekyll or Hyde. He feels depressed and helpless. Repeatedly, Jimmy is told that there is something wrong with him and that he, not she, needs to be in therapy.

When Jimmy confides his feelings, observations and suspicions to a close friends or family members, they tend to disbelieve him because Carla usually 'behaves' like a sane, friendly and loving person around other people. But in Carla's twisted reality, Jimmy is a homosexual, child molester, cruel, and has multiple affairs during the five-minute drive or walk between work and home. No amount of denial suffices. "It happened. End of discussion. I want a divorce." Those are her demands…for his infidelity and cruelty and non-support of her goals to do what she damn well pleases.

Based on Carla's erratic behavior, moodiness and instability, Jimmy distances himself from his relatives, friends and peers in an effort to convince others that his marriage is normal. Yet, Jimmy feels that he is trapped in a no-win marriage – "I hate you. You're unfaithful; a pervert; sinful. I love you. You're wonderful; great. I want a divorce…but, not now…not while I'm having this affair with my therapist, my cousin, or with whomever I damn well please. Besides, my therapist needs the insurance money."

It is Jimmy who is in tears while Carla smiles a sinister smile and threatens to kill him while he sleeps and take all that he cherishes; his children. She says that "it's the medication that she is currently taking," but Jimmy knows by now, after years of repetition, that it will not get any better; only worse. Things will never change. They never get better, no matter what the therapists say or what medication she is currently prescribed. Meanwhile, the medical bills mount exponentially because Carla always discovers ways to "escape" from her repeated commitments to a mental hospital ward.

Carla blames her family, the doctors and therapists, Jimmy's family, friends and peers when things do not get better, never once taking responsibility for her own behaviors. When things do not go her way, Carla leaves for several days, using the family credit cards. Returning home, she once again becomes a violent, raging and abusive wife. She has, Jimmy eventually discovers, a borderline personality disorder, one of the most untreatable situations known to man and does not usually change enough so that the problem goes away.

Emotionally traumatized, nearly financially bankrupt, confused, and no apparent support from the psychotherapeutic community, Jimmy briefly contemplates suicide by biological toxins while attending medical school. Each day simulates walking on highly sensitive land minds, or a fragile tightrope. Little does he know of the trauma that his children suffered at the hands of their birth mother while Jimmy is away at work or furthering his studies at the university – Carla shuts them in a closet during the day; pushes their heads under water during baths; screams and throws dishes and other objects at them; informs the authorities that the children should be locked up for using or selling illegal drugs; threatens to accuse Jimmy of incest if she does not get her way.

A Tear in the Summer Canvas

Jimmy attempts marriage counseling with little success. Ending the marriage in divorce does little to end the nightmare. Jimmy divorces Carla in the summer of 1975. He is granted custody of his children, and makes plans to enter medical school. But, shortly after the divorce Carla kidnaps Jimmy's two infant children - a fifteen-month-old daughter still in diapers and a three-year-old son. Carla leaves no written or phone messages. Two days later she calls in a fit of hysterics, "Jimmy, you've got to come get your kids! I can't explain now, but something terrible has happened." It is 4:00 o'clock in the afternoon and Jimmy just arrived at his parents' home after teaching in a local high school.

Jimmy has a sinking feeling because his ex-wife has made many threats against him and his children. Jimmy tells his parents that he is leaving to retrieve his children and begins the all night drive.

Upon arrival at the address given to him, Jimmy rushes in asking for the whereabouts of his two children. Carla says that they are in the bedroom and she points in that direction. Jimmy finds his daughter lying on a bed, shaking and crying. "What happened?" he asks. Carla says that the infant daughter was crying and would not stop. She goes on to say that her brother, recently home from his second tour of duty in Vietnam began spanking Jimmy's daughter. Seeing bruises on the back of his infant daughter, Jimmy removes her diaper and discovers that her buttock is covered with bruises. He then looks for bruises on his son. There are no bruises.

"Why?" Jimmy asks, "For God's sake, she's just a baby!"

"Because she would not stop crying," Carla calmly replies.

Jimmy knows that he has few choices – to permanently end the gene pool of the family that has physically and emotionally traumatized his daughter (and son emotionally), to report the abuse of his daughter to the local authorities, or to remove his children from this place and be a full-time father once again. Quickly, he decides and acts.

It would be another thirty years before Jimmy would learn that the man he had forgiven was not the perpetrator of the physical abuse of his daughter, but Carla, his ex-wife. The witness, present at the time of the physical abuse, would turn out to be none other than Jimmy's son, who remembered that his birth mother threatened to kill both him and his sister rather than return them to their father. Jimmy's infant son had blocked it from his childhood memory all those years.

"In all things give thanks," Jimmy kept repeating to himself over the next thirty years. "In all things give thanks." His children were alive and thriving, for which he continues to be thankful.

Human beings can be thankful that they can feel pain. Pain, unavoidable pain, is a gift. Unavoidable pain is emphasized here because if pain is avoidable, the sensible thing to do is to avoid it. A masochist does not. In the end, Jimmy acknowledges, experience is not what happens to an individual; experience is what one does with that which happens to him. But, in the case of his infant children thirty years earlier, they had no choice; they had no power to prevent their mother's abuse.

It takes nearly ten years for psychotherapists to diagnose the illness of Carla. Worse, they never inform Jimmy to not ever leave his children or grandchildren alone with Carla. Had Jimmy made audio recordings of Carla's raging fits, threats and demands, the trauma for both him and his children would have ended much sooner. Whether it was fate, faith or a combination of both, Carla opted to give Jimmy full custody of his children, but it came with a price – repeated late evening calls from his ex-wife to his son of feigned illnesses and suicide threats.

Absent Fathers

Many of the problems that face the youth in the world today can be linked to the absence of fathers, and in particular the absence of elder-facilitated rite of passage. If the youth are not provided the experiences of the latter, they will seek to create it for themselves. Such pursuits in the absence of elders are dangerous, intense, and edgy. They pursue it through indiscriminant violence, risk-taking behaviors such as drug and alcohol abuse, casual and careless sexuality, and bodily mutilation. Youth do not possess the wisdom or cosmology to carry out initiation of their peers in contained and meaningful ways. Only initiated elders are capable of providing this.

In this context, the goal of working in this book is to make it possible for individuals to live and unfold the infinite meaning potentials of their being in terms of the wholeness of their inner nature, rather than in terms of a partial or fragmented aspect of their outer life. Losing an arm or a leg, sight or hearing, a marriage or friendship, a job or contract or the death of a loved one does not eliminate those potentials. On the contrary, hardship, pain, temptation, suffering, desolation, and even death may be life's calling for individuals to 'let go, let be, and let grow,' or in the words of Viktor Frankl, a calling for individuals to 'embrace experiential, attitudinal and creative values.'

The Discovery of Meaning Just Takes a Little Longer:
The physical dimension is not always the thing that got broken. Knowledge is learned. Wisdom is discovered. By embracing the brokenness in our life, be it physical or emotional, we begin the healing process while discovering our purpose and meaning potential.

- Write a short autobiography using only six words.
- Write a short paragraph about a reoccurring dream.
- List four significant life-changing events you've experienced.
- List four unusual childhood experiences that make you *unique*.
- List four meaningful goals that you most want to pursue in life.
- List four life experiences which appear to have potential meaning.
- List four challenging struggles you've overcome despite initial hesitancy.
- Write a short paragraph about a meaningful volunteer activity you pursued.
- Write a short paragraph about experiential pain and suffering that made you stronger.

III.
Pain: The Gift that Nobody Wants

Pain is not the enemy, but the loyal scout announcing
the enemy... Pain truly is the gift nobody wants.   - Paul Brand

Dan Millman reminds us in *The Way of the Peaceful Warrior* that "pain is relatively objective, a physical phenomenon," and that "suffering is our psychological resistance to what happens. Events may create physical pain, but they do not in themselves create suffering. Resistance creates suffering. Stress happens when our mind resists what is...The only problem in our life is our mind's resistance to life as it unfolds."[51] And Carlos Castaneda noted in *The Teachings of Don Juan* that "the basic difference between an ordinary man and a warrior is that a warrior takes everything as a challenge, while an ordinary man takes everything as a blessing or a curse...The trick is in what one emphasizes. We either make ourselves miserable, or we make ourselves strong. The amount of work is the same."[9]

Veterans - Broken by Wars

Doug Pringle is a veteran. He is determined not to let the loss of a leg during the Vietnam War mar his enjoyment of winter sports or any other activity. He disciplined himself to ski on one leg in 1968 and went on to win several gold medals in the Winter Paralympics. Stating that "it is one of the best things to happen to me," he organizes summer and winter sports programs for similar afflicted veterans returning from never-ending war fronts of Vietnam, Iraq, and Afghanistan. "The loss of my leg in Vietnam has taken me in directions I could not have imagined prior to the war," says Doug. He became the president of Disabled Sports USA Far West, the first of 88 chapters he helped organize nationwide beginning in 1970.

Disabled Sports was founded by World War II veterans in 1967. In addition to working with the local chapter, Doug also represents the national organization on the US Olympic Committee. The motto of Disabled Sports is "If I can do this, I can do anything." He won three national slalom championships and was one of the first amputees certified as a ski instructor by the Professional Ski Instructors of America in 1972. Doug is inducted into the Ski Hall of Fame in 1990 and the Disabled Ski Hall of Fame in 1997 for contributions in the development of adapted skiing nationwide. In September 2001, he is awarded California's highest honor, the Governor's Trophy. This award is given to a Californian with a disability for "outstanding achievement in the world of work and significant contributions that increase public awareness of the experience of disability." He was elected to the Board of Directors of the U.S. Olympic Committee in 1998 and is a senior fellow member of the American Leadership Forum.

Disabled Sports USA provides *meaningful* opportunities for people with disabilities to develop physically, mentally and emotionally through our therapeutic recreation and sports rehabilitation programs. It is the lead agency for providing therapeutic sports and recreation rehabilitation to the soldiers wounded in the Iraq and Afghanistan wars, including cycling, snow sports, waterskiing, golf and adaptive adventures such as four-wheel drive outings, white water rafting, camping, and water sports. Disabled Sports serves anyone with a disability including autism, developmental disabilities, paraplegics, quadriplegics, amputees, stroke survivors and people with visual impairments, cerebral palsy, multiple sclerosis, spina bifida, head injury and muscular dystrophy.

Modern Day Leprosy

Human beings have a remarkable ability to shut down pain. Americans, comprising only five percent of the world population consume over 60 percent of the illegal drugs, one-third of which work on the central nervous system, and over 30,000 tons of aspirin a year. Not advertised is the fact the aspirin causes the stomach to bleed two teaspoons of blood, while Tylenol causes deterioration of the liver when combined with alcohol or a case of hepatitis. If leprosy is the inability to feel pain, then alcohol and drug addiction, which deaden pain, are forms of modern day leprosy.

Every human being has experienced pain, is experiencing pain or will experience pain. If you are now or about to be released from the war front or from a hospital trauma and physical therapy unit or about to be released from jail or prison or drug rehabilitation center, you are being asked what you wish to do with your life at this fork or chapter of your life, a chapter in a novel potentially greater than any ever written. When you come to a fork in the road, the path you choose has consequences. Once you have made a choice, you can never return to that fork. However, there will be infinitely many other forks in the road of life that require wise and meaningful choices.

A 16-year-old girl smiles as she cuddles one of twin newborn goats in her arms, not knowing that one is infected with the potentially deadly E. coli bacteria. Within a few days the E. coli begins to take its toll and she is taken to a local hospital. Her parents are told that she will be fine and to take her home. Eventually, the young teenager develops a staph infection; then, gangrene in her lower left leg. The gangrene begins to rapidly spread, killing the tissue for lack of blood supply. She will die if drastic medical measures are not taken. A decision is made; the leg is amputated at the upper part of her thigh and she begins the long road of painful recovery that would take years. She takes up photography as a full-time career goal that begins to put a measure of meaning back into her life.

An 18-year-old woman is injured by a gunshot while walking to the grocery store. A quadriplegic, she can only accomplish various tasks by means of a mouth stick. Meaning and purpose enter her life as she watches for stories about troubled people in local newspapers and television stations. She writes to them, typing with the mouthpiece, and provides them with a measure of comfort, encouragement and meaning.

A nurse student of Viktor Frankl is assigned to a 31-year-old mechanic who had both arms and legs amputated following high-voltage electrocution. Paralyzed from the neck down, this young man learns to use his teeth and, after hearing Frankl's *Man's Search for Meaning* read to him, begins to discover the meaning in his suffering. His favorite memorized quotation is the statement: "It is the spiritual freedom which cannot be taken away, which makes life meaningful and purposeful." He opens a small business that supports his family. Later, with a specially equipped car, he drives his wife and two children on a tour of the United States. He states that his life was empty before the accident, but now knows true happiness having squeezed meaning out of suffering and turned tragedy into triumph.

Joseph Fabry points out that Logotherapy cannot prevent unavoidable pain and suffering, but it can keep people from despair.[17] He says, people "can assume meaningful attitudes towards events that in themselves are meaningless." Pain and suffering become meaningful when they are transcended. Events and circumstances can break one's body and mind, but they are not able to break the spirit. Human beings can become strong at the broken places. Carl Jung states that "meaning makes many things, perhaps even everything, endurable and bearable." And Nietzsche says, "If you have a why to live for, you can put up with almost any how." It is a principle that applies to all inescapable pain, suffering and brokenness.

There is not one person who has not experienced pain, is experiencing pain or will experience pain. Pain, unavoidable pain, we are told, is inevitable, but misery is an option. Furthermore, Paul Brand states that unavoidable "pain is a gift that nobody wants."[8] Transcendence begins with discovering its meaning through the attitude an individual takes when he/she is faced with a situation in which he/she can do absolutely nothing, as in the case of an incurable disease, an inoperable malignancy, or being stricken with blindness or deafness, or losing an arm or leg.[20]

Viktor Frankl's attitude towards unavoidable pain and suffering is one of his most valuable contributions to the art of living, a contribution tested and validated in the harsh and inhumane conditions existing in the concentration and death camps of Auschwitz, Belsen, Treblinka and Dachau during the Holocaust. Frankl and others imprisoned there were stripped of their identity, not only of their possessions and clothing, not only of their hair and dignity, but also of their name. In return each incarcerated human being was given the cast-off clothing of a man already a victim of the gas chamber and a number was tattooed on their forearm. Thin people were given clothing from an overweight person; an overweight person was given clothing from a thin person; tall individuals were given clothing from short individuals; and short individuals were given clothing from tall individuals. Men and women were stripped of clothing were forced to march in front of each other or forced to wear clothing of the opposite sex. Nobody was given a choice in any of the daily details and activities of prison life in the death camps.

What is pain? Pain is an unpleasant sensation that may be associated with physical injuries, illnesses or feelings and emotions. It may be a pain that signals a decayed tooth, a cut finger, an upset stomach, a tumor disrupting the functioning of an internal organ or a break-down in our body. It may be an annoyance that produces painful tension in our neck muscles or stomach. It may be a signal of too much guilt, too much conflict and threat with those close to us, a dreaded necessity to make a decision, a feeling of emptiness and futility to the daily routine, a fear of aging or death of a loved one or us, or intolerable loneliness.

Pain is the voice of our inner life, the wisdom of our body, crying out for attention, for remedy. On the other hand, pain suppressors are life suppressors and tranquilizers are signal deniers. They come in the form of 'magic pills, powders or potions.' But much of that experienced pain is self-induced. Why self-induced? Research (*The Power of Positive Self-Talk*) indicates that over eighty-seven percent of self-talk, the internal sensory chatter tends to be negative in nature – www.wallace.edu. Coincidentally, over eighty-seven percent of illnesses tend to be psychosomatic, that is, self-induced.[39] And as much as eighty percent of this experienced pain is the result of our resistance to the 20 percent of real pain.

Pain is an inescapable and unavoidable theme in every person's journey in life. The journey traveled is a difficult one, in a mysterious, spiritual and paradoxical way. It is often filled with fatigue, boredom, depression, despair, apathy, and suicidal ideations. Ernest Hemingway states, "The world breaks every one and afterward many are strong at the broken places."[30] There are no favorites; the very young and the very old are equally affected. A broken bone, once mended, becomes the strongest part of a bone, but its mending is not a 12-Step program.

Brokenness is also an undeniable fact of life. Viktor Frankl tells that when he was brought to Auschwitz, he was taken to the showers after being selected to live. His manuscript of all of his scientific work, his life's work, was taken from him and thrown onto a fire. At that moment he felt that his personality was being erased…totally disintegrating and smashed to bits. This sensation redoubled when he left the showers, having had his hair shaved and being deloused. Everyone appeared shaven, naked and broken, as though they had undergone a total metamorphosis of personality; utterly robbed of everything except of his tragic humanness.

After receiving his clothes – and the Germans made sure that short, thin people received long, wide clothes and that tall, broad people received short, narrow clothes as part of the attempt to grind down the personality and turn the individual into a ridiculous automaton – Frankl put his hand in the pocket of his jacket and found a piece of paper. It was a legacy from the former owner of the garment, who had been separated from his clothes before separating from the world in the gas chambers. This piece of paper was the page of a Jewish prayer book which bore the verse, "Here O Israel the Lord our God the Lord is One." In that second, his perception of his personality came back to him.

By Viktor Frankl's definition despair is caused by suffering in which the sufferer sees no meaning. "Suffering in itself has no meaning." Fabry furthermore states that "we can assume meaningful attitudes towards (painful) events that in themselves are meaningless." These events can come without warning, as in the case of Frankl's tragic triad of death, guilt and suffering.

Aaron Kipnis states that when a child's world lacks secure and insightful parents, it becomes a dangerous world filled with losses, disappointments, unrealized dreams, loss of confidence, lowered self-esteem, depression and anger resulting from the wounds of rejection, neglect, and abuse. In the actual or emotional absence of parents, especially fathers, young children learn to numb their pain, withdrawing into an imaginary world of a calloused mind, or resorting to magic pills, powders or potions. Negative-attention-seeking behavior increases despite ever-increasing hostile punishment. Their minds and bodies become more callused to the physical and mental pain. They become cold and distant, as if meaning had been sucked out of them. They become more depressed and unable to respond to emotional and physical stimuli. Unresolved childhood pain becomes a formidable force with the power to capture and hold children's fullest attention well into middle adulthood.[35]

Extreme challenges to the human spirit are hardly limited to concentration camps. The examples of genocide from Rwanda to Bosnia, the suffocating poverty in Bangladesh, the self destructive alcohol and drug culture found in every corner of the world, the intense suffering of incapacitating diseases and terminal illnesses, compel us to confront the fact that there is no escape from troubles which can overwhelm our defenses. Not only in the extremes but in the surfeit of ease can come a crisis of meaning.

Frankl warns that many "people have enough to live by but nothing to live for." He identifies all these troubles as the tragic triad and asks, "How is it possible to say yes to life in spite of all that?" Responding from the depths of personal experience with unimaginable horror, Frankl suggests "optimism in the face of tragedy and in view of the human potential which, at its best, *always* allows for: turning suffering into a human achievement and accomplishment; deriving from guilt the opportunity to change oneself for the better; and deriving from life's transitoriness an incentive to take responsible action." Being open to the spiritual value of death, guilt and suffering does not mean that individuals will realize the meaning immediately, be it as simple as falling off a bicycle, or as complex as a relationship that ends tragically, or haunting war memories, a prison sentence or a diseased body and mind.

Meaning, Frankl emphasizes, is unique for each individual and varies from moment to moment and from experience to experience, never to be repeated. Meaning appears to us unexpectedly as an "aha" experience, providing clues of "what can be done about a given situation... discovering a purpose or intention in a given moment in time." Frankl suggests three avenues to actualizing meaning potential: creating a work or doing a deed; experiencing something or encountering someone; and facing and growing beyond the self.

The first two sources of meaning are active: creating, doing, experiencing, and encountering. The first might be called meaning through work. The second might be called meaning through relationship or love. The third source of meaning is active but in a paralyzing situation of tragedy, pain and suffering. Frankl explains the third in these words: "Even the helpless victim of a hopeless situation, facing a fate he cannot change, may rise above himself, and may grow beyond himself and by so doing change himself."

Americans spend tens of billions of dollars annually suppressing and denying pain, both real and self-inflicted. They live in a culture that has a remarkable ability to shut down pain in their lives. People in North America, comprising only five percent of the world population consume over 60 percent of the illegal drugs and over 50% of all manufactured drugs, one-third of which work on the central nervous system, and over 30,000 tons of aspirin annually.

When an individual has a headache what does he take for it? He takes aspirin, a magic pill that causes the stomach to bleed two teaspoons of blood. He may switch to Tylenol, informed that it does not make the stomach bleed, but not knowing that, when taken with alcohol or having alcohol in your system causes chemical reaction that slowly destroys the liver. Likewise, Tylenol should never be taken by hepatitis-infected individuals.

We are the most advanced society in the world in terms of suppressing pain. Yet the more we try to shut down pain, the more pain strikes back. When we refuse to listen to the pain in our body, we invariably begin to destroy the wisdom of its healing powers within. Consider the number of famous baseball, football, basketball and hockey stars who continue to damage themselves for life by going out on the playing field, still injured, with the help of painkiller injections.
Pain, the Gift Nobody Wants

Unavoidable pain is the gift that nobody wants! Dr. Paul Brand uses his knowledge of leprosy (a disease that causes a person to go numb and lose all sensitivity to pain) to point out the need for pain.

Leprosy is a terrible disease, but more terrible than that is what happens when lepers stop feeling pain. Rats eat fingers off while lepers are sleeping; hands burn against oil lamps without them noticing, leading to third degree burns; and bones break just because they are tightening a loose bolt on a car engine. Dr. Brand says that human beings need only fear the lack of pain, not pain itself. Pain lets them know they are alive, and that they are wonderfully well-protected through a natural mechanism created by God.[39]

Pain is a signal that something is wrong in our life system. It is an unpleasant sensation that may be associated with physical injuries, illnesses, or feelings and emotions. It is the wisdom of the body that signals a decayed tooth, a cut finger, an upset stomach, a tumor disrupting the functioning of an internal organ, or a break-down in the body.

Pain may be an annoyance that produces painful tension in the neck. It may be a signal of too much guilt, conflict or threat. It may be a dreaded necessity to make a decision, a feeling of emptiness and futility to the daily routines. It may be a fear of the aging affects on the body and mind, or the death of a loved one or oneself, or intolerable loneliness.

Pain is the voice of the inner life force, the wisdom of the body and mind, crying out for attention for remedy, for artificial cogitation (the intellectual equivalent of artificial respiration). On the other hand, pain suppressors are life suppressors and tranquilizers are signal deniers. Much of experienced pain is self-induced through negative self-talk or life style.

Pain: the Gift Nobody Wants by Dr. Paul Brand describes research on the pain-nullifying effects of leprosy. Paul Brand is a world-famous leprosy surgeon, who has spent most of his life caring for the forsaken lepers in India. He has performed countless medical miracles, enabling people with leprosy (Hansen's disease) to live healthy and productive lives.[39]

One of Brand's greatest breakthroughs is the discovery that people with leprosy do not have 'bad flesh' that just rots away for no apparent reason. In fact, their flesh is just as healthy as other individuals. They are usually not even contagious. What they lack is the ability to feel pain. As the blood flow is cut off from key parts of their body, their nerve endings die. With the death of their nerve endings comes the death of their ability to sense danger to their bodies. Leprous people live a virtually pain-free existence. Many individuals would do anything to live a pain-free life. Yet in fact, the absence of pain is the greatest enemy of the leper. Again and again they wound and impale themselves. Yet they don't feel a thing.

Brand speaks about a four-year-old female patient, Tanya with dark, flashing eyes, curly hair, and an impish smile. She seems fine as an infant. But when she is 18 months old, her mother observes her daughter finger-painting red pictures on the floor of her playpen. Suddenly her mother realizes that her daughter has bitten off the tip of her finger and, in the process of attempting to wipe her finger clean, notices that she could 'paint' with her own blood. Because of her leprosy, the infant feels no pain even when she damages herself.

Individuals normally blink because of the pain caused by impurities accumulating on the surface of the eyes. Blinking acts to wash away impurities. Brand discovered that leprous people go blind because they feel no pain that comes from microscopic impurities building up on the cornea, and thus do not blink. The absence of pain actually makes them go blind. Brand solves this blinking problem of lepers by surgically attaching the chewing muscle to their eyelid. Every time a leper chews gum or food, his eyelids blink, thus preserving his eyesight.

One of the greatest mysteries that Brand faced was why leprous people kept mysteriously losing their fingers and toes. He was certain that the fingers and toes didn't just shrivel up and fall off. But no one could ever find what happened. Finally Brand decided to have people stay awake all night watching the leprosy patients sleep. To their surprise, they discovered that rats were coming in at night and nibbling off the fingers and toes of leper patients. Because the patients felt no pain, they never woke up and brushed away the rats. To save their extremities, leprosy patients are now required to take cats to bed with them, wherever they plan to sleep.

Baby Ashlyn never cries, even with severe diaper rash or a massive corneal abrasion. Ashlyn suffers from a condition called Congenital Insensitivity to Pain with Anhidrosis, or CIPA. Incurable, untreatable and so rare that only three dozen cases are known in

America, CIPA makes Ashlyn completely unable to sense pain or extreme temperatures, and thus utterly vulnerable to a wide range of injuries and infections.

Ashlyn slams into walls and shrugs at the blood on her face. As a toddler, absent-mindedly she bites her skin just for fun. At five, she burns her hand by leaving it on the muffler of a gas-powered motor, has her fingers crushed in a door frame and, on one terrible occasion, walks into her home and announces she can not get the dirt off her skin. The dirt turns out to be hundreds of fire ants biting her. She has badly bitten her tongue, cheek and lips, and begins knocking out her front teeth by crashing into walls or biting down on a bottle. Later, she begins to comprehend that she is different from her friends. CIPA is a genetic mutation shared by both her parents. It results when a particular type of nerve cell fails to develop normally. Not only does the absence of pain make her brain slow to respond to injuries, it can take twice as long as normal to heal. Damage to the joints is typical.

Gradually, Ashley begins to comprehend that she is different from her friends. CIPA caused by a genetic mutation shared by both her parents, results when a particular type of nerve cell fails to develop normally. The absence of pain makes her brain slow to respond to injuries, which can take twice as long as normal to heal. Damage to the joints is typical, since people with CIPA unknowingly put weight on injured ankles and knees. Professional sports player suffer the same damage, artificially pain-numbing injections.

Pain of Childhood Abuse

Childhood pain is generally never openly talked about in families due to feelings of guilt and shame. Being a molest victim does not fit in with the stereotype of masculinity. Victimization implies powerlessness, helplessness, and lack of control, which flies in the face of society's demand that males maintain personal, physical and sexual power at all times, even during childhood. Boys who are sexually abused by women think that they are not men enough as adults. Societal expectations of manhood and maleness create a critical snag in the boy's perception of events. It is common to think, "Even if I didn't cause it, I should have prevented it. I'm a male; I'm supposed to deal with things; to always be in control." Another reason sexual abuse is not always called abuse is due to a simple anatomical reality: To have sex a man must have an erection. A boy sees his own body responding. It is right before his eyes and he feels his body has betrayed him. More difficult to deal with still, he may ejaculate. None of that means that a boy or girl 'wanted it.' Willingness or compliance is often confused with 'willing victim.' There is no such thing as a willing victim.

Ward is a 12-year-old boy visiting his incarcerated father. He is one of two sons who were taught all the criminal vices of their father. Looking at the granite walls of the 150-year-old prison, Ward casually states, "This is a great place, Dad. I can't wait to come here one day and share a cell with you!" His 17-year-old son sits in court, being tried for murder. The odds of a child of a recidivist father to enter the judicial system are as high as 92 to one. It is not unusual for several generations of sons to be jailed or incarcerated, and being angry for their father's criminal choices.

The physical and emotional absence of fathers appears to be the engine driving social breakdown, social pathology and social costs. Nearly three million children have a parent in state or federal prison. Nationally, one in three kids live in a fatherless home, a much larger percentage in African-American homes. More than four in 10 kids live in homes without their biological father. As the incidence of father-absence grows, community disintegration and crime, especially youth crime, continue to grow.

Absent fathers are linked to grim statistics: two of every three youth suicides, nine out of every 10 homeless and runaway youths, more than eight of every 10 children who exhibit behavioral disorders, seven out of every 10 high school high school dropouts, youths in state institutions, and adolescent patients in substance abuse centers. The Child Welfare League of America reports that children who have been abused and neglected are 67 times more likely than other children to be arrested between ages nine and 12. And these children typically are found in fatherless homes. It's no wonder that children living under these circumstances look outside the home for answers to their existential vacuum.

A child's evolving addictions and violence become not just diversions of choice, but as pseudo-lifeboats necessary for his or her very survival. They provide something in which the victim can believe in order to live and survive. They provided predictable relief and power in an unpredictable and painful world that was often difficult and seemingly unfair, especially when it involves physical punishment in the home of school. It is highly unlikely that any incarcerated individual has never experienced childhood trauma in the form of physical, sexual or long-term emotional abuse.

Jimmy's grandfather, Bill was horse whipped daily up to the age of fourteen when he ran away from home, never to return. Bill passed on that legacy to his son, the father of Jimmy. Most physically abused children do survive and wear their survival as a badge of courage justifying its use in each successive generation. Several countries have passed laws forbidding the physical punishment of children in the home, school or public. Only thirty states in America have passed laws to end corporal punishment of children in schools. In all probability, the United States will be among the last countries to pass such legislation, replacing abuse in all forms with kinder, gentler forms of discipline.
Reflection

On the last day of 1917, Matisse's friend George Besson took him to visit Pierre-Auguste Renoir at a home in nearby Cagnes-sur-Mer. Although Renoir had suffered from crippling arthritis for many years, he still painted every day except Sunday. Matisse admired the old painter's fortitude and unshakable dedication to his art. Matisse brought some of his recent paintings for the master's critique on a second visit in January 1918. They became good friends and Matisse returned twice again later in the year. He called on Renoir frequently during early 1919 when the old painter lay ailing and near death. Matisse would never forget Renoir's words: "The pain passes, Matisse, but the beauty remains" (quoted in H. Spurling, *Matisse the Master: A Life of Henri Matisse, Volume Two*, New York, 2005, p. 217). Matisse also suffered from chronic pain. His art was in part a response to the pain he experienced in much of his life.

Meaning Can Come Unexpectedly at the Broken Places;
Do the Unexpected:

- *Paint a canvas, regardless of your skill, with acrylics, oils, pastels, watercolors, crayons or colored pencils. Remember, practice makes for improvement.* For many artists, 1,000 paintings would probably represent a body of work spanning a lifetime. But for Los Angeles artist Robert Thome, that milestone took only 20 years to achieve, and that feat is made all the more impressive considering that Thome paints by using a brush held in his mouth. Thome, a quadriplegic since age 15, suffered a spinal cord injury that paralyzed him from the neck down in a football accident. The accident broke his neck; it did not break him. He taught himself how to paint with a brush held in his mouth and now creates 50 paintings every year. He has also participated in more than 200 exhibitions. "I just feel this is the best way to express myself," he says. "It seemed natural to paint with my mouth, because I just had to paint. I knew I would find a way to do it."

- *Look for and compliment the good in others.* Take 'The 40-Day Love Dare' by Stephen Kendrick & Alex Kendrick. This forty day journey cannot be taken lightly. It is a challenging and often difficult process, but an incredibly fulfilling one. To take this dare requires a resolute mind and a steadfast determination. It is not meant to be sampled or briefly tested, and those who quit early because of relationship strife will forfeit the greatest benefits. If you will commit to a day at a time for 40 days, the results can change your life, friendships and marriage. Consider it a dare, from others who have done it before you.

- *Celebrate and embrace the unexpected.* These give you an opportunity to grow and become strong at the broken places. Liz Murray's life is an example; going from *Homeless to Harvard* - see her life story on DVD; also discussed in Chapter X. Make a list of unusual events, circumstances and experiences for which you discover unexpected gifts.

- *Aim for goals that others believe is unattainable for you.* Nobody rises to low expectations. What was is not what can be. "There is no try; you either do or do not" (Yoda in *Star Wars*). Johann Goethe states that "if you treat a man as he is, he only becomes worse. But if you treat a man as he can be and ought to be, he will become that which he can and ought to be." The same principle applies to how an individual treats himself. Viktor Frankl emphasizes what exists in all human beings, but in particular, in a young person's "will to meaning" that, if not recognized, contributes to making him worse, contributes to his frustration. Presupposing a spark of the search for meaning in the young person, in spite of being driven by the will to pleasure, power or prosperity tends to aid him in becoming what he in principle is capable of becoming. Make a list of goals that others believe is unattainable. Then, take steps to achieve them – one small step at a time; one day at a time.

- *Just do it.* Failing is about taking risks and learning from them. We fail again and again. That is how we learn and discover truths. A naysayer would have you believe that uncharted fields are filled with landmines. Something scarcer and rarer than ability is the recognition and pursuit of it to the fullest. The ultimate responsibility rests entirely in your hands. Achievement of goals begins with taking an initial step. Sometimes, an individual must be creative in his pursuit. For example, there is the story of a child who arrives late to school one morning. His teacher asks for his excuse. The child says that due to ice-covered sidewalks, every step forward resulted in two back-sliding steps. His teacher, disbelieving the response, asks how the child arrived at school when every step forward resulted in two steps backward. The child simply says that he changed directions, noting that for every step toward home resulted in two steps closer to school!

- *Give thanks in all things, not just for the good.* All that human beings experience helps them to grow in strength, character and wisdom one unique experience and encounter at a time. It takes no character to give thanks for pleasure, power and prosperity. The *real heroes* are those who have been traumatized, broken and survived. The *real heroes* are those who give of their life without others knowing that they have done so. You play the cards that you are given. It takes no skill to play a winning hand. It takes great skill to play a losing hand. Every human being has been broken, is being broken or will be broken. How can that brokenness become strength?

- *Laugh often every day, and if need be, for no reason whatsoever!* A good book, movie, family, friends and pets provide endless hours of joy and laughter. Kindergartners do it very well, but preadolescent girls surpass them. Children do it about 400 times daily. Adults, for the most part, do not do it very often or very well. Laughter is a total body experience, influencing our circulation, muscles, breathing, and your endocrine and immune systems. But it is the effect on the endocrine (hormonal) and the immune (disease fighting) systems that may be the most surprising findings from laughter research. Following happy and joyous laughter while watching a baby or puppy there is a change in the cellular and chemical aspects of your immune system, with an increased circulation of antibodies and increased vigor of certain white blood cells that fight off invaders like bacteria. In fact, studies show that the increase in disease-fighting cells lasts for up to 36 hours after you have regained your composure. Laughter also influences your ability to feel pain. It reduces stress, enhances creativity and helps solve problems. A sense of humor is the ability to look at things from a different perspective. It means taking your problem and, paradoxically, imagining how much worse it could possibly be. The goal is to shift to a bigger perspective, which reduces tension. When you laugh, you loosen up and are able to listen better.

- *Make a list of positive events, circumstances and experiences that followed a traumatic Steppingstone you listed at the end of Chapter II.* Steppingstones are essentially markings which enable you to retrace the pathways of your experiences. Each includes a composite of events and experiences which took place before and after the markings themselves occurred, and which comprise a full unit of life in which many varied experiences are contained. Each evokes to memory the totality of a Steppingstone Period.

IV.
For Sale – Combat Boots – Worn Once

In war, there are no unwounded soldiers.   - José Narosky

Jimmy suddenly comes under a vicious fire-fight in a combat zone. He watches not only his closest friend die in front of him but every member of his platoon, men who shared their hardships, dreams, and family letters and pictures from home. Jimmy is hit by several bullets that seem to be coming from all directions. It reminds him of being in the middle of a swarm of killer bees; the attack is vicious, continuous, and comes from all directions. One bullet shatters his femur; another glances off his forehead and he slips into unconsciousness. He is hit twice more as he lies there unconscious on the battlefield with blood covering his face. The Viet Cong weave through the bodies, insuring that each is dead. Jimmy is left for dead and wakes the next day in a battlefield triage unit.

The memory of that event stays with Jimmy, troubling him for the rest of his life. Post-traumatic Stress Disorder (PTSD), once known as a psychological disorder associated only with veterans of wars, is now being considered in relation to many trauma-inducing experiences such as genocide and the Holocaust, rape, abuse, disasters, accidents, and torture. The result has been a literal explosion of information on this psychological disorder both in scientific and popular literature. Thousands of journal articles have been written on PTSD spawning several specialty journals such as ***The Journal of Traumatic Stress and PTSD Research Quarterly***. In addition, many books have been published on PTSD, particularly in the last four decades.

History of PTSD

Post Traumatic Stress Disorder (PTSD) is a natural emotional reaction to a deeply shocking and disturbing experience. It is a ***normal*** reaction to an *abnormal* situation. In the first edition of the ***Diagnostic and Statistical Manual***, published in 1952, stress response syndrome - "shell shock," "war neurosis," "traumatic neurosis," "combat trauma," or "combat fatigue" - was listed under the heading of "gross stress reactions." In the 1968 second edition trauma-related disorders were conceptualized as just one example of situational disorders.

Finally, at the persistence of forensic psychiatrists, ***DSM-III***, published in 1980, listed PTSD as a subcategory of anxiety disorders. In the most current edition of ***DSM-IV***, published in 1994, the Advisory Subcommittee on PTSD was unanimous in classifying PTSD as a new stress response category. PTSD has achieved increasing respect in the psychiatric community and continues to evolve in terms of it's classification in the ***DSM***.

There are those who argue that the origins of PTSD can be found in the hysteria research conducted by Sigmund Freud and Pierre Janet in the late 1800's. Reaching back to studies done on railroad accident survivors of the 1700's, Trimble explored the biological components which produce PTSD symptoms.[5]

Vietnam War Veterans

More has been written about PTSD with reference to war veterans than any other group. The psychological problems experienced by veterans of the Vietnam War provided a key catalyst for the inclusion of PTSD in the nomenclature of the DSM-III. Most of the theory and research for PTSD has been done on combat veterans, particularly veterans of the Vietnam War. As a result, many important and influential works have been written on the severe impact PTSD has had on Vietnam veterans who experienced severe psychological conflicts and guilt feelings, including substance abuse, insomnia, emotional numbing, and a sense of purposelessness and existential vacuum.

In Vietnam the dead bodies of soldiers were quickly whisked away from the combat field and almost immediately sent back to the states, leaving their comrades little opportunity to mourn the dead or engage in any meaningful death ritual, explaining why Vietnam veterans have had so much difficulty with their war experience. Additional hardships were experienced as a result of being condemned for serving while war resisters were condemned for their lack of participation - labeled anti-American and cowardly.

Genocide & the Holocaust

Millions die every year of tuberculosis, malaria and diarrhea. Countless others die of natural and manmade disasters. But tens and hundreds of thousands of others die as a result of genocide, millions as a result of holocaust, targeted because of their skin color, or ethnicity, or religion, raped, brutalized and slaughtered. We are familiar with the events and places – the rape of Nanking; the Holocaust in Auschwitz, Dachau, Belsen, and Treblinka; Algeria; Darfur; Rwanda; Nigeria; and Somalia. The victims may suffer a lifetime of PTSD.

Those responsible for committing genocide go around burning fields of staples and villages. Family members carry off their wounded to temporary safe shelter. Women are raped in front of their husbands and children, followed by the massacre of the family members in front of the brutalized women before they too are finally mutilated. Children are thrown in the wells to poison the water. Hungry dogs carry off arms, legs and other human body parts following machete attacks and decomposition. The only fellow human beings who feel a sense of mission are the survivors of genocide.

Genocide survivors seek safety in camps sponsored by the United Nations, but are profoundly demoralized because they feel that they are in one big prison. Security exists only to the perimeter of the camp enclosure. U.N. soldiers never accompany villagers to gather firewood or water to earn extra income for fear of being killed themselves by the perpetrators of genocide. The moment an individual leaves a camp, he is vulnerable to being shot if a man, raped and beaten up if a woman, kidnapped if a child and forced into drugs, war, violence and killing as a child soldier. Gunshots just outside the camp are a constant reminder of the threat hovering over the whole camp that is encouraged by whatever government is in power. It is clear to the survivors of genocide that the authorities control the situation, and if they simply apply the same rules to the perpetrators of genocide that they apply to the survivors, the genocide would be over quickly.

Rape of women is a calculated effort by perpetrators of genocide to get rid of long-term tensions between two groups of people, culminating with the rise of a rebellion and an insurgency in the area. The aggressors decide that the easiest way of getting rid of a selected population is to de-populate large areas by any dehumanizing means. Based on past responses to aggression resulting in genocide, the aggressors know that there will be a certain number of objections from other nations. But based on the fact that the aggression is a remote area, it will take other concerned governments a while to notice, and their objections probably will not be too pronounced.

The aggressors believe this is the best way to go about eliminating a selected population. From their same point of view, one of the most effective ways is rape. The aggressors reason if they kill people, then bodies will turn up, infuriating the international community. On the other hand, when perpetrators of genocide go around raping women, then the victims usually keep silent because of the stigma. Everybody else in the community knows what has happened. Consequently, it terrorizes people, driving them away, not wishing to expose their women to rape or their children to being traumatized, kidnapped or murdered.

So, rape of the weak is a very evil and traumatizing weapon used to terrorize people and drive them out of contested areas. Rape in armed conflict always constitutes torture. It is cruel, inhuman and degrading treatment of the weakest among us. The international community calls it genocide, but next to nothing is done. There is never any great solution and invariably, because there is no perfect solution, and there is no maximal solution, so the international community ends up doing nothing at all except to pay lip service.

Disaster Victims

Many disaster victims also experience symptoms associated with PTSD. Disasters such as earthquakes, avalanches, airplane crashes, and toxic chemical spills, and the general nature of traumatic response to these disasters can generally be buffered by talking the survivor through the incident. Therapists can clarify what actually happened to the survivor and educate him about normal psychological reactions to such events. These can provide effective protection against full-blown PTSD, as well as the provision of social support for primary victims and early intervention to help survivors express emotions about disasters.

Childhood PTSD

War veterans are not the only ones to suffer from PTSD. Parents who have lost a child in war often visualize that day's events frozen in time, played over and over in their mind. So too does the sole survivor of a traumatic accident or wartime firestorm that decimates an entire platoon. In the absence of an advocate – a wise elder, a teacher, or some other positive mentor – many children resort to drugging, diverting or burying their childhood pain – victims of extreme abject abuse of a physical, sexual or verbal nature, or neglect by caregivers. Over the last 15 years, over two million children have been killed in conflict. Over one million have been orphaned, over six million have been seriously injured or permanently disabled and over ten million have been left with serious psychological trauma in the form of childhood PTSD.

War affects every aspect of a child's development. Children affected by armed conflict can be injured or killed, uprooted from their homes and communities, internally displaced or refugees, orphaned or separated from their parents and families, subjected to sexual abuse and exploitation, victims of trauma as a result of being exposed to violence, deprived of education and recreation, at risk of becoming child soldiers. Children living in conflict areas are routinely deprived of basic needs such as shelter, food and medical attention. In addition, relief for children tends to be the last priority in war, resulting in insufficient or no protection for them. Besides, children are, due to their physical constitution and growth, most vulnerable to being deprived of food, medical assistance and education, which has a severe and lasting impact on their development.

The traumatic scars left on children in war-torn countries are just one of a vast aftermath of post war problems: refugees, food shortages and mourning for lost relatives. Former child soldiers may at best have their needs forgotten and at worst be blamed by their communities for what happened.

Children from poor and disadvantaged families who are seeking physical support, revenge for their losses or the sense of belonging are particularly vulnerable to exploitation during war. Other children are kidnapped and forced to become fighters. Children are deliberately targeted as they are manipulated more easily than adults and can be indoctrinated to perform crimes and atrocities without asking questions.

Virtually every incarcerated man, woman and youth has experienced some form of childhood trauma – mourning the death of a loved one; witnessing a horrific event; growing up in the home of a physically or emotionally absent father; or experiencing physical, emotional or sexual abuse or neglect during childhood. Tragically, childhood sexual abuse is the predominant form of abuse experienced by incarcerated women, exacerbated by spousal abuse in adulthood.

A few weeks before release from prison, Joe asked to talk to Jimmy in private. "Doc" asked Joe, "my mother began sexually molesting me when I was four years old. Was it my fault?" Up to that moment, there had never been a wise mentor, a minister or therapist to intervene on his behalf and provide him the tools that would enable him to discover his meaning potential. During his quest for a spiritual healing of his wounds he discovers that alcohol and drugs readily numb the pain, guilt and shame, albeit temporarily. They cover the traumatic experience like a Band-Aid.

When drugging with a magic pill, powder or potion fail to numb, when diverting fail to work, Joe resorts to burying his pain with expensive "wants" and to surrounding himself with peers of similar abusive pasts temporarily anesthetized by wants. But the pain signals from guilt and shame only grow stronger than his ability to self-medicate. So Joe continues to compulsively increase his abuse of alcohol and drugs until the behavior results in repeated stays in jail, followed by incarceration in a youth facility and prison. Nothing appears to provide him long-term relief. He suffers an "existential frustration" or "vacuum," a failure to embrace values that lead to the discovery of the "meaning" of these tragic chapters.

A child may have a parent participating in a wartime conflict and be concerned for his or her parent's safety. The child may experience increased irritability, fearfulness, sadness, anger, agitation, insomnia, poor academic record, clinging behaviors at home, not wanting to go to school, and complain about physical problems. He/she may suffer from PTSD following the death of that parent on the warfront. Everyday news from the warfront or news that a parent died in combat only exacerbates the problems.

The surviving parent or guardian needs to respond to the child's concerns. Parents can teach their children good listening and communication skills, respect and support for differing opinions. They can teach ways for their children to manage fears and anxieties by taking the time to listen, observe, and talk to them about what is happening around them.

Children want to be included in family matters, including when a parent must go to war, and they want to be listened to and understood. Parents can talk about war, using language that is understandable, does not hide the truth, and is consistent with values they want their children to learn. Ultimately, children must be protected from unnecessary worries and concerns and provided with a sense of security and safety. Parents can serve as an active buffer against undue anxiety and distress for the child, encouraging him to freely express his concerns and feelings.

Children are not free of trauma. Contrary to what we now know, they have often been presumed to handle stressors much the same way as their adult counterparts. Single traumatic events are rarely forgotten, while prolonged childhood trauma is often repressed and dissociated. The younger a child is at the time of the trauma, the more likely he or she is to develop PTSD.

There are a number of traumatic events that have been shown to cause PTSD in children and adolescents. Studies document PTSD in child and adolescent survivors of: natural and man made disasters such as floods; violent crimes such as kidnapping, rape or murder of a parent, sniper fire, and school shootings; motor vehicle accidents such as automobile and plane crashes; severe burns; exposure to community violence; war; peer suicide; and sexual & physical abuse.

There are three factors that have been shown to increase the likelihood that children will develop PTSD: the severity of the traumatic event, the parental involvement in or reaction to the traumatic event, and the temporal proximity to the traumatic event. In general, most studies find a strong relationship between children's reports of trauma severity and PTSD. As would be expected, children and adolescents who report having experienced the most severe traumas also report the highest levels of PTSD symptoms. Family support and parental coping has also been shown to effect PTSD symptoms in children. Studies show that children and adolescents with greater family support and less parental distress have lower levels of PTSD symptoms. Finally, children and adolescents who are farther away from the traumatic event report less distress.

Treatment of PTSD in Children & Adolescents

Although some children show a natural remission in PTSD symptoms over a period of a few months, there are a significant number of children for whom PTSD persists for years if untreated. Few treatment studies have been done examining which treatments are most effective for children and adolescents. A review of the adult treatment studies of PTSD shows that cognitive behavioral treatment (CBT) is the most effective approach. CBT for children generally includes: exposure (child directly discusses the traumatic event), anxiety management techniques such as relaxation and assertiveness training and correction of inaccurate or distorted trauma related thoughts.

There is some controversy regarding exposing children to the events that scare them. Nevertheless, exposure based treatments seem to be most relevant when the child is distressed by trauma-related memories or reminders. Exposure can be done gradually and can be paired with relaxation such that children can learn to relax while recalling their experiences. Through this procedure, they learn that they do not have to be scared of their memories. CBT also involves challenging children's false beliefs such as the belief that "the world is totally unsafe." The majority of studies that have been conducted using CBT for children with PTSD have found that it is safe and effective.

CBT is often accompanied by psycho-education (i.e., education about PTSD symptoms and its effects) and parental involvement. Psycho-education is the process of learning about the symptoms of

PTSD. It is equally important for parents and caregivers to understand the effects of PTSD. In addition, research shows that the better parents cope with the trauma and the more they support their children, the better their children will function. Therefore, at times it is important for parents to seek treatment to develop the necessary coping skills to support their children.

Several other types of therapy have been suggested for the treatment of PTSD in children and adolescents. Play therapy can be used to treat young children with PTSD who are not able to deal with the trauma more directly. The therapist uses games, drawings, and other techniques to help the child process their traumatic memories.

"Psychological first aid" has been described for children exposed to community violence and can be used in school as well as traditional settings and involves: clarifying trauma related facts, normalizing the children's PTSD reactions, encouraging the expression of feelings, teaching problem solving skills, and referring the most symptomatic children for additional treatment.

Eye movement desensitization and reprocessing (EMDR) has been used which combines cognitive therapy with directed eye movements. While EMDR has been shown to be effective in treating some adults with PTSD, studies indicate that it is the cognitive intervention rather than the eye movements that accounts for the change. Medications have also been used with some children with PTSD. However, due to the lack of research in this area it is too early to evaluate its effectiveness.

Finally, specialized interventions may be necessary for children exhibiting particularly problematic behaviors or PTSD symptoms. For example, a specialized intervention might be required for inappropriate sexual behavior or extreme behavior problems.

Combat-Related Post-Traumatic Stress Disorder (PTSD)

Joey is serving his second tour of duty in Vietnam. It is the beginning of the hot, rainy season. He and his squadron are on a mission north of Da Nang when they come upon a village seemingly abandoned. A village dog is barking, perhaps warning the Vietcong of their presence.

Suddenly, a small child cries out from within one of the hutches. One of the soldiers enters the hutch and sees a baby lying on the floor, swaddled in a blanket in a reed basket. The soldier reaches down to pick up the baby. At that same instant, Joey yells out for the soldier to stop, but it is too late. There is an explosion. Joey is thrown back from the impact of the blast. Blood and body parts were strewn everywhere. Forty years later Joey can still hear the baby's cry; he can still see and smell that moment; the smell of the baby; the smell of death.

Upon returning from the war front things usually go bad when one or more of three major stress factors erupt: relationships, finances and legal problems, usually in that order. PTSD is an anxiety disorder that can develop after exposure to a terrifying event or ordeal in which grave physical harm occurred, was threatened or was observed. Traumatic events that may trigger the disorder include violent personal assaults, natural or human-caused disasters, accidents or military combat on the war front.

PTSD was not officially named until 1980, but the first documented case was reported nearly 4,000 years ago in Egypt by a physician who noted a victim's "hysterical" reaction to a traumatic event. After the American Civil War it was called "soldier's heart." After World War I it was "shell shock." In World War II it was known as "battle fatigue."

By whatever name, the symptoms are the same: nervousness, anxiety, depression and insomnia. Similar symptoms plague survivors of terrorist attacks, rape and childhood abuse as well as war front and emergency room nurses and physicians; even social workers who are exposed to traumatic stories from clients.

Combat-related PTSD is often highly debilitating and affects nearly all areas of psychosocial functioning. Veterans with PTSD who returned from Vietnam, the Gulf War, Iraq and Afghanistan Wars re-experience their war-time traumas in the form of haunting intrusive memories, nightmares and flashbacks, and have chronic difficulty modulating arousal. PTSD veterans do their best to avoid those memories, but still fall victim to debilitating nightmares and other unwanted trauma-memory intrusions, and concurrent intense body fear arousal. They may experience numbness, anger, and jump when somebody slams the door. They appear hyper-vigilant, scanning or looking around always, as if somebody is behind their back following them. For some, the stress simply grows too great.

Compared to the past, a larger percentage of returning soldiers are physically or emotionally wounded. That's because vast improvements in body armor and battlefield medical care are saving the lives of thousands of American soldiers who would have died in previous wars. The negative consequences are that they are coming home with the memory of it all, often resulting in skyrocketing rates of divorce, homelessness and suicide. Many have lost arms, legs, fingers, toes, sight and bodily functions. Some will need tubes and machines to keep them alive. Hundreds and thousands are disfigured by burns and mangled minds. They will show the psychological scars of these wars for years. They are America's war wounded, a toll that has received less attention than those killed in the wars or in the attack on the Twin Towers.

Time usually heals wounds, but PTSD wounds may not heal over time without intervention. Trauma memories may remain fresh years after the fact. Decades after they served in Vietnam, thousands of veterans suffer the trauma-linked PTSD symptoms. Nearly two million men and women served in Iraq, Afghanistan and the Horn of Africa Theater. The Department of Veterans Affairs says at least one in five returnees suffer some PTSD symptoms. Mental health experts estimate it could be as high as one in three.

As a way to cope with these symptoms, many survivors live isolated and avoidant lives, avoiding visual, auditory or kinesthetic experiences that trigger wartime memories. Many others self-medicate with alcohol and substances of abuse, and numb themselves to emotional experiences and relationships with family and friends. Many end up in psychiatric wards, substance abuse clinics, jail and prison, and divorce and bankruptcy court. Others choose to live among the homeless on city streets or along rivers and streams in mountainous regions.

Many combat veterans self-report survivor guilt, having survived a fire-storm battle. Others report depression, anger or behavioral outbursts at home, in school or on the job, destroying or throwing objects, aggressive towards self or others, and threatening to kill oneself. Those veterans with the highest risk for suicide are veterans who are white, college-educated and living alone in a rural area, most often in a Southern or Western state. Veterans were half again more likely than non-vets to kill themselves with guns - Non-veterans generally commit suicide by drug or alcohol overdose, or suicide by cop, or drive while intoxicated. Some veterans express an altered world view in which they view their fate as uncontrollable and their life as devoid of meaning.

Chronic PTSD is difficult to treat, particularly for veterans whose daily activities are limited by physical or mental impairments. Numerous therapeutic approaches have been tried in this population – exposure therapy, cognitive processing therapy, hypnotherapy, beta-blockers, virtual reality therapy, and neurofeedback. However, even when their symptoms respond to treatment, many are left tormented and hopeless with existential questions related to the loss of meaning in life.

PTSD and Peniston-Kulkosky Protocol

For more than twenty years neurofeedback has proven to greatly relieve the effects of PTSD and the endless cycle of addiction by increasing healthy brain function.[52] Thirty years ago EEG feedback was of major significance in the field of biofeedback. In 1989 Dr. Eugene Peniston[53] focused on a population of alcoholics, all of whom had been difficult alcoholics for more than twenty years and had been in rehabilitation unsuccessfully several times. Using his protocol of alpha-theta brain wave training combined with imagery of desired outcome, Peniston was able to show reduction to elimination of craving for alcohol. The original research population continues to show better than eighty percent success rate more than twenty years later.

In 1991 Drs. Peniston and Kulkosky[55] expanded their research to a population of Vietnam veterans who were hospitalized for PTSD and were having nightmares, flashbacks, and many other problems, dysfunctions, and diagnoses. By the end of the research protocol, the symptoms of this population appeared to have resolved. They were no longer having nightmares and flashbacks. Whereas all subjects were on medications at the beginning of the study, only one was on medication by the end of the study and his dosage had been reduced by one-half. Tests were given before and after the Peniston-Kulkosky Protocol training. Respected instruments such as the Minnesota Multiphasic Personality Inventory (MMPI) and MCMI demonstrated that measurable personality shifts occurred in those who went through the training. In fact, most of the pathology of these personalities had normalized.[54]

The Peniston-Kulkosky Protocol begins with several sessions of thermal biofeedback and autogenic training prior to EEG feedback. In the original research the protocol involves fifteen 30-minute sessions, typically performed twice a day, five days a week, on Veterans Administration Hospital in-patients. In the field today there are many versions of this original protocol, with the most common employing the original thermal and autogenic training followed by approximately thirty EEG feedback sessions, including an imagined scene of the rejection of the undesired behavior and imagery of desired outcome, which are introduced at the beginning of each EEG session and repeated in each session throughout the treatment.

In the initial stage of this protocol, a layman's explanation of the brain, the limbic area, the neurochemistry, and its process to effect change is believed to offer the patient both a conscious and an unconscious program to follow and, along with the clarification of goals, to create a clear intention for the desired outcome. The subsequent development of imagery of the desired outcome apparently enhances the result. According to studies published in peer reviewed journals, over eighty percent of patients whose initial tests showed sociopathic personality traits had test outcomes after training which are within normal ranges.

Hand warming with autogenic training and temperature biofeedback follow as the next step of this protocol. Hand warming has been used in the field of biofeedback for many years as an effective tool to correct hypertension and other symptoms of sympathetic over arousal. It is helpful in teaching one to relax and be calm in any situation. Hand warming involves the circulatory aspect of the sympathetic branch of the autonomic nervous system involved in the "fight or flight" response.

In the fight or flight response, the body is alerted and blood flow is increased to the major organs. This can become a chronic stress response. To counter this state, as the peripheral circulation is increased with training, the body relaxes. Hand warming also is a way of teaching the body to respond to cues from a tangible feedback to which the patient can easily relate and acts as a bridge to lower arousal states as pre-training to eventual achievement of alpha and theta EEG frequencies.

Autogenic training exercises are used in combination with the temperature biofeedback training to achieve further relaxation of the body and a quiet, inward turned state of mind. In addition, rhythmic diaphragmatic breathing is taught to still body functions and focus attention.

During the initial sessions of thermal feedback and autogenic training exercises, the patient and his or her therapist develop a graphic, detailed visualization of the desired outcome, including a scene rejecting undesired behavior or a "clearing" of the condition to be altered. This final state visualization also involves the image of being already healed, which is believed to avoid the problems of potential harm that might result from imaging the healing process incorrectly, and is designed to reprogram the "unconscious" in a desired direction. "Programming the unconscious" with mental rehearsal of new images and intentions of desired change seems to effect healing and change both physiologically and psychologically. Imagery is one of the earliest forms of healing. There is archaeological evidence suggesting that the techniques of the shaman using imagination for healing are at least 20,000 years old, with vivid evidence of their antiquity in the cave paintings in the south of France. Asclepius, Aristotle, Galen, and Hippocrates, often regarded as the fathers of medicine, used imagery for diagnosis and therapy. [1]

This protocol seems to represent a therapeutic approach designed for the induction of higher states of consciousness and insight, and one's relationship to the world is altered by these insights. It is a therapy that contains elements of the five senses, but its very nature takes one beyond the five senses to abilities that may lie latent within us all. It is a transpersonal therapy.

Neurofeedback is a subtle brain exercise that effectively tunes veterans' brain to function better by training it toward particular brainwave patterns, which will produce more activated and more restful states. Both are needed for good brain function. The process involves observing the brainwave activity as it occurs, and rewarding the brain whenever it changes in a favorable direction. When these positive changes are repeatedly reinforced, learning occurs. The brain is drawn naturally to better functioning. As it functions better, it never lets go of its new abilities. Human beings continue to do that which they are good at, and the same holds true for the brain.

"Homecoming for Veterans" is a national outreach program to provide neurofeedback therapy and rehabilitation for all veterans dealing with the effects of Post-traumatic Stress Disorder, stress and anxiety, addiction, and brain trauma. It seeks to link arms with health care providers from all medical and alternative health backgrounds to support increased mental health through neurofeedback, psychiatric, pharmaceutical and behavioral/societal conditioning. It is a non-profit venture of The EEG Institute and is committed to providing relief for veterans from the mental devastation of war (www.homecoming4veterans). With a network of hundreds of generous clinicians and through dedicated efforts, the organization is dedicated to raising awareness about the prevalence and seriousness of these problems, their effects on the lives of veterans and their families, and society.

PTSD and Virtual War

Scientists hope the "Virtual Iraq" (VI) experience and a new use for an old drug will help the one-third of the soldiers returning from Iraq and Afghanistan recover from the trauma of war. Virtual reality exposure therapy has been used to battle post-traumatic stress for more than a decade. Similar to the Logotherapeutic technique of *paradoxical intension*, it is considered effective because it gradually desensitizes patients to specific fears. One study found that Vietnam veterans' symptoms were reduced by 34 percent when they were treated by psychologists using a "Virtual Vietnam" developed at Georgia Tech.

Virtual Iraq is different. It is designed to prove that virtual reality (VR) can work better and faster when subjects take a drug once widely used to treat tuberculosis. The drug, d-Cycloserine or DCS, affects a region of the brain called the amygdala that processes memories and emotional reactions like fear. Mounting research on PTSD and other anxiety problems show that the drug can also decrease fear.

A 2002 study demonstrated that patients treated with DCS tend to be less fearful of electric shocks. In a 2004 Emory study, twenty-eight people terrified of heights took DCS or a placebo before donning virtual reality goggles that zipped them skyward in a virtual glass elevator. Those who took DCS enjoyed a significant reduction in their fear of heights that lasted at least three months. Boston University investigators found that DCS helped people with anxiety disorders learn to overcome fear of social situations, such as public speaking.

DCS tends to make therapy work better and faster. It is not a tranquilizer, like Xanax, which provides a temporary balm for anxiety. DCS appears to open up channels in the brain that allow more chemicals to flow that are involved in memory and emotion. It only works on fear in conjunction with exposure therapy. The pill alone has no effect. The virtual reality module may help people make the connections with traumatic memories faster.

Soldiers who don the VR helmet to experience Virtual Iraq see themselves behind the wheel or in a passenger seat. They hear explosions, or see hostiles popping up and firing with AK-47s, or grenade launchers. They see planes and helicopters flying over and rising smoke. A Nintendo controller lets them steer, but not fire back.

Apparently, the details do not have to match perfectly, but rather be close enough to cue each veteran's individual experience and allow them to fill in their own details. They learn that their anxiety goes down with repeated exposure to their traumatic memory. This decrease in fear makes the memory easier to control and allows them to be more at peace with the memory. They do not have to avoid it at all costs because it is too painful to think about.

PTSD and Logotherapy

More recently, Logotherapy or "healing through meaning" has been successfully used in the treatment of combat-related PTSD. Viktor Frankl developed his meaning-centered psychotherapy prior to World War II, but found his convictions later "tested" in the harshest of circumstances as a slave laborer and inmate for three years in four different Nazi concentration camps. His experiences were first recorded in his book *Man's Search for Meaning.*[19] Being future-oriented, Logotherapy focuses on an individual's personal strengths and places responsibility for change on him. Frankl used Logotherapy on a daily basis while imprisoned in the concentration camps that led to the survival of him and his fellow prisoners during the Holocaust.

Viktor Frankl was one of the first mental health professionals who worked with and wrote about victims of trauma and terror. His existential treatment approach with Holocaust survivors has considerable value and usefulness with other kinds of PTSD clients. In Franklian psychotherapy, the PTSD client is helped to remember the details of their trauma experiences to identify meaning opportunities embedded in memories of trauma and terror and to make use of such meaning opportunities for self-transcendent giving to the world.

Logotherapy is considered an adjunctive therapy, enhancing rather than supplanting other treatment approaches. Logotherapy focuses on a client's strengths and his search for personal meaning and purpose in life. Loss of personal meaning and purpose in life has pronounced effects on all areas of psychosocial functioning. Logotherapy promotes the adoption of an optimistic view of human potential and the ability to transcend the self through the pursuit of meaning that is specific to one's life. It employs specific techniques, such as self-distancing, paradoxical intention, Socratic dialogue, and dereflection, to be discussed in Chapter IX. Frankl says that man can discover meaning in a deed, work, or love, or by the attitude that one adopts to a predicament that cannot be changed.[27]

Logotherapy addresses a number of problematic symptoms experienced by veterans with PTSD, including a sense of foreshortened future, an external locus of control, guilt and survival guilt and existential loss of meaning. Veterans with PTSD feel that death is imminent; feel unworthy of treatment or a better life; feel that they have no power to change because life is controlled by fate; or that participation in therapy would be pointless. Many live with profound doubts about the meaning of life dominated by death, guilt and suffering, but are eager to discuss their existential struggles and be understood. Logotherapy provides an opportunity for spiritual healing and growth.

When veterans discover greater meaning fulfillment, they appear more accepting of and less deterred of their symptoms. Ultimately, many begin to see their wartime experiences as a gift that enabled them to grow stronger at their broken places.

PTSD and Cognitive Behavioral Therapy

In cognitive therapy, the therapist helps an individual understand and change how he thinks about his trauma and its aftermath. The goal is to understand how certain thoughts about trauma cause an individual's stress and makes his symptoms worse. Cognitive behavioral therapy is used particularly for drug and alcohol abuse, depression, and anxiety disorders.

He learns to identify thoughts about the world and himself that are making him feel afraid or upset. With the help of his therapist, he learns to replace these thoughts with more accurate and less distressing thoughts. He also learns ways to cope with feelings such as anger, guilt, and fear. He learns to transform those feelings creatively, socially, spiritually and existentially.

After a traumatic event, he might blame himself for things he couldn't have changed. For example, he may feel guilty about decisions he had to make during war. Cognitive therapy, a type of CBT, helps him understand that the traumatic event he lived through was not his fault.

PTSD and Exposure Therapy

In exposure therapy the goal is to have less fear about memories. It is based on the idea that people learn to fear thoughts, feelings, and situations that remind them of a past traumatic event. Like phobias, the more an individual tries to avoid situations that bring on the feeling the stronger the fear becomes. Paradoxical intension is a Logotherapeutic tool that enables a person to overcome phobias by pursuing that which one fears. For example, if I fear public speaking, I might attempt to be the worst public speaker ever. In the process, to the point of being ridiculous, I overcome it.

By talking about trauma repeatedly with a therapist, an individual learns to get control of his thoughts and feelings about the trauma. He learns that he does not have to be afraid of his memories. This may be hard at first, like any physical or mental exercise. It might seem strange to think about stressful things on purpose. But he begins to feel less overwhelmed over time.

With the help of the therapist, an individual can change how he reacts to the stressful memories. Talking in a place where he feels secure makes this easier over time. In the beginning, he may focus on memories that are less upsetting before talking about worse ones. This is called "desensitization," and it allows him to deal with bad memories a little bit at a time. His therapist also may ask him to remember a lot of bad memories at once. This is called "flooding," and it helps him learn not to feel overwhelmed.

He also may practice different ways to relax when he is having a stressful memory. Deep breathing and visualizing exercises are sometimes used for this. For example, he may visualize ocean waves rolling toward a shoreline, pausing and then receding over and over again.

PTSD: Eye Movement Desensitization & Reprocessing (EMDR)

EMDR is a fairly new therapy for PTSD. Like other kinds of counseling, it can help change how an individual reacts to memories of his trauma.
While talking about his memories, he begins to focus on distractions like eye movements, hand taps, and sounds. For example, his therapist will move his or her hand near the patient's face, and he follows this movement with his eyes.

Experts are still learning how EMDR works. Studies have shown that it may help individuals have fewer PTSD symptoms. But research also suggests that the eye movements are not a necessary part of the treatment.

Treatment with the Drug RU38486

Current medications are often ineffective in controlling PTSD symptoms and so in the 2009 February 1st issue of Biological

Psychiatry, published by Elsevier, a group of basic scientists shed new light on the biology of stress effects upon memory formation. They suggest new approaches to the treatment of the distress related to traumatic memories. Their work is based on the study of a drug, RU38486 that blocks the effects of the stress hormone cortisol.

Using an animal model of traumatic memory, investigators at the Mount Sinai School of Medicine show that treatment with RU38486 selectively reduces stress-related memories, leaving other memories unchanged. They also found that the effectiveness of the treatment is a function of the intensity of the initial "trauma." Although this particular study was performed in rats, their findings help to set the stage for trials in humans.

Group Therapy

Many people want to talk about their trauma with others who have had similar experiences. In group therapy, an individual talks with a group of people who also have been through a trauma and who have PTSD. Sharing his story with others may help him feel more comfortable talking about his trauma. This can help him cope with his symptoms, memories, and other parts of his life.

Group therapy helps individuals build relationships with others who understand what they've been through. They learn to deal with emotions such as shame, guilt, anger, rage, and fear. Sharing with the group also can help them build self-confidence and trust. They learn to focus on their present life, rather than feeling overwhelmed by the past.

Brief Psychodynamic Psychotherapy

In this type of therapy, an individual learns ways of dealing with emotional conflicts caused by his trauma. This therapy helps him understand how the past affects the way he feels now.
A competent therapist can help an individual:
- Identify what triggers his stressful memories and other symptoms.
- Find ways to cope with intense feelings about the past.

- Become more aware of his thoughts and feelings, so he can change his reactions to them.
- Raise his self-esteem.

Other PTSD Treatment Approaches

Counseling

Integrative counseling strategies are pointed to throughout because victims of violence often require a variety of support networks (e.g., crisis intervention, suicide prevention, substance abuse counseling, group counseling, etc.)

Psychoanalysis

The authors reject, as over-simplistic, the notion that the traumatic event in itself holds psychological meaning to the person experiencing it. Instead they argue that traumatic events shatter archaic and narcissistic fantasies which are central to the organization of self-experience, and, that in the subsequent faulty attempts to restore these fantasies lays the unconscious meanings of the traumatic events. The meaning that one attaches to the traumatic event is what actually changes the person's experience of self.

Self-Help Books

Although the lion's share of treatment oriented works on PTSD are written with the practitioner in mind, a handful of books have been written with the PTSD sufferers as their primary audience. Benjamin Colodzin's *Trauma and Survival: A Self Help Learning Guide* is an outstanding source for war veterans suffering from PTSD. Colodzin outlines a practical and compassionate program, drawing on both modern and ancient knowledge, for viable solutions for those suffering from traumatic experiences. This work is particularly useful in its examination of communication processes and anger. Colodzin writes this book with obvious care and compassion for PTSD sufferers. Raymond B. Flannery's *Post-Traumatic Stress Disorder: The Victim's Guide to Healing and Recovery* is written specifically for PTSD survivors and their families. This clear and insightful book describes PTSD, including the links between addictions and traumatic stress, and shows survivors how to master the skills of stress-resistance.

Barry M. Cohen's ***Managing Traumatic Stress through Art: Drawing from the Center*** provides another self-help approach for PTSD. Three art therapists have collaborated to produce this unique workbook. Designed for the trauma survivors, this work introduces inventive ways to understand, manage, and transform the aftereffects of trauma. This work could help survivors to explore the aftermath of trauma as it affects self-image, relationships with others and functioning in the world. Richard G. Tedeschi and Lawrence G. Calhoun's ***Trauma and Transformation: Growing in the Aftermath of Suffering*** provides another perspective for those recovering from trauma. Tedeschi weaves together material on the experience of personal growth or strengthening that sometimes occurs in persons who face traumatic events. Tedeschi posits that growth occurs because trauma leads to change in belief systems and these beliefs assist in relieving emotional distress and encouraging useful activity.

Exploding PTSD Cases among Veterans

American troops in Iraq and Afghanistan daily face the risk of death or injury — to themselves or their fellow soldiers — by homemade bombs and suicide attackers. So it is not surprising that post-traumatic stress disorder is a common problem among returning soldiers. But how many, exactly, are affected? Some estimate that one in five will return with PTSD symptoms; others suggest that it will be as high as one in three.

This question is key to determining how large an investment the Department of Veterans Affairs needs to make in diagnosing and treating the problem. The United States Army's Mental Health Advisory Team, which conducted a survey of more than 1,000 soldiers and marines in September 2006, found that 17 percent suffered from PTSD. Similarly, a Rand study put the number at 14 percent.

But these estimates do not take into account the many soldiers who will eventually suffer from PTSD, because there is a lag between the time someone experiences trauma and the time he or she reports symptoms of post-traumatic stress. This can range from days to many years, and it is typically much longer while people are still in the military.

To get a better estimate of the rate of PTSD among Iraq war veterans, two graduate students, Michael Atkinson and Adam Guetz, and Lawrence Wein constructed a mathematical model in which soldiers incur a random amount of stress during each month of deployment (based on monthly American casualty data), develop PTSD if their cumulative stress exceeds a certain threshold, and also develop symptoms of the disorder after an additional amount of time. We found that about 35 percent of soldiers and marines who deploy to Iraq will ultimately suffer from PTSD — about 300,000 people, with 20,000 new sufferers for each year the war lasts.

Consider that only twenty-two percent of recent veterans who may be at risk for PTSD (based on their answers to screening questions) were referred for a mental health evaluation. Less than 40 percent of service members who get a diagnosis of PTSD receive mental health services, and only slightly more than half of recent veterans who receive treatment get adequate care. Those who seek follow-up treatment run into delays of up to 90 days, which suggests there is a serious shortage of mental health professionals available to help them.

Proper PTSD care can lead to complete remission in 30 percent to 50 percent of cases, studies show. Thorough screening of every soldier upon departure from the military, immediately followed by three to six months of treatment for those who need it, would reduce the stigma that is attached to current mental health referrals. The Rand study estimates that treatment would pay for itself within two years, largely by reducing the loss of productivity. This is the least we can do for our veterans.

Symptoms of Post-Traumatic Stress Disorder

Individuals with PTSD exhibit four different types of symptoms, including:
1. *Reliving or re-experiencing the event* — symptoms include nightmares, intrusive thoughts, flashbacks and psychological distress and physical reactivity in response to trauma cues.

2. *Avoidance* — avoiding reminders of the traumatic event, including thoughts, emotions, people, places and conversations that may trigger memories of the traumatic event.
3. *Emotional numbing* — symptoms include feeling emotionally numb or having reduced emotional experiences, detachment or estrangement from others, and being less interested in previously enjoyed activities.
4. *Arousal symptoms* are very common in returning veterans, even in those who do not meet full criteria for a PTSD diagnosis. The most frequently reported problems are increased anger or irritability and difficulty sleeping. Other arousal symptoms include constantly being on guard, having difficulty concentrating and feeling jumpy or easily startled.

These symptoms cause difficulties in social relationships — with family, dating and friendships — and occupational functioning in work or school.

Although the symptoms and syndrome of PTSD have been observed in veterans for hundreds of years, PTSD was not formally recognized as a mental disorder until 1980, when it was included in the **Diagnostic and Statistical Manual of Mental Disorders** (DSM-III). Today, PTSD is the most commonly reported mental health diagnosis following deployment to the Middle East: 12 to 13 percent of the Marines and soldiers who have returned from active duty have screened positive, as reported by Hoge and colleagues.

In addition to military personnel that meet full criteria for a PTSD diagnosis, many others display some combination of PTSD symptoms as they readjust to the challenges of civilian life after functioning under the constant life-threat they experienced during deployment. It is common to have some PTSD symptoms at first, especially hyper vigilance, insomnia and nightmares as veterans try to integrate and process their war zone experiences. These symptoms are likely to be more intense for those who have returned recently, and many of these symptoms are likely to decrease over time as they adjust to civilian life.

One way to conceptualize many of these PTSD symptoms is to think of them as part of a stress-response continuum. At one end are individuals who are burdened by stressors at home at the same time that they are reminded of traumatic events that happened in the war zone, yet are coping well with few mental health symptoms and little functional impairment. These people are often able to reintegrate into their previous jobs with little disruption and return to their relationships, in which they can communicate about areas of difficulty. In the middle may be those who have a variety of PTSD symptoms, yet do not evidence clinically significant impairment in functioning. At the other end of the spectrum are veterans who are plagued with a host of PTSD symptoms and have difficulty functioning in their daily lives.

Despite this country's involvement in wars for hundreds of years, there has been little clinical research on the mental health impact of taking another life in combat among veterans, compared to the amount of research that exists about other potentially traumatic events that military personnel may experience in the context of war.

A few studies have detailed the elements of war-zone exposure that are necessary, but not sufficient, to create risk for chronic PTSD. In one study of Vietnam veterans, King and colleagues found that instances of traditional combat (e.g., firing a weapon, receiving fire), reports of atrocities/abusive violence (e.g., mutilation, killing civilians), feelings of fear and the degree to which soldiers experienced discomfort in a war zone were each associated with PTSD symptom severity.
In another study that examined killing in the context of committing atrocities during war within a larger model, Fontana and Rosenheck found a strong relationship between killing and PTSD. After taking killing into account, the atrocities variable no longer predicted PTSD symptoms, suggesting that killing could be the potent ingredient in predicting PTSD.

A third study conducted by MacNair involving Vietnam veterans also found a relationship between taking a life in combat and PTSD. Our preliminary results from a current study of Vietnam veterans have demonstrated that in addition to PTSD, killing is also associated with a number of mental health and functioning problems, even after taking exposure to general combat into account. Finally, we are currently in the process of conducting a study about the impact of killing on veterans returning from deployments to Iraq and Afghanistan.

We are not aware of any other studies that document this relationship in newly returning veterans.

Although soldiers are trained to kill, killing is quite difficult for most individuals. Prior to killing another enemy combatant or a civilian, there is generally some type of life threat. The circumstances of killing also generally involve either the person him or herself being injured or in danger of being killed and often others being killed. Pulling the trigger, even in self defense, is not easy and is often accompanied by a series of complex emotional reactions before and after taking a life. These may involve helplessness, fear and/or horror either during or after killing. While some may react in this way, others may not, which is why assessment of reactions to killing is quite important.

Also, it is important to remember that just because an individual experiences killing as a traumatic event does not mean that the person will inevitability develop PTSD symptoms or a formal diagnosis of PTSD. Killing is difficult for many soldiers who may not develop PTSD, and those issues are generally evaluated separately.

A recent RAND study found that one in five veterans deployed to Iraq or Afghanistan suffered from PTSD or major depression. These rates are somewhat similar to those reported in other scientific studies. An initial report by Hoge and colleagues indicated that sixteen to seventeen percent of returning Operation Iraqi Freedom (OIF) combat veterans and eleven percent of returning Operation Enduring Freedom (OEF) combat veterans met screening criteria for at least one mental health disorder.[30] In a more recent study, Hoge and colleagues found that the prevalence of screening positive for a mental health problem was nineteen percent among service members returning from Iraq and eleven percent after returning from Afghanistan.[31] Among OIF/OEF veterans seen at VA healthcare facilities, twenty-five percent received mental health diagnoses, with fifty-six percent of these meeting criteria for two or more mental health diagnoses.[55]

Mental health problems are related to impairments in physical health and general functioning. For example, those with PTSD often experience difficulties in many domains of functioning such as relationships and employment. There have also been several studies that document the relationship between PTSD symptoms and physical health. In one recent study of newly returning veterans, those with

PTSD also manifested more physical symptoms — greater symptom severity, lower ratings of general health, more sick call visits and more missed workdays — even after taking into account those who have been injured or wounded.[32]

Oftentimes, family and/or couples therapy can serve as a preventative measure, assisting family members with understanding the process of reintegration into civilian life as well as highlighting some of the readjustment symptoms that family members might observe in their loved ones. This process can also help the veteran learn how to reconnect and communicate with family members despite feeling like loved ones can never understand his/her experience. Working with the veteran and the family can decrease the process of isolation and avoidance within the family unit by opening channels of communication.

Going back to work or school can also be a challenging experience for veterans, especially as many might have difficulty relating to authority figures. Many have experienced situations in which they perceive that authority figures made decisions that were not in their best interest, and as a result understandably can be reactive in this context. Difficulties with concentration can also hamper work or school functioning, and therapies that help process the trauma can be helpful in this regard; providing the veteran with a space to process his or her experience ultimately can help reduce impairment in this arena.

Veterans who served as part of Operation Iraqi Freedom/ Operation Enduring Freedom can currently get five years of free treatment at their local VA hospital. Many VA hospitals have designated PTSD Clinical Teams (PCT) providing a wide array of treatments to returning veterans. At the San Francisco VA Medical Center, we offer a comprehensive PTSD diagnostic evaluation, skills-based therapy (for example, stress and anger management), exposure-based therapies (for example, Prolonged Exposure Therapy and Cognitive Processing Therapy), couples/family therapy and OIF/OEF adjustment groups. Prolonged Exposure Therapy and Cognitive Processing Therapy are two evidence-based treatments which have been shown to improve PTSD symptoms in veterans returning from war. There is currently a national effort to train mental health professionals across the nation to provide one or both of these treatments.

One of the biggest challenges that mental health-care professionals face in providing services to military personnel returning from deployments to the Middle East are obstacles related to stigma and barriers to care. In one study, among those who screened positive for a mental health disorder, only twenty-three to forty percent received professional mental health care in the last year and only thirty-eight to forty-five percent were interested in receiving help. Furthermore, those who screened positive for a mental health disorder were twice as likely as those who did not meet screening criteria to report stigma and barriers to care for seeking mental health care.

There are many reasons that returning veterans do not seek mental health care, including common fears of being seen as weak (sixty-five percent). One of the most important things that you can do if you know someone who is suffering from PTSD symptoms is to encourage them to seek treatment at their local VA hospital or at any facility that provides evidence-based treatments.

Soldiers returned home to their girlfriends, boyfriends, spouses and families unable to feel any emotions. When their kids got hurt, veterans don't get upset. Veterans take their children to the doctor but don't feel their hurt. Their emotions are completely buried.

They don't have close, non-combat friends. They don't want to get hurt. They might casually discuss what happened in Vietnam with a long-term friend and never hear from them again. Many still suffer in silence. They don't cry when their spouse, parents or child dies.

For mental health professionals, the needs and concerns of both Vietnam and Iraq/Afghanistan veterans are challenging and varied. Issues that arise again and again include morality in war, spousal abuse, social isolation, criminalization of substance abuse, the taking of a life in wartime, difficulty overcoming PTSD, psychic numbing, suicidal ideation, and transforming anger and rage.

It is *not* surprising that many therapists avoid treating veterans of the Vietnam and Iraq/Afghanistan wars. None of these issues alone is easy. The composite can be overwhelming. "It is foolish," writes Primo Levi, "to think that human justice can eradicate the crimes of

Auschwitz. Or that the human imagination can encompass and transfigure them. Some losses cannot be made up, neither in time nor eternity. "

Aaron Kipnis asks, "Can the victim of trauma who has offered himself as undeniable evidence of life's harsher realities through suicide, homelessness, and drug and alcohol abuse find meaning in a society that denies suffering and death?"[36] Many more Vietnam veterans will continue to struggle with survival unless and until they see a way to live in America. The sharing of PTSD has been a bond between war veterans and rape victims. They don't struggle with each other but with PTSD. Most will have been exposed to being attacked or ambushed, sought dead bodies and body parts, been shot at, and/or knew someone who was seriously injured or killed.

Research shows that some ten percent of those exposed to traumatic events suffer from PTSD. The National Institute for Clinical Excellence states that five percent of males and ten percent of females will develop PTSD in their lifetime. The current conflicts in Iraq and Afghanistan continue to generate PTSD in soldiers, as high as one in three, and they join the ranks of veterans of the Persian Gulf War, Lebanon, Vietnam, Korea and WWII as survivors of things that no man or woman should ever witness in a civilized world.

Millions of Americans get Post Traumatic Stress Disorder every year. A large number of those Americans are our combat forces serving in Iraq and Afghanistan. The Veterans Administration's almost immediate medical answer is to provide morphine-based drugs that numb the senses and create addicts. But, there are better, more creative ways for those who suffer from PTSD to find relief and therapy.

Beyond the increasing rate of veteran suicide, the dark side of PTSD for too many who serve their nation can be alcoholism, homelessness, drug abuse, depression, and sometimes destructive behavior.

Summary of PTSD & Other Disorders

PTSD is a natural emotional reaction to a deeply shocking and disturbing experience after which it can be difficult to believe that life will ever be the same again. The symptoms are surprisingly common and include sleep problems, nightmares and waking early, flashbacks and replays, impaired memory, inability to concentrate, hyper vigilance (feels like but is **not** paranoia), jumpiness and an exaggerated startle response, fragility and hypersensitivity, detachment and avoidance behaviors, depression, irritability, violent outbursts, joint and muscle pains, panic attacks, fatigue, low self-esteem, feelings of nervousness and undue anxiety. Survivors endure abnormal feelings of guilt, perhaps for having survived when those around them didn't.

It is very common to have PTSD at that same time as other mental health problems. Depression, alcohol or substance abuse problems, panic disorder, and other anxiety disorders often occur along with PTSD. In many cases, the PTSD treatments will also help with the other disorders. The best treatment results occur when both PTSD and the other problems are treated together rather than one after the other. Untreated, PTSD symptoms can last a lifetime, impairing health, damaging relationships and preventing people achieving their potential. Sufferers often find that knowledge and treatment of PTSD (and especially Complex PTSD) is difficult to obtain. However, prospects for recovery are good when an individual has the right counsel and is in the company of fellow survivors and those with genuine insight, empathy and experience.

Exercising in Response to PTSD:

Inactivity is associated with many chronic medical conditions, hypertension, heart disease, diabetes, obesity and osteoporosis. These conditions can add to feelings of depression and helplessness. Helplessness is an oftentimes expressed feeling of PTSD sufferers. Exercise can release endorphins into the bloodstream, acting as the body's natural painkillers and temporarily make one feel better between other PTSD treatments. Consult with your physician before you begin an exercise regimen.

V.
Death, Guilt, Suffering - Tragic Triad or Tragic Gifts

What does not destroy me makes me stronger. - Friedrich Nietzsche

Winter of 1970

It is the winter of 1970. Jimmy awakes to the sound of his wife moaning and in labor pain. She is about to lose their first child. The traumatic loss is unexpected. After all, a healthy pregnancy is not supposed to end this way. Later in the day, following the loss, Jimmy retreats to another room of their rental, an old Victorian structure on the grounds of a mental institution. It is a coincidence that his life is about to enter a chapter of craziness for which he is totally unprepared. That is a fact, not a complaint. His chest tightens as the tears begin to flow. "How can the loss of my child be meaningful?" he asks of nobody in particular as he prays for guidance.

Grief over the loss of a child at any point in its life is expected, but certainly not uncommon. Jimmy would experience an array of feelings - sadness, depression, longing, anger and resentment. Acknowledging feelings of loss is just one of several stages in the process of grieving described by Elisabeth Kubler-Ross.[41] Viktor Frankl quotes Nietzsche: "That, which does not kill me, makes me stronger." Jimmy's parents arrive a few hours later to comfort him in his loss. His mother can empathize with him; she too lost a child in a miscarriage.

Jimmy's life would take him around the world. He would experience the good, the bad and the ugly. He would learn that there is no joy without hardship; no happiness without pain and suffering. It would take many years, however before he would realize the "gift" of his first unborn child, a child who would not take its first breath of air, who would not take nourishment from his mother, who would not take his first step toward his meaning potential, but whose existential three-dimensional "canvas" was nonetheless a complete *masterpiece*; a gift from God. It is a masterpiece that does not begin and end on the first page. It is a novel that would far exceed the pages of *War and Peace*.

Each individual has a date with destiny that is potentially one of the most touching and heartbreaking novels ever written. He is not in control of the timeline; only the pursuit of his meaning potential from moment to moment. The transitoriness of his existence in no way makes it meaningless.

Jimmy's unborn child taught him a great deal about love, fatherhood, and being present during its short lifespan. Nobody can ever take those memorable experiences away from him. Jimmy can reflect with pride and joy on all the richness that he's experienced with each of his children. Sure, Jimmy experienced pain, grief and sadness during his first marriage. But, he also has the realities of his children, his friendships, his experiences and his current wife, met only as a result of having embraced and learned the meaning of the gift of his pain and suffering. It is these unavoidable life experiences, meaningful experiential brushstrokes, some bravely suffered, of which Jimmy is most proud.

Jimmy's first marriage was broken, but it did not break him. Kubler-Ross states that "if not for AIDS, would we notice our humanity is in jeopardy? If not for death, would we appreciate life? If not for hate, would we know the ultimate goal is love? If not for windstorms, would we realize the beauty of their carvings upon the Grand Canyon?" [42]

As individuals near the end of their life, some begin to contemplate its meaning. Elisabeth Kubler-Ross states, "Death is the final stage of growth." Death need not be a physical reality. It may be a traumatic assault on the body, mind or spirit. It may involve an unexpected and unavoidable loss – of a child, a job, a relationship, health or other. Death is a call to individuals to nourish the potential within relationships, jobs, children, and themselves and to continue to do so even when they do not see immediate results. *Mors inceptio solum est* – "Death is only (another) beginning."

Viktor Frankl suggests "living as if you were living for the second time and had acted as wrongly the first time as you are about to act now." It is about second chances not taken lightly. It is about gaining a perspective on where an individual is in the movement of his life and exploring the possibilities of his future in the context of his whole life. It is about discovering his purpose and meaning potential. It is recognizing that sometimes events that are meaningful for one's life occurs as coincidences or as synchronistic events with no apparent cause but nonetheless have a strong message for him. Pain and suffering tend to be our greatest teachers.

Viktor Frankl says that "life is not primarily a quest for pleasure, as Freud believed; it is not a quest for power, as Alfred Adler taught, but a quest for meaning. The greatest task for any person is to find meaning in his or her life." Frankl saw "three possible sources for meaning: in work (doing something significant), in love (caring for another person), and in courage (during difficult times). Suffering in and of itself is meaningless; we give our suffering meaning by the way in which we respond to it… Forces beyond our control can take away everything we possess except one thing, our freedom to choose how we will respond to the situation. We cannot control what happens to us in life, but we can always control what we will feel and do about what happens to us.[20]

In fact, the opportunities to act properly, the potentialities to fulfill a meaning, are affected by the irreversibility of one's life. But also the potentialities alone are so affected. For as soon as individuals have used an opportunity and have actualized a potential meaning, they have done so once and for all. They have rescued it into the past wherein it has been safely delivered and deposited. In the past, nothing is irretrievably lost, but rather, on the contrary, everything is irrevocably stored and treasured. To be sure, people tend to see only the stubble fields of transitoriness but overlook and forget the full granaries of the past into which they have brought the harvest of their lives: the deeds done, the loves loved, and last but not least, the sufferings they have gone through with courage and dignity."[20] These treasures, too often go to the grave without being put to paper, photo, recording device or canvas.

San Quentin

In May 1966, in the middle of a busy lecture tour in Northern California, Frankl is handed a note from the educational director of San Quentin Prison. The note is from Joey who has just finished reading *Man's Search for Meaning* in the prison library. He asks if Frankl would consider visiting him; he has unanswered questions that only Frankl, a survivor of the death camps of Auschwitz and Dachau can answer. Only Frankl, thought Joey, could comprehend what he was going through isolated from society for a crime against humanity. Only Frankl, thinks Joey, is capable of leading him to discover the meaning of a life possibly entering its final chapter. Frankl has a choice, as all do when they come to a fork in the road of life: To keep his speaking engagements or speak to the needs of a fellow human being incarcerated possibly for life or sitting on death row.

Frankl agrees immediately, although the sponsors of the tour are not very happy about having to rearrange his very tight schedule. His host, Joseph Fabry, a fellow survivor of the Holocaust, drives him north along the San Francisco Bay to the prison built on a rocky outcropping. Inside San Quentin Prison, Frankl speaks to Joey and, in a follow-up visit to a larger group in the institution's library. Frankl says that freedom comes with responsibility. Frankl tells the men, "'You are human beings like me, and as such you were free to commit a crime, to become guilty. Now, however, you are responsible for overcoming guilt by rising above it, by growing beyond yourselves, by changing for the better."[20]

Viktor Frankl listens as Joey shares his understanding of the book, *Man's Search for Meaning*, but he wants more. He wants to know that his life still has meaning in spite of all previous choices made in his life journey. Joey is not just hurting because something in his life sucks. He desperately wants to re-orient himself to once again discover meaning for what is happening in this chapter of his life. Finding meaning in suffering would necessarily bring him happiness, but happiness is not the point; it is a superficial thing, next to meaning.

Bicycle Metaphor

Individuals stuck in an existential vacuum or frustration want to escape, but are conditioned to believe that to pursue is to fail. Using the bicycle as a metaphor for life, most choose to ride it with the kickstand down. As a result, they're not moving despite the appearance of genuine movement. They settle for this charade because they don't want to go through the uncomfortable, frightening and sometimes painful 'wobbles' of learning from the forward motion in the lessons of life. In the process of letting go, these lessons enable them to ride authentically, to experience real freedom and joy, and begin to discover the meaning of their life.

It's perfectly fine to be temporarily off the mark, to envision, with the "kickstand down," a life scenario without all of the frightening and sometimes painful wobbling. But, sooner or later individuals must put the kickstand up and push off into the unknown, without the support of millennia of wrong thinking and behavior. Much of the thinking is ego-based. Nearly 90 percent of self talk is negative. Thomas Paine noted in Introduction to Common Sense, 1776, that *a long habit of not thinking a thing wrong gives it a superficial appearance of being right, and raises at first a formidable outcry in defense of custom. But the tumult soon subsides. Time makes more converts than reason.*

When individuals first hop on the 'bicycle,' they may feel clumsy and awkward as they find their own way. They want to do everything perfectly. But as long as they continue to do things perfectly, there is no growth. If individuals have never failed, they have never grown. Practice never makes for perfection; practice only makes for improvement. They can always improve upon their best efforts.

They might see someone performing beautifully that which they do not. Their self-talk proceeds as follows, "That's wonderful. It really appears quite *simple*, that thing that he is doing. And he seems to be really enjoying himself." They would like to do that too.

However, the moment they get on the 'bicycle' and attempt to perform an apparently simple act they immediately begin to feel awkward. They don't seem to be gliding along. They keep experiencing setbacks, falling down and getting seriously hurt physically and emotionally. They feel clumsy and, in that clumsiness state of mind, they become angry, a response to stress learned from birth and throughout childhood observing their adult roll models. They become impatient because they believe they're doing 'it' wrong. They would much rather look cool!

All compulsiveness is a state of wobbles and wobbling is the message that there's something to be learned. Wobbling does not imply that they're bad or that they're doing 'it' wrong or that there may be something wrong with them. What's wrong is that they simply haven't mastered everything and that's okay. Mastery is a process of *doing*. There's much that is wonderful and unique about them, even when they appear to be doing it wrong. All that's wrong with them is that they're slightly off course, slightly out of balance and that's just part of life and of being born in a particular point in time and space. And sometimes wonderful discoveries appear to them when they are doing it *wrong*.

Eventually they'll face the insecurity of "What's next?" not knowing whether they'll succeed. Sometimes it feels like they're being asked to move a seemingly immovable mountain. It seems impossible. But mountains can be moved – one stone at a time; one day at a time. It takes great courage to abandon the so-called security-giving life scripts. It takes great courage to wobble through life until authentic balance arrives, balance that equates to attaining true mastery of the physical, mental or spiritual dimension.

The Immovable Mountain

Each day in a small village in China a family had to climb over a mountain to get the rice fields to work. This had gone on for generations. But one day the elder in the family decided to move the mountain, one stone at a time. Each day he and his sons would go to the mountain and move stones from it.

One day a wise old man was passing by and questioned the elder's foolish notion of moving the mountain, "How can you possibly believe that you can move a mountain?"

The elder responded, "Perhaps I won't. But, my sons will have sons. And they in turn will have sons. There will be many generations of sons. And one day the mountain will be moved, one stone at a time." The elder has chosen to focus, not upon the obstacles or the destiny, but upon the journey.

It takes great courage to abandon the so-called security-giving life-scripts. It takes great courage to wobble through life until authentic balance arrives, balance that equates to attaining true mastery of this dimension, be it physical, mental and emotional, or spiritual.

In War All Men are Cremated Equal – Writing your own epitaph:

While appearing difficult, the purpose of this exercise is to look at your values from a different angle. In your mind's eye, see yourself going to the funeral of a loved one, one whom you have known your whole life. As you walk down to the front of the funeral parlor or chapel and look inside the casket, you suddenly come face to face with the deceased - you! This is your funeral, decades from today. All the people present have come to honor you, to express feelings of love and appreciation for your life.

As you take a seat and wait for the celebration to begin, you look at the program in your hand. There are to be five speakers. The first is a member of your family, immediate and extended – children and grandchildren, brothers and sisters, nieces and nephews, aunts and uncles, cousins and grandparents. The second speaker is one of your friends, someone who can give a sense of what you were as a person. The third speaker is from your work or profession. And the fourth is from your church or community organization for which you performed a service. The fifth speaker is a total stranger whom you casually encouraged once on a street corner many years ago.

Now, close your eyes while going within the well of your being. Remain there until the sensory chatter clears. Listen as the speakers begin to speak about you and your life. Write down what each is saying about you, as a husband or wife, a father or mother, a son or daughter or cousin. What are they saying about you as a friend or work associate? What do they see in your character, your contributions to humanity, your achievements, and the difference you have made in their lives?

Continue to jot down your thoughts, visions, and emotions. Then write the things that prevent you from being the kind of person you see yourself being – the obstacles. If you knew you were going to die in five years, how would you choose to live until then? In the next six months? In the next 24 hours? With whom would you choose to spend that time, living and deceased, talking about the meaning of life, boosting their self-esteem, dancing with them at the shopping mall or in the parking lot, hugging them or site-seeing. What can you now do to develop the courage to pursue and follow through on those visions and goals that would be most meaningful?

VI.
Stages of Grief - Stages of Growth

The task of grief is...to find meaning in the stories of the deceased person's life... There are no ends, only meanings that can be passed on from generation to generation...To honor the life of the deceased is to move beyond survivor guilt...to survivor responsibility...to transcend the circumstances of the incident and cherish the memory of the deceased.[25]

Elisabeth Kubler-Ross, well known for her work on death and dying, demystifies the psychological and medical role of death in our culture. She offers profound psychological and spiritual insights for the living and the dying. She teaches us not only to love, and to love what we are doing, but to experience our emotions without trepidation. She finds that people who are experiencing traumatic events, terminal illness in self or others for example, initially go through specific stages of potential growth - shock, denial, anger, bargaining, depression, testing and acceptance.

This grief model has been widely adopted by other authors and applied to many other situations where someone suffers a loss or change in social identity. The model is often used in bereavement work. Not all workers in the field agree with the Kübler-Ross model, and some critics feel the stages are too rigid, stimulating authors to develop other grief models with different numbers of stages. Regardless of whether you feel the stages are absolute, her book, *On Death and Dying* is a "must read" for anyone seriously interested in death and dying issues.

People who already have healthy coping techniques may go through these stages quickly. The stages are responses to feelings that can last for minutes or hours or days as one flips in and out of one stage and then another. We do not enter and leave each individual stage in a linear fashion. We may feel one, then another and back again to the first one. Others may linger in one or more stage. This is potentially unhealthy, whether it involves denial, anger, bargaining or depression. Becoming stuck means one is not moving forward or, perhaps even regressing. Being stuck in a grief stage can damage those around the one grieving, particularly children. It is good to know what to expect when grieving, in order to learn how to deal with these common stages of emotion, and thus teach children not only how to cope but also to grow. The following is a brief discussion of those stages.

Shock

The first reaction on hearing bad news is one of classic shock. Initially, however it may appear to the outsider that the affected person shows no reaction at all to the news. The person may nod and accept the news without appearing to be troubled by it. Inside, he has blocked out the news that has not really taken hold yet. To get the news through, he may need to be told several times. As the message slowly comes into view, it is followed by a more external shock, where there may be physical reactions such as paling of the skin, shortness of breath and physical numbness.

When shock occurs, a person may need to be sat down to prevent him from collapsing and given a drink of some sort to divert his attention. He may be shown sympathy and acceptance. If the shock is not a short-lived one, he may be escorted to a place where he can sit safely and let the news sink in.

A person can pre-empt shock symptoms to some extent by going to a place where he can safely hear the news. Especially if he is likely to move swiftly into more emotive stages, he will need to be in a private place, away from the embarrassment of public tears, and in the company of trusted friends or family.

Denial

The initial shock begins to merge into denial, where a person displays no knowledge of the news. He effectively closes his eyes and ears to any evidence, pretending that nothing has happened. Denial involves rationalizing and becomes a necessary mechanism of self-defense in helping a person cope and survive a horrible, unexpected, or sudden traumatic experience or loss. In this stage, the world temporarily becomes meaningless and overwhelming. Nothing seems to make sense. A person goes numb and questions whether he can go on with life. But denying feelings, and failing to work through grief, is harder on the body and mind than going through it. If he does manage to go on, he questions why he should go on. He tries to find ways to simply get through each moment, each day, each month and each year. Denial is a gift that helps a person pace his feelings of grief, letting in only as much as he can handle.

Typically, a person in denial will continue his life as if nothing has happened. In the workplace, he will carry on doing his job even if that job is no longer required. At home, he will continue to assume that his marriage is stable. Health problems simply do not exist. As he accepts the reality of his loss he begins to ask himself questions. Unknowingly, he is beginning the healing process, becoming stronger at the broken places in his life. As he does, denial slowly begins to fade and denied feelings begin to surface. A classic behavior here is a 'flight into health', where previously-perceived problems are suddenly seen as having been miraculously fixed.

Most people are unprepared for grief, since so often, tragedy strikes suddenly and without warning. The vast majority find emotional pain more difficult to deal with than any physical pain, often withdrawing from their usual social contacts. It takes a lot of courage to share pain with another. But that act of courage is the first step in really taking that painful problem and being very constructive in dealing with it. If good self-care habits are practiced, it helps them to deal with the pain and shock of loss until acceptance is reached. With good self-care habits and having a circle of family members or friends or mentors, grieving and its stresses pass more quickly. It also helps to eat a balanced diet, drink enough non-alcoholic or non–caffeinated fluids, and get exercise and rest.

Anger

"Anger," Danny Trejo says, "is inward fear directed outward," on loved ones, peers and total strangers. C.S. Lewis says that "men are not angered by mere misfortune but by misfortune conceived as injury. And the sense of injury depends on the feeling that a legitimate claim has been denied. The more claims on life, therefore, that man can be induced to make, the more often he will feel injured and, as a result, ill tempered."[43]

Mohammed went to a Circle K store the other day. He was only in there for about five minutes. When he came out there was a motorcycle cop writing a parking ticket. So Mohammed went up to the cop and said, "Come on buddy, how about giving a guy a break?" The cop ignored Mohammed and continued writing the ticket. So Mohammed called him a pencil neck. The cop glared at Mohammed and started writing another ticket for having bald tires. So Mohammed called him a horse's ass. The cop finished the second ticket and put it on the car windshield with the first ticket. Then, he started writing a third ticket. This went on for nearly a half-hour. The more Mohammed verbally abused the cop, the more tickets that were wrote. Mohammed did not give a damn. His car was parked around the corner! Imagine the shock experienced by the owner of the car…with all the fix-it tickets.

Chronic anger can lead to an early heart attack; to an enlarged, less efficient heart; and to a depressed immune system, leading to more illnesses and longer recovery. Chronic anger displayed in the presence of children can lead to a lowering of the child's IQ by as much as 25 points; a lowering of his problem-solving ability by as much as 30 points; and, in the case of neglect, a reduction in the size of the child's cortex in the brain, or the thinking part of the brain.

Fear, spelled F.E.A.R., is often presented as an acronym that stands for *false evidence appearing real*. While vacationing in Atlantic City, Sally wins a bucketful of quarters at a slot machine. She wants to take a break from the slots for dinner with her husband in the hotel dining room. But first she wants to stash the quarters in her hotel room. "I'll be right back and we'll go to eat," she tells her husband and carries the coin-laden bucket to the elevator.

As Sally is about to walk into the elevator she notices two men already aboard. Both are black. One of them is big, very big and an intimidating figure. Sally freezes. Her first thought is: "Oh, my God. These two men are going to rob me." Her next thought is: "Don't be a bigot. They look like perfectly nice gentlemen." But racial stereotypes are powerful and fear immobilizes her. She stands and stares at the two men. She feels anxious, flustered and hopes they cannot read her mind. "But God, they must know what I am thinking."

Sally's hesitation about joining them in the elevator is all too obvious now. Her face is flushed. She couldn't just stand there. So with effort and will power, she picks up one foot and follows with the other foot onto the elevator. Avoiding eye contact, she turns around stiffly and watches the elevator doors as they close. A second passes and then another second and then another. Her fear increases. The elevator doesn't move. Panic consumes her. "My God," Sally thinks, "I'm trapped and about to be robbed!" Her heart plummets. Perspiration pours from every pore. Then one of the men says, "Hit the floor." Instinct tells her to do what they tell her. The bucket of quarters flies upwards as she throws out her arms and collapses on the elevator floor. A shower of coins rains down on her. "Take my money and spare me," she prays.

More seconds passes. Then, she hears one of the men say politely, "Ma'am, if you'll just tell us what floor you're going to, we'll push the button." The one who makes the request has a little trouble getting the words out. He is trying mightily to hold in a belly laugh. The woman lifts her head and looks up at the two men. They reached down to help her up. Confused, she struggles to her feet. "When I told my friend here to hit the floor," says the average-sized man, "I meant that he should hit the elevator button for our floor. I didn't mean for you to hit the floor, ma'am." He speaks genially.

He bites his lip. It is obvious he is having a hard time not laughing. Sally thinks, "My God, what a spectacle I've made of myself." She is too humiliated to speak. She wants to blurt out an apology, but words fail her. "How do you apologize to two perfectly respectable gentlemen for behaving as though they were going to rob you?" she ponders. She doesn't know what to say.

The two men gather up the quarters and help fill Sally's bucket. When the elevator arrives at her floor they insist on walking her to her room. Sally seems a little unsteady on her feet, and they are afraid she might not make it down the corridor. At her door they bid her a good evening. As Sally slips into her room she can hear the two men roaring with laughter as they walk back to the elevator.

Sally brushes herself off. She pulls herself together and goes downstairs for dinner with her husband.

The next morning flowers are delivered to her room – a dozen roses. Attached to each rose is a crisp one hundred-dollar bill. The card says: "Thanks for the best laugh we've had in years." And it is signed: Eddie Murphy & Michael Jordan.

A grieving person can be moved out of denial by deliberately provoking him to anger; sympathetically holding up the future so he cannot avoid or deny his circumstances. He can be told that his situation is not fair, that experience is not what happens to him but what he does with that which happens to him. Others can also show anger, thus legitimizing when he gets angry. Others may suggest that he "look for the gift within the loss" or other ways of cutting off difficult feelings, but their suggestions may cause him to feel pressured to hide or deny his emotions. Healing will thus take longer.

When the traumatized and grieving individual is angry, the best thing others can do is give him space, allowing him to rail and bellow. The more the storm blows, the sooner it will blow itself out. However, where anger becomes destructive then it must be addressed directly. As necessary, others may need to remind the traumatized and grieving individual of appropriate and inappropriate behavior. Attempt to reframe his anger into useful channels, such as problem areas and ways to move foreword. Beware of the anger becoming an argument for the individual may be pushed back into denial or cause later problems. Support and accept the anger; even let the anger be directed at others until it can be managed, then transformed.

Anger and –isms…sexism, racism, ageism tend to isolate and disconnect individuals from their fellow human beings. Beginning in infancy, children generally mirror their caregivers consciously until the behaviors become habitual. Paul T. P. Wong, a Ph.D. professor of Counseling Psychology at Trinity Western University, proposes that which is habitual can be transformed *over time* by way of four basic processes – creatively, socially, existentially or spiritually.

Angry feelings are transformed into something new, such as works of art, inventions, and other creations. When imagination is stimulated and powered by anger, anything can happen when it is transformed creatively. The creative process provides both an outlet and a goal for an individual's pent-up emotions. Some of the most memorable poems and music have been created out of the depth of suffering and anger. Some of the best ideas have been born in the crucible of despair and frustration.

Charlie Yardbird Parker experiences many personal difficulties throughout his life. Often in debt and addicted to alcohol and drugs, he endures broken marriages, suicide attempts, and imprisonment. His death at the age of thirty-four is the result of a number of ailments, including stomach ulcers, pneumonia, cirrhosis of the liver, and a heart attack. Parker once said that "if you don't feel the music in your soul, it's not going to come out of your horn."

Billie Holiday, whose mother is only thirteen when Billie is born, grows up in a brothel. It is there she first hears the music of Louis Armstrong and Bessie Smith on an old Victrola. Billie dies at the age of forty-four in New York almost unrecognizably thin, drawn, and haunted. She sells off her clothing to feed her habit and her little dog. Even on her deathbed, someone manages to smuggle heroin into her room.

John Coltrane, whose addictions lead to his early death, recovers in time to compose "A Love Supreme," a synthesis of music and religion to the glory of God. Coltrane says, "My music is the spiritual expression of what I am – my faith, my knowledge, my being… When you begin to see the possibilities of music, you desire to do something really good for people, to help humanity free itself form its hang-ups… I want to speak to their souls."

Rage has the potential of being transformed into social reform through activism and political struggles. Martin Luther King Jr. is a prime example. Social interest and acts of altruism can indirectly reduce one's angry feelings. Often, social transformation is a group effort, as oppressed individuals are galvanized and organized to fight for justice, freedom and a higher purpose; to make a difference in this world. A non-profit, gun-buy-back program is initiated in South Boston in order to curb the random killing by gang members. Resignation, cynicism, and bitterness can fester and destroy a person. But smothering anger can also spark the spirit of social reformation to fight against injustice, oppression and abuse.

Bitter despair can also be transformed existentially into wisdom, serenity and a higher purpose through enlightened acceptance, detachment and self-transcendence. Personal hurts often fade away when viewed against the backdrop of inevitability and immensity of human pain and suffering. To affirm the goodness of life in the midst of misfortunes can also make pain more bearable when one embraces experiential, creative and attitudinal values.[20]

Pain can be spiritually transformed into transcendental experiences through spiritual exercises, such as prayer, mediation, forgiveness and reconciliation. Human beings perceive that they are no longer alone in their efforts to control anger, because they can solicit divine help according to their beliefs and faith traditions.

When spirituality is an important part of our lives, and faith is one of our core values, we are more likely to succeed in transcending our plight and enter into a chapter in our life in which anger gives way to thanks. The development of spiritual maturity may lead to a state of total surrender to the wisdom within or divine higher power. Different from other processes, spiritual transformation needs to take place in the person first, before it can be practiced effectively.

Anger becomes part of the healing process when it is not only managed but also transformed through these processes. A grieving person must be willing to feel his anger, even though it may appear without end. Anger dissipates and healing begins when a person truly feels it. There are many other emotions under the anger and an individual will get to them over time, but anger is the emotion individuals are most used to managing. Anger has no limits. It extends not only to friends, doctors, family, self and loved ones who died, but also to God.

A grieving person may ask, "Where is God in this? The grieving person may even be angry with himself for letting the event take place, even if, realistically, nothing could have stopped it. The phrase 'Why me?' may be repeated in an endless loop in his head. A part of this anger is thus deflected, 'Why not you?' This only fuels the anger at those who are not affected or perhaps not as seriously so.

Underneath anger is pain. It is natural for a grieving and angry person to feel deserted and abandoned, but we live in a society that fears anger. Constructive anger can be strength. It can be an anchor, giving temporary structure to the nothingness of loss. At first, grief feels like being lost at sea with no connection to anything. Then the grieving person gets angry at someone, maybe a person who didn't attend a funeral, maybe a person who isn't around, maybe a person who is acting different now that a loved one has died. Suddenly a grieving person has a structure in the form of anger toward others. The anger becomes a bridge over the open sea, a connection from the grieving person to others. It becomes something to hold onto. A connection made from the strength of anger feels better than nothing. We usually know more about suppressing anger than feeling it. The anger is just another indication of the intensity of love.

Bargaining (with a Higher Power)

After the fires of anger have been blown out, the next stage is a desperate round of bargaining, seeking ways to avoid having the life-threatening or traumatic event happen. "God," we may bargain, "I will never be angry at my child again if you'll just let her live." After a loss, bargaining may take the form of a temporary truce. "If I devote my life to helping others, can I wake up and realize this has all been a bad dream?" We become lost in a series of "What if…" and "If only…" statements to the judge, the doctor or God.

We want life returned to what was. We want the health of our loved one restored. We want to go back in time, to be able to alter our course, to negotiate our way out of the hurt, to take a different path, make a different decision, discover a health issue earlier…if only, if only, if only. Bargaining is thus a vain expression of hope that the bad news is reversible, or at least survivable. When bargaining takes place in organizations, it may include offering to work for less money, offering to do supplemental work or accepting a demotion within the hierarchy.

One's loyalties, debts and dependants may be paraded as evidence of the essentiality of being saved.

When traumatized individuals bargain, others should not offer any false hope. Although there may be practical things the traumatized or terminally ill can do which others can offer them, others should never offer something that cannot be fulfilled. Sometimes the best others can do at this stage is point even more at the inevitable, even though this may well tip the traumatized or ill into depression which may well be a necessary move.

Guilt is often the companion of bargaining. "If only..." statements cause us to find fault in ourselves and what we believe we could have done differently. We may even bargain with the unavoidable pain; do anything not to feel the pain of loss. When the expression of anger is allowed to be experienced without guilt or shame, bargaining takes place, promises that are seldom kept, while the ante is raised each time.

When a person is in a bargaining mood, sometimes there are things others can offer him, such as support for change or new opportunities to embrace the inevitable in creative ways. In these cases others may be able to strike a win-win deal, where the grieving person gets an improved deal and others get collaboration or some other contribution. In a business setting, this may include finishing off some important work before leaving and receiving a special bonus for doing so.

Bargaining can sometimes simulate a spiritual quest to a Higher Power, even as the terminally ill seeks a magic pill, powder or potion to anesthetize the pain or cure the illness. Spiritual by nature, when we suffer physical, mental or emotional pain, we consciously or unconsciously seek a spiritual remedy, the spiritual dimension equivalent to a medicine chest. So, what are the implications?

Drug Religion

Every religion has four basic characteristics in common – a leader, sacraments, rituals, and jargon. When human beings suffer a traumatic event or life-threatening illness, they often seek out a leader of their faith – shaman, guru, priest, or imam - because they feel that s/

he has the answers, a remedy for taking away the pain and suffering. In the *drug religion*, for example, the person suffering the pain or illness may seek out an illicit drug dealer, pusher, bartender, or long-term addict. S/he seeks out this person because s/he feels that the chosen one has a remedy.

As in other religions, the pseudo drug religion also has sacraments – drug paraphernalia, things that are uniquely associated with its practice. It also has rituals, practices unique to an illicit drug culture that persons rehearse again and again until they feel fairly certain that they're not going to endanger themselves or embarrass themselves in the 'congregation' of the user/abusers. The drug religion also maintains a fluid jargon and code of 'ethics' spelled out in a bible which constantly changes to confuse 'outsiders' such as concerned parents and undercover narcotic agents. Rites that make one a member of the drug religion have the potential of being deadly when repeated again and again. Does this religious phenomenon affect other areas of society? I believe that it does.

War Religion

The *war religion* also has its leader, sacraments, rituals and jargon. The leader in the war religion is the Commander in Chief. The sacraments are the weapons of war - small, medium and large handheld weapons, short- and long-range ballistic missiles, armored tanks, jets and bombers; they also include biological, chemical and nuclear weapons. The rituals include military boot camp, parades, and war games. And the jargon includes identification of military maneuvers, the ever-changing secret code words to counter espionage, and military strategy documents.

Socio-Economic Religion

The *socio-economic religion* too has its leader, sacraments, rituals and jargon. The top five leaders in the world of capitalism include, Bill Gates, Warren Buffet, and Lawrence Ellison of the United States, Carlos Slim Helu of Mexico, and Ingvar Kamprad and family of Sweden. The sacraments include mega-mansions, limousines, land

and mineral rights, precious stones and intangible stocks and bonds. The rituals are the corporate ladders, the dance of intimacy, and other. The jargon includes the fluid and ever-changing vocabulary. Corporations no longer 'lay off' employees; they 'downsize.'

Neurotic Triad: Depression, Addiction & Aggression

After denial, anger, and bargaining, the inevitability of the news eventually, and not before time, sinks in. The grieving person reluctantly accepts that a traumatic event, such as death, is going to happen, but he feels cheated. From the animation of anger and bargaining, he slumps into a slough of despondency. He enters a deeper level, deeper than he ever imagined. The neurotic triad of depression, aggression or addiction becomes a vicious cycle. In deep depression, he sees only a horrible end with nothing beyond it. He feels numb, isolated, and empty, involving a loss of self-esteem, with anger and sadness lying just beneath the surface. He feels as though it will last forever. In turning in towards himself, he turns away from any solution and any help that others can give him. He sees no escape from his fate.

Depression may be seen in a number of passive behaviors. In the workplace, this includes physical absenteeism, long lunch breaks and mediocre work performance. It can also appear in tearful and morose episodes where the person's main concern is focused on his own world. The first thing others can do with people who are in depression is to be there with him, accepting him in all his misery. People who are depressed feel very much alone and the company of others, even though it may not seem that way, is likely to be welcome.

It's important to understand that this depression is not a sign of mental illness. It is the appropriate response to a great loss. A grieving person withdraws from life, left in a fog of intense sadness, wondering, perhaps, if there is any point in going on alone. Why go on at all? Depression after a loss is too often seen as unnatural: a state to be fixed, something to snap out of. The first question to ask oneself is whether or not the situation is actually depressing. The loss of a loved one is a very depressing situation, and depression is a normal and appropriate response. To not experience depression after a loved one dies would be unusual. When a loss fully settles in one's soul, the realization that his loved one didn't get better this time and is not coming back is understandably depressing. If grief is a process of healing, then depression is one of the many necessary steps along the way.

The second thing for a grieving person to do is to keep moving. It is easy to get stuck in depression, and the longer he stays there, the deeper into the mud he is likely to sink. So a steady stream of support is important to keep up, showing the grieving person that there is light ahead and encouraging him to reach towards it. In the workplace, provision of professional coaching, counseling and other support can do a lot to help a grieving person recognize his depression and find a way to clamber out of the pit of despair, despondency, and dysfunction.

Depression is a gift of life, a painful signal that a root situation has become unmanageable. However, when it gets covered over by pain suppressors, a grieving person never gets to the root of what's going on, or what's causing the pain in his life. Depression is a call for transformation to become the next possible self he can be in the ontological development and growth as a human being. But change can be frightening. His ego tells him that he appears to be losing his world – his current support system, and he doesn't know what he is going to become.

Depression provides an illusion of helplessness while addictions provide an illusion of control. Addictions transport an individual into a world where he seems to be in charge. They provide a predictable way of changing the way he feels about others and himself. They appear to provide predictable doses of relief and power in the midst of pain and helplessness. But in reality they are a house of mirrors, promising freedom and then trapping an individual with little hope of escape. The effect is always self-destructive bondage.

A grieving person needs a place where he can gather his thoughts in the absence of sensory chatter in the body, mind or spirit. So, when depression becomes too painful and difficult to handle, a grieving person often retreats back to the bargaining stage. That leads us to the third illusion, anger and aggression directed toward self and others. At first, using aggressive behaviors can help an individual feel that he is getting what he wants and that he can control other people. However, gradually this behavior may feel quite frightening and out of control, as he pushes people further away and feels more and more alone.

Sometimes what an individual puts in his body brings on depression. Diet and lifestyle account for about sixty to seventy percent of what can be done to treat depression and other mental imbalances. On the other hand, self-talk may account for nearly 90 percent of all psychosomatic illnesses. There are times when an individual simply needs to take a break from negative thoughts and images; this includes negative messages or unwanted obligations and 'would-of, should-of, could-of, and if-only' that may be coming from outside oneself.

Groundhog-Day Effect

Sometimes people habitually get stuck in one of these early stages, repeating it again and again. At other times the traumatized individual may appear to "bounce" back and forth between loss and anger, loss and bargaining or loss and depression. Their lives can be painful, spinning out of control unless and until they move to the healing stage – acceptance. Last night Jesus, in a drunken stupor, physically abused his wife and children. However, the very next day he experienced a "groundhog-day effect." All was forgotten and his family whom he abused seemed to have forgotten the incident. Therefore, Jesus is in the same position as he was before he got drunk and abused his family. He, like most human beings, is a creature of habit, and he instinctively struggles with change. He is literally trapped in a time loop, like Phil in the movie *Groundhog* Day, trapped by virtue of conditioning. When confronted with his addiction and aggression he responds with a built-up contempt, withdrawal or defensive mechanism, so whatever his wife learns about assertiveness and boundaries is futile. The "groundhog-day effect" is based on the movie *Groundhog* Day, a parable about personal transformation. It is the idea that the rewards and consequences of every action that one makes are not followed through the next day. If someone were to make a big choice, commit a crime, offend someone, make a mistake, or meet someone through out a period of a regular 24-hour day, the rewards and consequences for all of those actions are not carried through the next day. It is all forgotten. In other words, it's like yesterday never happened. Therefore this pattern can keep on repeating for an unknown amount of time as one questions how to get out of a rut, to find meaning and fulfillment, to reconnect with family, friends, and coworkers, and to create enduring change.

The groundhog-day effect says that every context for action is in some degree novel, if only because the individual has lived through all his previous experiences before the current situation arose. This point was made by the philosopher Henri Bergson and, perhaps, by others before him. More recently, it was used a plot device in the Hollywood movie *Groundhog Day*. The protagonist, Phil rises each day to find that it is precisely the same as the previous day. Every day is February second; every day is Groundhog Day. The townspeople are unaware of this and behave identically on each repeated day. But the protagonist is aware of the past Groundhog Days and behaves differently from repeated day to repeated day. Even in the fantasy setting of this Hollywood movie, every context for action is in some degree novel, if only because the individual has lived through all his or her previous experiences before the current situation arose. This insight is the groundhog-day principle.

So how does Phil Connors change in the movie? Ironically, Phil breaks free and changes his life by slowing down, varying his actions over time, sometimes slightly, sometimes radically. By doing the equivalent of going from fast-forward to pause, he can start to see an accurate image of himself. Forced to witness his life in slow motion and pay attention to all the effects of his thoughts and actions on himself and on others, he gains great self-awareness and changes from the inside out. His transformation is authentic and enduring, unlike so many of the fleeting, superficial changes gained at such a high cost in incarceration.

By the groundhog-day effect, Phil was always facing something at least a little bit new and unprecedented. Thus, he had to improvise even if only slightly. The groundhog-day effect tells us, then, that all action must be in some degree an improvisation. To improvise is to do something new and different. It is to innovate. Thus, all action is innovation. But an innovation implies a previous discovery of an opportunity. And such a discovery can be made only if the individual is alert in an uncertain world. Uncertainty is an important and necessary element of the world in which human beings act. It is important, therefore, to have as much clarity as we can about the nature of uncertainty and its influence on action. The future is unknowable, though not unimaginable.

Like Phil, each of us can begin by paying attention to the consequences of our actions and recognizing the power of the underlying patterns and conditioned responses that have determined most of our habitual thoughts and behaviors. Only then will you begin to break free of what is referred to as the groundhog-day effect. This is what keeps us stuck, like the mysterious power of frozen time in the movie. When we accept that the strategies that used to work for us are no longer working, when we confront and overcome the fears and negative habits that keep us stuck, we begin to free ourselves and make genuine, long-lasting progress rather than the temporary fix of addictions and aggressions.

Experiment each day with a new approach to life and measure the effect of changing just one variable of your thoughts and behaviors as Phil did. In changing the way he greeted Larry the cameraman, Phil was able to measure the results of that single modification. Over time he discovered his greatest power lay in his ability to choose how he responded to his predicament.

Each day, you also enjoy the choice of how to create your day even if you rarely exercise that choice. Like Phil, you can wake up to a new day and choose the most effective and fulfilling strategies to live a more meaningful life. You can accept what you cannot change, and focus on what you can.

Viktor Frankl emphasizes that meaning is discovered by embracing experiential, attitudinal, and creative values. By paying attention to our moment-to-moment experiences, we discover we have a wide range of meaningful options rather than restricting ourselves to our worn-out, habitual responses driven by the desire for pleasure, power or prosperity. We can generate new ideas, new thoughts, and new behaviors that are meaningful.

Every day we have an opportunity to press the reset button and start again. We can choose to repeat our yesterdays and relapse in our addiction, aggression or depression, or we can press the reset button and listen to the wisdom within and pursue a meaningful course at that fork in the road of life. We can choose to learn new skills and techniques, or stay stuck in what appeared to work for us ten, twenty, or thirty years ago yet increasingly delivers diminishing returns as we lose our freedom, our career, our home, our health and our family.

The most successful and fulfilled people tend to have the widest range of strategies, tools, perspectives, and skills. They focus on changing themselves rather than trying to change other people, society or the laws. They are more resourceful and able to find creative solutions to any challenge they face. Creativity begins when you simply make small adjustments to your daily routine, to your belief window, and start each day as a new opportunity to recreate yourself – like Phil does.

It is only when Phil becomes compassionate and devotes his life to serving others that he breaks out of the groundhog-day loop when pleasure and power are used in a meaningful way. He becomes emotionally engaged with life and other people. He releases his need to manipulate the world around him. This offers a profound lesson to those wishing to discover their meaning potential.

Viktor Frankl says that we can find meaning, purpose, and fulfillment through serving a cause greater than ourselves which inspires us, such as mentoring youths in at-risk environments. In applying the ideas of the movie to articulate a vision, set of values, and culture that helps people to make the shift that Phil does in the movie or when in doubt, you may ask yourself, "what would Phil do?" Creatively we achieve meaning, says Frankl, through creative works and deeds. Creative works may involve a paper, wood, or metal project, making a flower arrangement, mechanically working on our car, decorating our home, creating a song, a poem, a short story, or other hobbies and leisure activities. It generally involves something that we enjoy doing and gives our life meaning.

A third way to achieve meaning lays in the attitude we take toward unavoidable suffering or fate. The tragic triad that remains unavoidable includes death, survival guilt, and unavoidable pain. It is not so much what happens to us that counts however, but the attitudes we take toward what happens to us. It is useless to ask why things happened to us; the useful approach is to ask what we can do in the situation in which we find ourselves.

Testing

The next stage is one of cautious testing, seeking realistic solutions. Even in the pit of depressive despair, reality eventually starts to bite and the individual realizes that he cannot stay in that deep, dark cesspool of despair forever. He thus starts looking for realistic things that he can do. These may be taken on as 'experiments' to see if doing these things help the situation in any way. As this activity starts to work, at least in some ways, it is found to be preferred to the neurotic triad (Frankl 1959) and so the person crawls out of that dark hole.

This escape is often done with the support of friends, family and professionals who specialize in helping people in whatever situation arises. In medicine, hospices help the terminally ill face their short futures with courage. In organizations, counselors and outplacement consultants help individuals move on to other work.

When an individual reaches out towards the road to acceptance, he is at last on his way out of the mire. Others may help him try different solutions and to see that he can, after all, have an effect on his future. Hand as much control to him as is measurably possible, as this gives him a lifeline of stability on which to pull himself forward.

Acceptance: Let Go; Let Be; Let Grow

The year is 1501. A gigantic slab of marble has stood gathering dust in the workshop of a Florentine cathedral for nearly forty years. The Renaissance sculptor Agostino de Duccio left it there, only partially worked, where locals referred to it as "the Giant," and deemed it little more than a future ruin.

Enter Michelangelo, to whom the head of the Florentine government entrusted the flawed marble slab, and who over the next four years will carve it into a statue of *David*, a masterpiece. An admirer asks Michelangelo how he sculpted the famous statue.

States Michelangelo, "I fixed my attention on the slab of raw marble. I studied it and then chipped away all that wasn't David."

He worked undistracted by all the extra material, peering through the unformed shape into what the figure it would become. Michelangelo intimately knew David - his age, how he was positioned, the shape of his torso, and the curved left arm just below his chin. Through the amorphous mass of rock, a clear form crystallized in his imagination. The marble would only need gradual chipping away. Michelangelo saw through the raw material, through all the chipping away, to its ultimate perfection. He created the statue of David through what he removed, through what he negated. Put simply, he created by accepting what was within, letting go of that which was not meaningful. It is a story of *acceptance.*

Acceptance is often confused with the notion of being "all right" or "OK" with what has happened. This is not the case. Most people don't ever feel OK or all right about the loss of a loved one. This stage is about accepting the reality that our loved one is physically gone and recognizing that this new reality is the permanent reality. We will never like this reality or make it OK, but eventually we accept it. We learn to live with it. It is the new norm with which we must learn to live. We must try to live now in a world where our loved one is missing.

In resisting this new norm, at first many people want to maintain life as it was before a loved one died. In time, through bits and pieces of acceptance, however, we see that we cannot maintain the past intact. It has been forever changed and we must readjust. We must learn to reorganize roles, re-assign them to others or take them on ourselves. Finding acceptance may be just having more good days than bad ones. As we begin to live again and enjoy our life, we often feel that in doing so, we are betraying our loved one. We can never replace what has been lost, but we can make new connections, new meaningful relationships, and new inter-dependencies. Instead of denying our feelings, we listen to our needs; we move, we change, we grow, we evolve. We may start to reach out to others and become involved in their lives. We invest in our friendships and in our relationship with ourselves. We begin to live again, but we cannot do so until we have given grief its time.

The final stage then becomes one of accepting what is a fact. It means facing inescapable physical or emotional pain, and 'listening' to the *meaning* lying within. Facing that which cannot be changed thus diminishes the negative powers that confront an individual. In the case of traumatic physical pain associated with disease or illness, the responsible thing to pursue is to transcend the pain through how an individual thinks, the attitude he embraces, and how he feels. Terminally ill persons begin to put their lives in order, sort out wills and help others to accept the inevitability that they now have faced. In the workplace, people who have lost their jobs actively seek an alternative career or entrepreneurial venture, whilst others who have had their work changed tidy up and get ready to move on.

Acceptance is typically visible by people taking ownership both for themselves and their actions. They start to do things and take note of the results, and then changing their actions in response. They appear increasingly happier and more content as they find their way forward. Acceptance is surrendering to what is; letting go. Acceptance of impending death, physical brokenness or traumatic illness takes place slowly as an individual quietly makes necessary plans and performs tasks that enable him to grow strong at the broken places. It takes place as he begins to embrace experiential, attitudinal and creative values[20] – letting be, letting go and letting grow.

Individuals affected by depression need a place where they can gather their thoughts in the absence of external and internal sensory chatter; chatter can take place in the body, mind or spirit dimension, the latter having the potential to heal. Each dimension is capable of reflecting like a mirror what is going on in another dimension. The body mirrors what is going on in the mind. When an individual goes back and catches the negative thoughts that are causing pain, he begins the process of healing.

There appears to be a strong relationship between health and illness in the body and mind. Diet and lifestyle can have both negative and positive impact on depression and other mental imbalances. Self-talk may account for most psychosomatic illnesses. There are times when an individual simply needs to take a break from thoughts and images – obligations, would-of, should-of, could-of, and if-only situations driven by internal or external sources.

If individuals are allowed to express their anger, to cry and grieve, to finish their unfinished business, to articulate their fears, to work through the stages of shock, denial, anger, bargaining, depression and testing, they will reach the last stage of acceptance. They won't be happy, but they will no longer be depressed or angry. Acceptance is a period of quiet, meditative resignation, of peaceful expectancy.

The previous struggle begins to disappear, replaced by the need for lots of rest and sleep.

Acceptance is when the anger, sadness and mourning have tapered off. The person simply accepts the reality of a loss and enters three sub stages of *letting go, letting be,* and *letting grow* – the equivalent of embracing experiential, creative and attitudinal values.[19] Acceptance is recommitting to one's life purpose, coming out of a new situation. Acceptance is a willingness to converse in depth about one's present awareness of memories, dreams and hopes while remaining fully cognizant of the present realities. Acceptance is a willingness to enter into peer-type relationships with other people instead of remaining in self-pitying relationships or loneliness. It is the capacity to take an interest in more than one's body, prestige, or material possessions.

Letting Go: Embracing Experiential Values

Elisabeth Kubler-Ross emphasized that "We need to teach the next generation of children from Day One that they are responsible for their lives. Mankind's greatest gift, also its greatest curse, is that we have free choice. We can make our choices built from love or from fear." We always remain free to reject and transcend those conditions, to move toward something positive. Letting go means that we are free to make choices, which carry a certain amount of responsibility. Even here, freedom is not freedom from responsibility, but freedom to be responsible for choices made. We must, says Frankl, accept our responsibleness in the three ways in which meaning may be discovered: 1) by doing a creative, meaningful deed, 2) by experiencing a value, such as a work of art or nature, or by experiencing someone through love, and 3) by how we suffer.[20]

Kubler-Ross further states that *"There are no mistakes, no coincidences. All events are blessings given to us to learn from."*

Acceptance is unconditional surrendering; letting go; a rite of passage. Letting go becomes more formidable if an individual is also carrying an assortment of phobic baggage. Being told to let go can be one of the most frightening suggestions that an individual will ever hear. It means letting go of old support systems, trusting that new support systems will be there when an individual needs them.

Human beings are born with two fears, the fear of sudden loud noises and the fear of falling. All other fears are learned. And being told to let go can be one of the most frightening suggestions that an individual will ever hear. It's like standing at the doorway of an airplane flying at 15,000 feet and being told to jump with a parachute packed by an unknown person with unknown packing skills. Letting go means being stripped of all beliefs, principles, friends, family, former occupation, clothing and even the roof over an individual's head that makes him feel comfortable, loved and secure.

Most indigenous cultures have elaborate initiation procedures for their youth during the age of puberty. However, in the modern world, one does not have to be a member of an indigenous community to experience initiation. In fact, Carl Jung asserted that initiation is an archetype or fundamental motif inherent in the human psyche. We want and expect engagement in the initiatory process, not only at the age of puberty, but throughout our human experience. The process is so fundamental, Jung believed, that even if we do not participate in a formal rite of passage ceremony as we transition from youth to adulthood, our human journey will provide us with initiatory events for the purpose of deepening our humanity and our connection with the cosmos and something greater than the human ego.

Examples of initiatory events which humans frequently encounter are loss of meaningful work, loss of livelihood, loss of home, loss of health, loss of relationship, loss of future security, loss of life, or loss of place. Loss is the hallmark of modernity. The irony is that civilization has promised us inestimable gain but fundamentally delivered infinite loss at every turn of our path toward embracing its demands.

Among Kikuyu and Tembu tribal cultures where formal rites of passage are practiced, it is understood that life on earth is fraught with loss-that in fact, loss is the hallmark of human experience but that the bone-marrow ordeal of the initiatory process grounds the young person moving toward adulthood, by way of loss, into his or her permanent place in the community. Thus, regardless of what losses one may endure, for the initiated man or woman, one's connection with community and with the sacred are constant. As a result, one is equipped to face and navigate loss with remarkable fortitude and grace, not alone, but supported by elders and peers in the process.

Nelson Mandela, former president of South Africa was born in Transkei, South Africa. His father was Chief Henry Mandela. Prior to Nelson Mandela's rite of passage ceremony at the age of sixteen he had to let go of all things meaningful - family security, food, sleep, and even his clothes. Standing with all his peers in front of his village, stripped naked except for the white, chalky substance on his body, an elder takes out a very sharp knife and passes before each youth to perform circumcision on each. Each cut child then is taught ancient songs, ceremonies and shared responsibilities. That is the essence of letting go, of embracing experiential values.[20]

In certain cultures, those chosen to be royalty are wounded in some way that is outwardly apparent; the chosen one may have an ankle or leg broken by the elders that causes him to limp. The basic premise is that a wounded person would find it more difficult becoming a tyrant.

Rites of passage as initiatory experiences come in many forms: The arrest and imprisonment of Nelson Mandela, Russell Means and Aleksandr Solzhenitsyn for their beliefs; the full scale battle on the shores of Normandy; a firestorm battle in the rice paddies in Vietnam; the equestrian accident that paralyzed Christopher Reeves; a stroke that paralyzes the powers of speech of a orator; the incurable but painless disease of the nervous system, amyotrophic lateral sclerosis, that paralyzed the body of Stephen Hawking; the inhumanity and childhood abuse suffered by Maya Angelou and Eleanor Roosevelt; the loss of mobility suffered by Senator Max Cleland following the loss of an arm and both legs in Vietnam War; each of these experiences propelled individuals into the next chapter of their lives. As discussed in Chapter II, initiatory experiences share universal characteristics:

- They need be experienced only once.
- They are those in which we start to figure out which god is there in our lives.
- Individuals do not know where they are.
- Individuals must accept an unknown outcome.

- Individuals feel exposed, vulnerable, naked, and completely unprotected during the rite of passage ceremony; traumatized, some may even die.
- Individuals are not given a choice about turning back once they've entered the ceremony.
- The ceremony involves the physical body and all the senses.
- Individuals are made to feel exposed and the walls of vulnerability are broken down.

Individuals will be forced to face their worst fears and pain, sometimes fasting for several days and nights and put through sleep deprivation. With repeated practice at facing what individuals fear, their fears are gradually reduced (habituation). Viktor Frankl states that the way to reduce fears, anxiety, distress and doubt is to face the fear, anxiety, distress and doubt. It can be a difficult journey that requires a lot of dedication, courage, persistence and support.

Once individual youths have survived the rite of passage, they are taught myths, stories, and songs of their ancestral fathers, which embody not only the male competitive values in work, sport, battle, and sexual conquest, but spiritual values about soul, nature, tenderness, health, body, sexuality, desire, dance, poetry, beauty, deep feeling, suffering, weakness, fear and failure. Also, following the rite of passage ceremony, there may be a scar, a mark (tattoo), a new behavior, attitude, or some other evidence that change has taken place and can be seen by others.

The initiated youth comes out of the ceremony more alive, more involved in his life than before, and more willing to embrace experiential, attitudinal and creative values. He is ready to pursue his meaning and purpose; he shifts from his self-centeredness to a sense of community connectedness.

Jimmy's two children had embraced most of his values in their daily life by the time they were teenagers. They had become gifted climbing up and rappelling down mountains, riding trail bikes, and other adrenaline-producing activities. They knew the difference between living life vicariously and pursuing it in a clean and sober state. Jimmy's son was even beginning to understand the 'gift' of lessons learned from having entered several dysfunctional relationships. And his daughter was preparing for the ultimate adrenaline rush.

Jimmy had ridden on the Drop Zone several times but had no desire to skydive. The Drop Zone ride was simply a ride that involved a 22-story drop. The thought of skydiving, on the other hand, led to racing thoughts, increased heart rate, rapid shallow breathing, feeling dizzy or faint, sweating, shaking, nausea, fear, doubt and uncertainty. Any attempt to reduce his discomfort only reinforced and strengthened his fear of skydiving.

One day during her sixteenth year, Jimmy's daughter approached him with a request to go skydiving. "What an adrenaline rush that would be!" Jimmy responded. "Of course, I give you my blessing, but I want you to wait until your eighteenth birthday."

So, on the morning of her eighteenth birthday Jimmy's daughter approached him once again with the request, "Dad, remember the promise you made to me two years ago? You promised that I could go skydiving on my eighteenth birthday."

"Yes, I remember. What an adrenaline rush that is going to be. Of course, I give you my blessing. When do you want to go?"

"Today, Dad. I want to go skydiving today."

"Do you know where skydiving is offered?"

"Yes, I do. And I want it videotaped. It is part of the package."

"Great. I can't wait until I see that videotape."

Jimmy's daughter looked at him in disbelief, shaking her head. "But, Dad, I want you to accompany me; I want you to go skydiving too!"

Jimmy quickly responded, "Nope, not today." Jimmy's mind quickly hit the f*** it wall. Even though he had given his blessings to his daughter to skydive, he rationalized in his mind's eye that he was not ready to die. For him there were only two realities when it comes to skydiving: "She lives; I die."

Acceptance is a form of skydiving. Letting go amounts to overcoming the fear of skydiving and Jimmy had barely overcome his fear of great heights when he worked atop 90-foot oil- and gas-drilling rigs. He was not ready to skydive with his daughter; to let go and trust that it would all come out okay! In his mind, to suggest that he go skydiving was equivalent to hitting an overwhelming wall of FEAR – *F*alse *E*vidence *A*ppearing *R*eal.

When Jimmy watched the video of Jimmy's daughter sky-diving, he noticed that his daughter appeared to be talking to the other person tandem to her. Jimmy asked his daughter what she was saying to the man on the videotape. She stated that she was simply telling the professional sky-diver "This is fantastic!" and suggested, "Don't pull the cord on the parachute!" She was 'in the zone!'

Now, this scenario may seem both awe-inspiring and humorous because we may all hear the sound of our own voice in Jimmy's response to his daughter to go skydiving. It may be that we lack the courage to let go and say what we often think when we begin to hear the phrase "let go" in our own lives. We 'hit' that all-too-familiar wall, and we respond with, "Not now, thank you," or in other words, "never!"

This may be the story of just one of many peak experiences in an individual's life and of an invitation to take a different journey. Letting go frightens most. So they continue to hang onto whatever baggage, or whomever, for dear life. They fear the necessity of letting go of their long-held principles of what they feel are right, good, and normal, but they are often those of the organization, group or gang they've joined. They fear losing things, thoughts, friends, and their grasp on the meaning of life, or our life itself.

Together with the fear of loss comes the fear of the unknown on the other side of the experience of "letting go." Fear of the unknown tends to make individuals think that what they are clinging to is much better than a promise that seems beyond their reach, or their comprehension.

Intertwined with the fear of dying, the fear of loss, and the fear of the unknown is the fear of not being in control and the depression that accompanies it. Individuals are taught from birth to pursue happiness and to not relinquish control, even their control of others. When they are not happy, they've been brainwashed into believing that there is a magic pill, powder or potion, a wonderful woman or man, a residential area, or job that will make them happy. They avoid, at all costs, not being in control. Even thinking about "letting go" is depressing for many. Letting go can be very painful, but pain, unavoidable pain is the gift that nobody wants.[7]

When life is inviting individuals to let go, they must have the courage to obey, to face the pain, to trust the promise, and to embrace the paradox of living creatively by freely letting go, as in when indigenous children are asked to let go just before they participate in the rite of passage from childhood to man- and womanhood.

Letting go in no way lessons the experience of painful endings. A sprained ankle can be quite painful; so too can a broken leg, but upon healing it can become stronger at the broken places. In fact, letting go tends to intensify physical, emotional and spiritual pain, and to give it a deeper than personal meaning and direction. And in the process of letting go, individuals can become stronger at the broken places. Take for example the painful endings that begin with a commitment to remain clean and sober.

In letting go individuals begin to embrace experiential values, understanding that experiences, loves and encounters with others benefit us in some, not so obvious ways.[20] The gifts are not always immediately obvious. In fact, some may not be realized for months, years or even decades; perhaps not until an individual reaches the end of his/her life, looking back and receive that 'aha' realization. It was that way for Jimmy.

Jimmy lost his first child, but it would take several years for him to realize the 'gift.' His first wife threatened to abort any pregnancy beyond the second live birth. If Jimmy's first child had survived, he might not realize the many gifts experienced with his daughter, born third. "In all things give thanks" now made sense; Viktor Frankl's "experiential values" became all the more meaningful. Decades of gifts began to flood his mind. He no longer felt the victim; he was now not only the survivor, but also the victor. Unavoidable experiences were embraced with increased enthusiasm.

Letting go may sometimes require that an individual forgive another person or group of fellow human beings. There are gifts in every moment, but the paradoxical gifts of forgiveness often come unexpectedly. In Chapter three, you may recall Jimmy's divorce from his first wife, followed by the near-tragic attack on his baby daughter's life, the ensuing trauma endured by both she and his son, and Jimmy's decision to forgive all alleged parties involved in the incident. Jimmy's children needed him; and he needed them… more than they will ever know. Only later would he learn of their fears of being bathed by their mother during infancy, of being traumatized when she shut them in an entry closet, and many other unsold abuses.

Letting Be: Embracing Attitudinal Values

In letting be, individuals have a positive expectancy that their life moves in a direction uniquely meant for them. They embrace attitudinal values, the gifts of each lessons learned. In letting be, they embrace attitudinal values.[20]

Sam is an elderly man who lives in the projects of Compton, California. He is revered by all in the neighborhood as an honest, wise, old man. His reputation is beyond reproach. He survives on a limited pension and social security benefits that barely meet his living needs.

One day a young girl, who lived in the same neighborhood, was found to be pregnant. She was only sixteen years old but was nearing completion of her high school education. She would be the first in her family to enter college on a full scholarship. Her father was furious. He insisted that she tell him who was the father of the baby. She knew that she couldn't tell her father; he would certainly kill her boyfriend, she thought. The girl resisted for as long as she could, but finally she admitted, "It is the old man who lives on the corner."

On the day of birth, the girl's father immediately took the baby to the house of the old man "who had gotten his baby girl pregnant." "You hypocrite!" he shouted. "You have violated my child. This is your baby; she is your responsibility."

"If that's your position, so be it." The old man replied as he took the baby on a journey of care. He understood that life often presents us with unexpected tasks. Rabbi Hillel says, "if not me, then who? If not now, then when?"

From then on, whenever the old man would walk through the neighborhood to beg for baby food and clothing, he would carry the baby girl with him. The people in the neighborhood cursed him, mocked him, and gave him next to nothing to feed and clothe the baby.

Several weeks went by. The young girl, now a high school graduate and about to enter college, could bear it no longer. "Father," she said, "I have lied to you. The old man is not the father of my baby." Then she told him the name of the baby's father, a young college student whom his daughter would soon marry.

The girl's father was overwhelmed with shame. He went to see the old man. "Please forgive me," he said. "I have done you a terrible wrong. You are not the father of this child."

"If that is so, then let it be." The old man replied. Then he gave the baby back to the girl's father with his blessing.

If individuals have listened to 'let be' in their own lives, this story tends to be a wisdom story. It celebrates the courage of an old man who has learned to let life be. The old man in this story is someone who has 'let go' of his need to deny responsibility. He does not defend or justify himself. He does not blame the young girl or contradict the irate father. With knowing compassion, he simply lets life be. He has the extraordinary courage to affirm what 'is' so that, in time, it may take its next step and become what it is really meant to be. He has embraced attitudinal values.[20]

Letting Grow: Embracing Creative Values

In letting grow, individuals pursue the unique creative human being that they are. By embracing creative values, they pursue that creative element within that makes their lives meaningful. If an individual is mechanically inclined and enjoys working with hand and power tools, she must pursue it for her life to be meaningful. If he is musically inclined, his life can be meaningful only through the pursuit of music. If he is a father, he must choose to be present in parental ways even when nobody is looking. Fatherhood is not a one-night stand; any male can father a child; it takes a man to be a dad. These are only two examples of creative values that must be embraced in order for life to be meaningful. When individuals, through poor choices remove the opportunity to pursue *that which they are*, life slowly becomes meaningless, hardly worth living. It is actions, not words that tell others what is meaningful.

Summary

Every traumatic life experience or encounter with others allows an individual to pass through some or all of the stages of life described by Elisabeth Kubler-Ross: shock, denial, anger, bargaining, depression, testing and acceptance. An individual may respond directly to a stressful event with denial, or anger, or bargaining, or depression. Life experiences continue to benefit every individual in some unique way except when the individual chooses not to learn the lesson or lessons of the moment. When he chooses not to learn from and embrace the unique lesson intended for him the symbolic lessons will continue to be repeated again and again with potentially negative consequences, i.e., addictions, divorce, disease, jail and prison, bankruptcy, dishonorable discharge, underemployment, and social isolation. However, through unconditional 'acceptance' an individual is able to continue on his path toward higher spiritual lessons, wisdom and freedom. But freedom not used responsibly will only widen the existential vacuum and frustration.[20]

Many of the young today are acutely suffering existential frustration and desperately seeking to fill it with drugs and alcohol, rebellion and violence, material things and a supporting group of people. It takes the courage of a warrior to enter the stage of acceptance. It takes courage to suffer gracefully. It takes courage to accept that a relationship cannot be salvaged. It takes courage to face man-made fears. It takes courage to honor the timing that healing behind unavoidable pain and suffering require. To be human is to feel pain. It takes courage to 'let go' of the secure feeling one feels aboard a plane at 15,000 feet to skydive in a parachute packed by an unknown packer, knowing that he/she can never return to old 'support systems,' not knowing whether the parachute will open!

There are no mistakes, no coincidences. All events are blessings given to us to learn from.

- Elisabeth Kubler-Ross

Reflection Exercises on Death, Dying and Grief: Grief is a natural process to death and dying. It is not pathological in nature, but rather, is a necessary response to helping heal from the overwhelming sense of loss when a loved one dies. It is important to understand grief as part of the human experience. If you are grieving, some things you can do to help yourself include:

- *Attend an Intensive Journal workshop*
(See www.intensivejournal.org for schedule and location).
This program is what can keep you going through a difficult time. It can give you strength by being your support system in a sense. Not only can it help you to value the time you have left with your dying friend or family member but it can also help you to better communicate with him or her. This method can help you to heal. Even after your friend's or family member's death you still can use this method in your everyday life. It can help you to not only live in the here and now but also to understand that it is possible to live with the pain, see the beauty in things and become stronger in the broken places.

- *Attend support groups* in your area. Many communities have secular and faith-based support groups that focus on sibling, spousal, parental and child death. You do not need special gurus to help you understand death. Teachers come in all forms and disguises – children, the terminally ill, a cleaning woman, the taxi driver, a pet. Psychotherapists or ministers may not help anyone as much as one fellow human being unafraid to open his or her heart to another.

- *Therapy* with a Logotherapist, a psychotherapist, psychologist or other qualified mental health professional therapy can be helpful in many ways, especially when combined with a support group.

- *Nutrition Supports Good Mental Health.* It is important to eat healthy foods and take supplements.

- *Exercise Daily.* Take power walks or work out with aerobics or a spring-cleaning week (any time of the year). Physical exertion is a great stress reliever and may afford you some time alone to gather your thoughts in the process.

- *Sleep Six to Eight Hours.* Grief drains your emotional battery. You will need to recharge more often.

- *Read and Learn* about death-related grief responses. Knowledge helps people regain a sense of control over their experiences and helps reduce feelings of vulnerability.
- *Seek Solace* in the faith community – church, synagogues, temple, mosque and other.
- *Connect with Others* who have gone through a similar tragedy – stillbirth, infant or toddler death, spousal or parental death, or death of a loved one as a result of homicide or DUI. It is important to realize that children mourn, too. They may not express their feelings of loss in the same way as adults. There are helpful books and organizations to help grieving children.
- *Seek Comforting Rituals* – funeral, memorial service, plant a garden or tree as memorial to deceased, donate to a cause, comfort others who have lost a loved one.
- *Cry & Laugh*: Tears can be healing; so can laughter, remembering a time you both had together.
- *Avoid major changes* in residence, job or marital status which can be too burdensome during grief. Wait for about one year after the death of a loved one before making any major changes.
- *Volunteer* in a worthwhile cause.
- Live out the *Balance* of your life so that, in looking back over your life, you do not regret having wasted it.
- *Live your life honestly, fully and without regrets* not having lived it differently.
- *Make a list* and consciously practice creative, social, existential and spiritual transformation of stress-related anger.

VII.
Addictions, Aggression, Depression –
The Neurotic Triad in One's Spiritual Quests

A LOVE LETTER

You are more precious to me than any living creature.
Reposing in a small cavity near my heart I take comfort.
With my lips, I caress you more than I do my family.
When I awake, my thoughts constantly turn to you and
Remain there every conscious and unconscious moment.
You are there in my dreams, in my hopes, and in my goals.
I worship at your shrine with burnt offerings
Every waking and slumbering moment of the day.
At my desk, the fires seldom go out on your altar.
I joyously share the incense of your being
As I scatter it in the faces of my loved ones.
I need not call upon my creator to comfort me,
For you have always comforted me in times of need.
I therefore devote more offerings to you
Than to both churches and charities combined.
My devotion to you is stronger than my devotion to my life,
To my spouse, to my children, to my loved ones, or friends.
My devotion to you is stronger than my need to live,
To love and be loved, to feel important, or for variety.
In return for having loved you and risking my health,
I risk one chance in eight of having lung cancer
And double my chances of dying from heart attack.
I bear on my body the marks of my devotion to you –
The color of my fingertips, my lips, my tongue, and skin.

I cover my body – inside and out – with your incense.
Many hold their noses and walk away
When your essence seeps from the pores of my body.
But they do not love you as I do; they do not embrace you.
A new light is dawning; I have become your lover and slave.
I work tirelessly, thankful for your ever presence;
Then bed with you, suckling the essence of you on one end
While your love for me burns at the other.
I have become a sucker of a love gone wrong!

[The above is an adaptation of a letter in Coping Successfully with Stress and Distress, by Dr. Desmond Ford. In it Dr. Ford reminds us that 75 percent of diseases are diseases of choice. These diseases spring out of wrong 'loves' and 'wants' that we won't surrender. They are loves and wants that ultimately lead to overwhelming stress. The love-addiction to nicotine leads to the death of over 500,000 people in America, over 800,000 in India and over two million in China each year.]

When Human Beings Lack Meaning

Contrary to the stereotype that an addict is a male from a lower socio-economic background, poorly educated, ghetto-barrio-Chinatown bred, and socially disenfranchised, studies indicate that there is an increased or overrepresented drug and alcohol abuse among the most intelligent, skilled, and talented individuals of our society suffering from existential vacuum or frustration. Physicians, nurses, and those with high IQ are six to eight times more likely to be addicts than are members of the general population. Addiction to drugs, especially heroin and cocaine, is of epidemic proportions among the most academically and artistically talented. Priests seem more prone to alcoholism than others. The most gifted and highly motivated youths go on to higher rates of suicide and drug abuse. The answer for addicts, alcoholics, and others suffering existential frustration, says Viktor

Frankl, lies in providing them the tools for discovering their meaning, *not* in building more prisons and passing harsher penalties.

Consider the fact that over 15,000 people die each year in the United States from cocaine and heroin overdose. On the other hand, over 125,000 die from alcohol, including half of all murders and a fourth of all suicides. And over 425,000 deaths a year are attributable to tobacco (possibly millions more annually in China and India). Taken together, that's nearly 600,000 lives lost to drugs and alcohol each year in America, equivalent to the population of a large city and over eleven times the number of lives lost in the Vietnam War, at a cost of over $250 trillion. That's an enormous price to pay for those who suffer an existential vacuum from a loss of meaning.

Loss of meaning comes in many different forms. As early as the 1930s, Viktor Frankl warns that meaning crisis of the young often leads to the adoption of dangerous beliefs and to dangerous actions. Among the beliefs about which Frankl expresses concern are:

- Nihilism: The belief that life has no meaning or future. Nihilism, despair, gang formation and violence are particularly prevalent among a billion people residing in the world's slums. Second and third generation gang members do not know the meaning of a steady job. They share a fatalistic outlook on life, having had little future orientation. They also share a willingness to engage in very risky behavior, including nihilistic violence, a common sense of hopelessness, grinding poverty and oppression.

- Hedonism: The belief that life is short. Those who hold this belief feel that the search for meaning is a waste of effort. They tend to be driven by the want for pleasure, power and prosperity. They prefer pleasure, power and prosperity over existential pain, behaving the way they do because they believe the way they have chosen to behave will bring them more pleasure than pain.

- Pan Determinism: A Pan determinist believes that certain forces, such as genes, psychological drives, one's past, predeterminism, and the stars determine his life and its meaning; that there is no point in struggling for meaning because something is always controlling him.

- Reductionism: Anyone holding this belief feels that he is nothing but an animal that can be trained, a thing that can be manipulated, categorized and predicted. He believes that society placed him in a caste from which there is no escape, be it welfare, indigenous neighborhood, ex-felon, gang member or drug addict status, or racial boundaries.

- Conformity: A conformist believes that he does not have the capacity to find meaning, and thus he does what other people want him to do; he surrenders to cults, gurus, gang cliques and dogmas. His behavior resembles that of several processionary caterpillars which move through pine trees feeding upon pine needles in a long procession, one caterpillar leading and the others following, each with his eyes half-closed and his head snugly fitted against the rear extremity of his predecessor. Through sheer force of habit, each follows the same path in the same finite neighborhood while ample opportunities are close at hand and plainly visible, but outside his circle of concern. He continues along the beaten path of habit, custom, tradition, precedent, past experience, standard practice, or whatever you choose to call it, but he is following it blindly. He mistakes activity for accomplishment; meaning well, but getting no place.
- Fanaticism: A fanatic believes that only his path to meaning is right, and he does everything he can to force others to follow his path.

Add to that the number of children who have lost their lives to those attempting to divert their pain: nine of ten murdered children under age twelve and six in ten murdered children age twelve to seventeen were killed by grown-ups diverting their fear, anger and pain onto their own children, not by other children, and not by auto accidents. Over 100,000 children are sexually abused each year in America. Children are far more likely to be household-violence victims than adults. And yet, our top political leaders continue to be engaged in a relentless campaign to scapegoat children for an array of social ills.

In the last decade, millions of children were recruited as soldiers in genocide and gangland wars resulting in the killing of nearly two million children worldwide and over one million children orphaned or separated from their families. How many more must die?

In the last quarter century, drug abuse by the middle-aged has risen enormously causing a dramatic increase in deaths and hospital emergencies form overdoses of heroin, cocaine and prescription drugs. There are no easy solutions to growing old. There are no easy solutions to dealing with increased physical pain, alienation, loneliness, isolation, grief, oppression, anger, frustration, underemployment, and relationship problems. These are all painful issues of a meaningless life.

Joseph Fabry states that we can "find the direction of our life by trying to find, from moment to moment, the meaning of our existence (while relying) on values handed down from generation to generation, by tradition, through such human institutions as family, church, school, and state."[16]

People can put intensity in friendships and marriage by ending tentativeness. They can help their friendships and marriage grow by stopping criticism, contempt, defensiveness, neglect and withdrawal that are so prevalent. They can remove the conditions they have previously set for bestowing their unconditional friendship and love. They can pursue the friendship and marital journey together.

Furthermore, they can put intensity into their life by committing to working with children who are in need of a mentor to guide them in discovering their meaning potential. They may commit themselves to children who have never been told that they are worthwhile human beings. They may help the mentally and physically handicapped, the terminally ill to understand that their lives still have meaning. They can put intensity into their life by teaching a skill to others; spend some time reading or talking to the blind; to "live as if (they) were living a second time, and as though (they) had acted wrongly the first time."[20]

Joey's Trauma

Joey starts shooting cocaine shortly after the unexpected death of his daughter. There is the slightly bitter taste sensation and hissing roar in his ears, and the pounding heart and sweats. The cool rush of cocaine seems to help ease the pain of his loss initially. But he continues to stick needles in his arms, continuing long after his sorrow and grief subside.

Later, Joey switches to speed to keep costs down. Then, one day he looks out the window and realizes that he has fired up crank every day for seven years straight and is using and dealing in methamphetamine. He can't figure out why he is experiencing underemployment; why his wife left him; and why his health has deteriorated greatly from what it once was. His next "fix" results in a prison sentence.

Even in prison individuals are not subject to the conditions that confront them there. Rather, these conditions are subject to their decision to discover the meaning of their life. The irony is that the more persistently they offend, the more likely they are to be sentenced to longer terms of imprisonment and the less likely they are to increase their sense of purpose. And so the more likely they are to continue offending when released.

It is a known fact that if you lead a horse to a food trough filled with unlimited oats, it will eat itself to death. When it is eating itself to death, it is getting both pleasure and pain signals. The pain-signals from its swollen belly eventually become stronger than the pleasure of eating and so it compulsively eats until it drops dead. It is using the cause of the pain as the cure for the pain so dies. In much the same way, the addict eventually winds up leading a miserable life yet still continues to use the drug or behavior that is causing the miserable life as the cure. An addict does not attempt to escape or avoid pain, the gift that he avoids at all costs. Instead, he attempts to fix, solve, control, to change his pain. He does not want a cure; he just wants some relief; wants to feel different.

The *want* to feel different can be taken to absurd extremes. In 2007 the Fort Lauderdale police department reported that the house of Nathan Radlich's was burglarized. The burglars left his TV, VCR and even left his watch. What they did take was a "generic white cardboard box filled with grayish-white powder." A spokesperson for the police department explained that the grayish-white powder "looked similar to cocaine and they probably thought they'd hit the big time." Then Nathan stood in front of the local TV cameras and pleaded with the burglars to "please return the cremated remains" of his sister, Gertrude, who had died three years previously. Well, the next morning, the bullet-riddled corpse of a drug dealer known as Hoochie Pevens was found on Nathan's doorstep. The cardboard box was there too, with about half of the remaining ashes of Gertrude. On the box was a note. It said: "Hoochie sold us the bogus blow, so we wasted Hoochie. Sorry we snorted your sister. No hard feelings. Have a nice day."

An addiction is an ongoing compulsive pattern of behavior that a person continues to engage in despite destructive consequences. People can't let go of addictive behaviors. They become agitated or upset if someone else or circumstances prevent them from engaging in the usual behavior. At some point, addicts are forced to choose between their addiction and those who love them. They know what they desperately want. They don't want to lose those they love, but they don't know how they could survive without the "toxic-friend" that is destroying them. They feel trapped in an addictive cycle. By far the best predictor of continuing criminal or health-harming behavior and recidivism or diminishing health is the degree of self-understanding and spiritual quest, not family climate, educational or social experience, neighborhood or cultural influences, health history, hereditary background, or any other aspect of their life.[20]

Sigmund Freud postulates that mankind is driven by the desire for pleasure, a drive that can lead to addictions. Addictions often begin as pursuit of pleasure to numb the discomfort of painful losses. But, we soon discover that addictions multiply the pain. In time, it becomes worse than the pain we were trying to relieve. Then, we find ourselves needing relief not only from our inescapable losses but also from the shame of our own foolishness. We feel shame for trusting addictive behavior that made our problem worse.

Addictions also provide an illusion of control. They transport us into a world where we seem to be in charge. They provide a predictable way of changing the way we feel about others and ourselves.

Addictions are attractive because they appear to provide predictable doses of relief and power in the midst of pain and helplessness. But in reality, they are a house of mirrors promising us freedom and then trapping us with little hope of escape. The effect is always self-destructive bondage.

What we find out too late is that in exchange for relief and control, our addictions master us. Even though we tell ourselves we have everything under control, experience tells us otherwise. We'd quit if we could. But, we become slaves to our own desires for pleasure, power and prosperity. We want our addiction more than we want to quit. We believe we need and deserve the relief and the power our addiction provides. In the beginning, pleasure holds us in the addiction. In time, shame has the same effect. In their own ways, both are deceptively effective pain relievers. Pleasure is filler; shame is a killer. Pleasure is a distracter; shame is an assassin. Both attach to our addictions. Both combine with our obsessions to numb our hearts not only to the harm we are doing to others but also to our own longing for love and relationship.

Ironically, shame ends up being even more useful than pleasure in providing relief from our pain. Shame causes us to feel unworthy to give and receive love. Shame deadens our longings for relationship. Shame becomes a powerful painkiller not merely by lessening our pain but by deadening our hearts until we feel nothing at all. When our hearts are deadened, we don't hurt. We don't long to give and receive love. Neither are we able to feel the harm we are doing to others. Yet using our addiction and its resulting shame to feel nothing seems preferable to bearing the sorrows of life. Being spiritual we seek spiritual answers for the sorrows of life. When guidance from wise elders is lacking, "street drug culture" is more than willing to provide answers.

Pseudo Religions

Religions make human beings feel safe. It gives them hope. It gives them comfort, a feeling of acceptance, and guidance. It gives them something in which to believe. It gives them a high. Religion serves a serious purpose in the lives of those who practice it.

The great religions are often spoken of as paths or ways of life. Gandhi said, "Religions are different roads converging upon the same point." Christians speak of themselves as *people of the way.* Buddhists speak of *the path of the Buddha.* In Chinese, the *Tao* means *way, path,* or *street* in a literal as well as a metaphorical sense. The Japanese word is *michi*. Muslims speak of the *straight path*. The world's religions are truly *paths of faith*, paths laden with pain.

Viktor Frankl refers to the physical, emotional/psychological and spiritual dimensions of human beings. The 'spiritual' dimension and the need for spiritual answers to unavoidable pain influence every aspect of our existence. Pseudo religions become a part of our lives when we suffer. Spiritual by nature we seek spiritual answers, answers often discovered in our religious practice. World religions, like all good things, can be corrupted. Though religion can be liberating, it can also be oppressive. Religion can bring health and wholeness, but tragically, it can also be toxic and destructive. Perhaps the best way to distinguish between true religion and pseudo religion is by evaluating the fruit of both paths: True religion creates compassionate, loving, life-filled people.

Quasi-religions, which have some of but not all the traits of religion, also called substitute religions, may be defined as systems of allegiance which function religiously, in part or in whole, in the lives of their followers but are not recognized by them as religious. They now constitute some of the strongest rivals to the traditional faiths for human allegiance.

A substitute cult-religion provides a functioning system of life orientation for many people and, practiced as such, is as religious as any sanctified religion in the world. The gang functions as a kind of cult whose leaders function sometimes as prophets. The neighborhood emerges as a safe haven to which the faithful go to pay honor to, to practice ceremonies or rituals.

Cult-like Practices

No group wants to be called a cult. Whether it's the culture of drugs, wars, or socio-economics, each may come to simulate a cult by virtue of its practices. When an organized group "disciplines" its followers in order to keep them under control, including physical force or threats of loss of life it may be a cult. When it protects itself through isolation from the outside world it may be a cult. When it pursues wealth and power for its leadership through political, judicial or international corruption it may be a cult. When it rationalizes its conduct without resorting to a transcendental belief system it may be a cult. When it informs its recruits that they will undergo strenuous basic training, get little sleep, and receive verbal abuse, for example, prior to being indoctrinated it may be a cult. When it is riddled with secrets it may be a cult.

Secrecy in recruiting hides unattractive aspects of cult routine. Its belief systems may discourage or forbid discussion of any doubts new or old members might have. Members must keep full knowledge of its inner workings from the less initiated, purportedly so as not to jeopardize their indoctrination. Secrecy is heightened if there are real or imagined battles with nonmember "enemies." Secrecy allows the moral banality of it to fester at all costs. Each is uninterested in altruism as a moral imperative. Most have self-serving moralities to benefit the organization and its leadership in particular. Individual fulfillment is irrelevant. Each does not want its inner workings exposed, although sophisticated organizations may curry media interest or even employ public relations consultants and ad agencies to manage their image.

Religion, as an ultimate concern, is a perennial and undeniable feature of human life and provides a functioning value system which people need to render life meaningful. The practice of drugging pain exhibits many of the features of a traditional religion, ranging from a leader surrounded by a context of ritual and myth, to total devotion to the cause on the part of faithful followers, even into death. Pseudo religions create petty, demanding, legalistic people. Every place and time is an opportunity to do the right thing. When religion facilitates this, bringing all things to this goal, then it is healthy, good, and right. When it does not, it becomes toxic. And worst of all, it does under the banner alleging doing "what is right." This is the worst form of hypocrisy.

Every community or neighborhood has its functioning religion. A spiritual life of some kind is absolutely necessary for psychological well being. The human need for religious practices shows no sign of abating. People still need some faith to guide the course of their lives, to provide them with life orientation. But, if overt religious forms or symbol systems are denied them, or if these do not speak with light and power, they will cleave to covert religions which are excessive and ungrounded spirituality. These pseudo religions will be dangerous religions, leading to all kinds of compulsive and even violent behavior. Indeed, the chief contender for the allegiance of human hearts, for ultimate commitment and concern today, when meaning is lacking, are not traditional faiths but the quasi-religions of the drug culture that sprang up in response to the *wants* and *needs* not being met by community elders and mentors. All studies point to the fact that the numbers of 'faithful' in these substitute religions is greatest in spiritually impoverished, white, suburban and middle class neighborhoods.

When religion becomes a means to avoid or control life, it becomes toxic. It traps believers in an addictive practice of religion that leads to addictions, aggressions and depressions. When people are excessively/compulsively devoted - sacrificing family, job, economic security, relationship with their higher power, their body or mental health - to a substance, relationship or behavior; when people suffer from not knowing they are unique, secure and significant, suffer an existential vacuum that demands to be filled, the pain intended to drive them to their God, they avoid listening to the pain by playing self-protective games. Along the way, they often find patterns of behavior that dull the pain, thus making it easier to live with. These can be virtually any substance, legal or illegal, relationship or behavior that provides relief.

When a person develops a pathological (abnormal) relationship to a mood-altering experience or substance that has life-damaging consequences, addiction exists. These addictions can be divided into three basic types: substance addiction (e.g., drugs or alcohol), emotional addiction (letting an emotion run your life e.g., aggression, anger or depression), or process addiction (e.g., work, religion). Addiction is ultimately idolatry, that is, the worship of a relationship, substance or behavior. Eventually, it leads to lost or dysfunctional relationships, underemployment, bankruptcy, divorce and declining health.

Irrational Thinking Patterns in Cult-Religious Systems

Pseudo religious systems tend to think in extremes, driven by an all or nothing, black or white mentality. There are no gray areas. Consequently, invalid conclusions, not based in reality, tend to be drawn. Members of the 'congregation' tend to filter out the positive or negative and distort reality. They selectively hear only the negative or positive (to shield their already low self worth) about everything. They allow in themselves what they would condemn in others. Feelings become the basis for reality. Self condemnation results from a feeling of not being able to measure up. They feel responsible for everything and a need to in control. They tend to be compulsively driven by and addicted to power, purging the congregation of anybody who would upset the status quo. The ministry appears negative and punitive to outsiders.

Many religious addicts are physically, emotionally and spiritually ill, lacking in values, looking to the pseudo religious leader for guidance and well-being. Communication with those outside the congregation is strictly forbidden. Communication is from the top down or from the inside out, with little regard for the needs of the members. It is a congregation that slowly becomes more and more ineffective and out of touch with the people. The addicts on the inside no longer care about the needs of the people on the outside. Someone in the system has the job of shielding the leadership from the truth by placating those who disagree and satisfying those who want a direct voice to the leadership. The lieutenant, or second in authority is never to tell the leader anything but what he/she wants to hear. Performance is everything. The pseudo faith flourishes because there is no objective accountability.

Labels become rallying points under which the other followers can be moved to action to squelch a revolt. Once the label is in place, it becomes more difficult to see that person as a human with real needs and the potential for good judgment. Labels are used to polarize the opponents and energize the followers to fight against those opponents. The enemy is "shot" so the underlying issues that need to be considered can be avoided.

Roles of Cult-Religions

A healthy system is made up of individuals with a full range of emotions, intellect, free will and the ability to function independently. In a dysfunctional system, each individual plays out a role needed for the system to function. Since individuals lack the ability to function independently, they depend on one another to play out their roles and allow the system to continue. Those roles have to be played so that those in the system can remain in their denial and avoid the overwhelming fear of insignificance.

In a dysfunctional system, roles evolve to support the system. Each person must be willing to play the roles which become more keenly defined as the addiction intensifies. Individuals become trapped in predictable, toxic behaviors that remove God and faith, replacing them with a dependency on a set of rules.

As a person's behavior lines up with one of these predictable roles, any deviation from that role is a sign of rebellion from the system and is dealt with quickly through shaming and rejection. Although each role is difficult to maintain, it is even more difficult to leave the safety and predictability of the role and act independently. A person who takes this step back toward reality becomes an outcast of the system. Outcasts may be dealt with harshly.

Ten Rules of a Pseudo Religious System
1. The leader must be in control of every aspect at all times.
2. When problems arise, find a guilty party to blame immediately.
3. Don't make mistakes.
4. Never point out the reality of a situation.
5. Never express your feelings unless they are positive.
6. Don't ask questions, especially if they are tough ones.
7. Don't do anything outside your role.
8. Don't trust anyone.
9. Nothing is more important than giving money to the organization.
10. At all costs, keep up the image of the organization or the family.

America's Drug Cult-Religion

Religion is our human response to the dual reality of being alive and having to die. Knowing that we must die, we therefore question the meaning of life. Viktor Frankl states that the tragic triad includes death, guilt and suffering. Everybody will die; not everyone lives to his fullest potential, however. Ernest Becker states that the denial of death is motivated primarily by our anxiety toward death.[6] Elisabeth Kubler-Ross refers to death as the last stage of growth. For Becker the function of culture and religion is to help us lessen the anxiety we feel toward death, which is made more intense given the fact that our intellectual and spiritual endowments, which seem to have the quality of immortality, seem inescapably caught in the web of our own mortality. Becker suggests that authentic life in the face of death requires considerable courage. We deal with our anxiety toward death in different ways.

"In my belief," states Arnold Toynbee, "every human being has a personal religion, and every community has a collective religion, whether the person or community is aware of this or not... Spiritual nature, like physical nature, abhors a vacuum. If we succeed in repudiating the religion that we have inherited, we shall inevitably acquire a substitute for it" and practice it religiously, be it a drug, war or socio-economic religion.

Carl Jung states that the key motivating factor in the beginning of an addiction is the seeking of spiritual answers to pain and suffering. An alcoholic wraps her car around a tree in a drunken haze. She has "hit bottom" and vows never to drink again. A methamphetamine abuser – 'meth tweaker' - has not slept in three to fifteen days and is irritable and paranoid. Unable to achieve his original high, frustrated, unruly, disoriented and unstable behavior he is arrested. In jail, cranked to the gills on speed, he pledges to go sober, starting right now. A cigarette smoker stumbles to bed after a typical two-pack day, coughing, throat burning, reeking of tobacco, and swears, that upon waking, his remaining cigarettes will go out with the trash and his life as a human ashtray is over.

In America many wake up with a cup of Espresso coffee or a line of cocaine. They take a break with a cigarette or a beer. They relax after work with a shot of hard liquor or a joint of marijuana. They self-medicate in order to sleep or to stay awake. They use drugs or alcohol to change the way in which they feel: to feel good, to feel bad, or just to feel different. They go on religious crusades to get their sacrament, their drug of choice, and practice their rituals religiously, leading to a kind of spiritual paralysis or death of the inner life. I emphasize religiously because the practice closely parallels that of all world religions.

All world religions have four things in common. They all have a leader, sacraments, rituals and jargon. In the addict's spiritual quest the *leader* is none other than the drug pusher, the cook, or the bartender. His *sacraments* include drug paraphernalia: the needle, spoon, roach clip, and shot glass, as well as so-called magic pills, powders and potions. He practices his *rituals* so that, when he returns to his *congregation*, he will no longer feel out of place, uncomfortable, or stupid; he will feel like one of the members. Some rituals, if not practiced correctly, may result in death. Finally, his spiritual quest consists of fluid *jargon*, greetings, words and a doctrine of salvation, a code of conduct scribed in a 'sacred' text, that constantly changes due to the fact that there are concerned outsiders, like parents, undercover narcotic agents and the like, who are always attempting to infiltrate the 'congregation.'

Examples of historical religious texts include the Koran, Bible, Holy Scriptures of Judaism, and Bhagavad Gita of Hinduism. The doctrines of criminal gangs inform its members how to conduct their lives. It instructs them how to act toward their leader and toward one another; whom they may marry; what jobs they may hold; and what foods they may eat. Membership may be prescribed for life. the weaker the traditional family unit, the stronger the gang becomes in influencing the individual. Dropping out may be forbidden. Those who attempt to drop out may be influenced to return when the life of a family member is threatened or taken.

Often, addicts choose to live out their lives inside a crack den or a rehabilitation center or a cell. Sometimes, they try to escape their nightmarish existence by joining the Armed Forces to travel to foreign countries where drugs are cheaper and more available. They choose their drug of choice over their health and that of their family. "Thou shall have no other gods before me," says our drug of choice. "Thou shall honor me before thy father and mother." They choose to die a slow death coughing up parts of their lungs or stomach as a consequence of tobacco or alcohol cancer. The crippling bad magic of addiction is the image of the addict's god, be it an addiction to drugs, alcohol, sex, anger and violence, or the rush of going through a stoplight or running away from the cops. Everything is sacrificed on the altar of the inner craving to mask their inner pain and fear.

The Ten Commandments of the Drug Addiction Cult-Religion
 1. Thou shalt have no other gods before me.
 2. Thou shalt honor me before thy father and mother.
 3. Thou shalt not question me.
 4. Thou shalt suspect everyone but me.
 5. Thou shalt kill any who threaten our relationship.
 6. Thou shalt set aside time to worship me.
 7. Thou shalt make large financial offerings to me.
 8. Thou shalt sacrifice thy children to me.
 9. Thou shalt seek forgiveness only through me.
 10. Thou shalt never forget me.

Addictions and aggression are not just diversions of choice. Addicts often see them as pseudo-lifeboats necessary for their survival, giving them something they believe they must have in order to live and survive. They provide predictable relief and power in an unpredictable and painful world that is difficult and seemingly unfair. And as much as eighty percent of experienced pain is the result of resistance to the twenty percent of real pain. The result is that they end up with the most inhuman kind of pain, an anesthetized self. Life requires that they learn to distinguish two contrasting circumstances: those that they cannot change and those that they can change. Even when they encounter uncontrollable circumstance they still have freedom to choose the attitude that they adopt toward that situation.

Sigmund Freud considered the desire for pleasure to be the highest motivational force behind human behavior, a force often driven by the ego. When faced with a loss of health, when haunted by harm done to others, when hounded by the rejection of a parent, a spouse or society, it is natural for human beings to try to relieve the pain. We hate feeling guilty, disconnected, empty and alone. We long for acceptance and love. Our addictions provide a remedy that helps us to forget the pain, at least for a little while. And the answer may be as near as the pharmacy, or bar, or drug pusher in the form of an alleviative, lenitive, anodyne, paregoric, analgesic, anesthetic, narcotic, morphine, Novocain, codeine, wine or alcohol, or sleeping pill.

One person justifies his use, noting "I can drink a couple of beers every day after work. Now, the guy who drinks two six-packs of beer is abusing." The next guy notes, "I can drink a couple of six-packs of beer and hard liquor every day after work. It's the guy who uses pot who's abusing." The guy who smokes pot says, "I don't have a problem with a little pot and beer. It's the guy who snorts cocaine who is abusing." The cocaine addict says, "I can handle a little magic powder. That's no problem, but those idiots who smoke it are the abusers." Those who smoke cocaine imply that IV-users are the abusers and the IV-users suggest that the real abusers are the ones who overdose; "If you die, you have abused."

So, everybody draws the line a little bit differently. The truth is: an addict is an addict is an addict is an addict. Addictions are a health issue that affects family, friends, co-workers, strangers and society-at-large and each has the right to draw the line where they want it saying, "You can do whatever you want, but we have the right to set boundaries when you've entered our space. If you want to share our personal space, you must respect our limits, our boundaries."

Both pleasure and power is important, noted Viktor Frankl, a student of Sigmund Freud and Alfred Adler. We do act to find pleasure and to achieve power. But, according to Frankl, "pleasure is not a primary goal. It is a by-product of having done something meaningful. And power is not an end in itself, but only a means to an end that is attained by using power in a meaningful way. Meaning is neither a by-product nor a means to an end. Meaning is the ultimate goal. If our will to meaning is ignored or repressed, we tend to feel empty. We are then tempted to fill the void with the will to pleasure, power and prosperity that often lead to addiction, aggression and depression.

Virtually all who resort to pleasure to fill an existential void in their lives note that meaning and purpose are absent. Alcoholism tends to drown sorrow. Drug addiction turns lows to highs. Compulsive overeating fills emptiness. Obsessive work replaces insecurities with a sense of accomplishment. Sexual addiction mimics adventure and intimacy. Addictions have profound ways of taking addicts where they do not want to go, like the emergency room, the probation office or court, jail or prison, or funeral parlors and graveyards.

The health problem will still be with us, even if state and national policies do not change. Addressing this as a health and education issue seems to make more sense. A drug offender, who might have had an exemplary life before going to prison, comes out of prison where he or she, having never participated in an effective drug rehabilitation program, but learning how to be a more effective criminal. On the other hand, the same individual, like an alcoholic, who receives treatment for an addiction can resume his or her life in society with a clean background. The health of our nation (and the world) depends on this issue, and the country needs something positive, progressive, and forward thinking dealing with this serious issue.

The only real response to life's ultimate questions is not, "How can I avoid pain and suffering so I can be happy?" Rather it is, "Now that I experienced this traumatic event, how will I respond?" It matters not what happens to individuals, but how they respond to that which happens to them. Those who are able to overcome adversity can be strengthened by their experiences. Injury and healing, defeat and triumph, and fear and courage go hand in hand – be it abuse, family disruption, delinquency, health problems and natural disasters. Without minimizing the destructive impact of these events, human beings have remarkable potential for survival, healing and becoming stronger at the broken places. In the most difficult situation lies some opportunity for growth. All humans have potential for resilience, for they are all descendants of survivors. They carry in their genetic code powerful brain-based programs motivating them to form attachments, to achieve, to develop autonomy, and to support each other in altruism.

The War Cult-Religion

America appears to have an addiction to unnecessary *wars*. These wars appear to adhere to a basic five-part pattern according to John Harper: (1) Each has been fought in the name of a broader mission that Providence has allegedly chosen the United States to carry out; (2) Self-deception has been at the heart of the decision to go to war; (3) Each has been the handiwork of a small, determined 'war party;'

(4) Congressional opposition has been weak and the party in power calculates "that successful military action…[would] pay dividends at the polls;" and (5) "More often than not, they have failed to advance the interests of the individuals and political parties who have advanced them."[29]

The leader of the war religion in America is the Commander in Chief. The sacraments include weapons of mass destruction: tanks, guns, nuclear and bio-chemical bombs, missiles, jets and battle ships. The rituals include military parades and war games, games that have serious objectives and often result in the death and the physical and psychological (PTSD) maiming of millions of innocent civilians and expendable soldiers. The fluid jargon are the secret and top secret code words that routinely change because of the concern that spies may infiltrate the military congregation; jargon also includes a "sacred" text devoted to the conduct and strategies of war, including secret code words devoted to protect vital information.

The Socio-Economic Cult-Religion

The 'religious aspect' affects all dimensions of American society. The leader of the socio-economic religion in America includes Bill Gates, Alan Greenspan, Donald Trump, Warren Buffet and other billionaires. The sacraments include mega-mansions, private jets, Mercedes Benz, expensive jewelry, stocks and bonds, offshore accounts and other paraphernalia thought to be important. Rituals have been developed at the expense of fellow citizens. Socio-economic jargon also remains fluid, constantly changing. Companies which once spoke of 'lay-offs' now use the term 'downsizing' to refer to the widespread firing of employees.

David Cay Johnston says in his book, *Free Lunch* that "many hundreds of billions of tax dollars have been diverted to the rich, leaving our schools, parks and local government services starved for funds. Jobs and assets are going offshore, sometimes to the detriment of not just the economy, but national security. We pour billions into subsidies for sports teams and golf courses. Our health care system costs us far more than that of any other industrial country and yet we live shorter lives than the Canadians, Europeans, and the Japanese.

We stand alone among modern societies in making tens of millions of our citizens go without health care, many of whom die or become disabled because of this nutty idea that medicine is a business, not a service. We have erected obstacles to the earnest but poor who seek to better themselves through library study and higher education." The jargon is likewise fluid, constantly changing. Corporations no longer lay off employees; they "downsize!"

The defiant power of the human spirit refers to the human capacity to tap into the spiritual part of the self and rise above the negative effects of situations, illness or the past. Spirit refers to one of the multiple dimensions of humanity. Spirituality is manifest in a person's quest for meaning. Religion encompasses the ultimate meaning, super-meaning as well as God.

The Evolution of Viennese Psychotherapy

Both pleasure and power is important, noted Viktor Frankl, a student of Alfred Adler and Sigmund Freud. We do act to find pleasure and to achieve power. But, according to Frankl, "pleasure is not a primary goal. It is a by-product of having done something meaningful. Power is not an end in itself, but only a means to an end that is attained by using power in a meaningful way. Meaning is neither a by-product nor a means to an end. Meaning is the ultimate goal. If our will to meaning is ignored or repressed, we feel empty. We are then tempted to fill the void with the will to pleasure that often leads to addictions, and the will to power often leads to aggression and violence, hurting those we love and who love us.

At some point, we are forced to choose between our addiction and those who love us. We know what we desperately need. We don't want to lose those we love. But, we don't know how we could survive without the "toxic friend" that is destroying us. We feel trapped in an addictive cycle. Joseph Fabry says that by far the best predictor of continuing pseudo religious practices "is the degree of self-understanding and spiritual quest, not family climate, educational or social experience, neighborhood or cultural influences, health history, hereditary background or any other aspect of your life."

Viktor Frankl clearly understood the importance of the spiritual dimension. Even in toxic surroundings, you are not subject to the conditions that confront you there. Rather, these conditions are subject to your decisions. Aleksandr Solzhenitsyn and Russell Means both understood the wisdom of life lessons learned in prison. Solzhenitsyn once wrote: "Bless you prison. Bless you for being in my life. For there lying on the rotting prison straw, I came to realize that the object of life is not prosperity as are made to believe, but the maturing of the soul." Means also noted that "the year [he] spent in prison was one of the finest of [his] life. On the physical side it was hard; [it was] hell. But on the spiritual side, it was a great year."

"Ultimately," noted Frankl, "a sense of purpose and the will to meaning are the strongest motivational forces to living and acting. Cultivating a sense of meaning is an important factor in preventing illness, in promoting health, and in successfully adapting to life's changing circumstance (resiliency as well as recovery). A lack of this sense of meaning can form the basis for such disorders and diseases as neurosis, depression, aggression, suicidal ideation, and substance abuse."[19] Seeing meaning in our life enables us to develop our capacities and endure hardships. Addictions, aggression and depression can never fill the existential vacuum; can never eliminate our frustration. What is the answer? It is meaning. Meaning cannot be given; it must be discovered, but how?

If we have meaning and purpose in our life, if you have a spiritual foundation, if we have a reason for living and getting up each morning, we can withstand almost any hardship. However, when we lack meaning and purpose in our life, consequences do not matter, no matter how harsh, and family and friends do not matter.

Adversities and suffering become more bearable when we have something that is worthy of living and dying for. In the past a trauma may have triggered a crisis of meaning. We may have been abused, neglected, traumatized or lost a loved one. Consequences are a matter of choice. And we are responsible for those choices. According to Viktor Frankl there are three avenues to achieving meaning; experiential, creative, and attitudinal values. Experiential values emphasize all that we experience, good and bad, are gifts that benefit us in some unique way. Creative values emphasize our pursuit of endeavors that are uniquely us, be they artistic, mechanical, paternal or other. Attitudinal values emphasize embracing a positive attitude toward those events over which we have no control.

Pain, the gift that nobody wants, grief and suffering can be transformed into a positive force for change through personal meaning. Pain is the voice of our inner life, the wisdom of our body, crying out for attention, for remedy. Pain suppressors, on the other hand, are life suppressors and tranquilizers are signal deniers. Much of our experienced pain is self-induced; self-induced through self-talk. Over eighty-seven percent of self-talk are negative and induces psychosomatic illnesses.

We spend tens of billions of dollars annually suppressing and denying both real and self-inflicted pain. We consume over sixty percent of all illegal drugs, one-third of which work on the central nervous system. We consume over 30,000 tons of aspirin a year. When we take aspirin for a headache, does anyone tell us that our stomach bleeds two teaspoons full of blood? No, nobody does. So, we replace aspirin with Tylenol because it does not make our stomach bleed. But, nowhere do they inform us that we must not take this magic pill if we have any alcohol in our blood because those two ingredients mix to form a third chemical that slowly destroys our kidneys and liver. Yet the more we try to shut down pain, the more pain strikes back.

Is pain really necessary? What would be the consequences of not feeling pain? It is a fact that people with leprosy do not feel pain; they do not feel pain because leprosy depresses their blood circulatory system. People with leprosy do not have bad flesh that just rots away. Their flesh is just as healthy as ours. What they lack is the ability to feel pain. When the blood flow is cut off from key parts of their body, their nerve endings die. With the death of nerve endings comes the death of their ability to sense danger to their bodies. They live a virtually pain-free existence. Again and again they would and impale themselves. Yet they do not feel a thing. Pain, unavoidable pain, is a gift nobody wants.

The best way to overcome pain, grief and suffering is to adopt a two-pronged approach, that is, to address both the specific trauma and the underlying lack of meaning. Self-medicating physical and emotional pain can do more harms than the isolated pain itself. Father

Joe Martin explains it best when he speaks of alcohol: "Alcohol is the world/s perfect solvent. It can take the varnish off the floor, paint off the wall, the wax off a table. It can also remove a son, a daughter, a wife, a family, friends, a car, a bank account, or a job. Everything it touches, it dissolves and destroys. It always has and it always will." On the other hand, people can transform anger and pain creatively, socially, spiritually and/or existentially. A crisis can be an opportunity for spiritual rebirth and a discovery of meaning for existence. Even in the most gloomy and hopeless circumstances, people can discover gifts of hope and grace.

The three-dimensional canvas of life is made up of a rainbow of experiential brushstrokes. Many dwell on the shadows and harsh brushstrokes of life. There is no cure without correct diagnosis. To be wrong about one's self is to be wrong about all else. The terrible shadow testifies to a light somewhere. There can be no evil unless there is good, no sickness unless there is health, and no darkness without radiance. The canvas that uniquely describes our life often remains unfinished; it is an unfinished masterpiece and you are the master painter – *"Good, better, best; never let it rest until your good is better and your better is best."* - [Mother of Tim Duncan]

In most cases, the pain we experience is probably at least eighty percent psychological and twenty percent physical. Two men look out of prison bars. One sees bars and the other stars. Two brothers can construe life very differently. One sees shiny new toys and arcade games as sordid and sorrowful, while the other working by his own private compass within a sea of horse manure is guided by shining orbed idealism. Its gleam transforms for him all that is dark, dingy, or foul manure and enables him to labor on, whatever the discouragement. His expectations are that where there's horse manure there must be a pony!

Not only beauty, but also truth is in the eye of the beholder. We habitually see with the eye and not through it. What is already present in the mind and heart determines what we make of all around us. Experience is not what happens to us, but what we do with that which happens to us.

Nothing ever happens by chance. Everything that comes into our life is there as a result of unvarying inescapable law. And the only operator of that law is none other than us. Consciously or unconsciously we have at some time or other produced every condition desirable or undesirable that we find in our life today. Yet there is a simple way out of those troubles. Learn how to think rightly instead of wrongly, and conditions at once begin to improve. Life need not be a battle; it can, and should be an adventure. Misguided attempts to escape from feelings of meaninglessness through the pursuits of pleasure, power and prosperity eventually lead to disillusion, despair and self-destruction over and over again. Such pursuits often turn pleasures into addictions, power into aggression, divorce and broken relationships, and prosperity into depression, underemployment and bankruptcy.

Unfortunately, we often forget to offer our gratitude to experiences and persons who have impacted and changed our lives. Experience is not what happens to us; it is what we do with that which happens to us. It matters not what city to which we are returning; it only matters *who* we take there. We and we alone are responsible for fulfilling our unique calling and for responding to the unique demand of meaning in every situation we encounter.

The meaning of life can be found in any situation. Life remains potentially meaningful, amid all the chaos, uncertainties and gloom of the world condition, be they pleasurable or miserable. That being the case, wisdom requires that we give thanks in all things, not just in good things, but in all things. Life requires that we move not to unavoidable and painful situations, but through those situations.

Most of us can do almost anything that we want to do, but it is that wanting that is so often missing. Needs are usually overridden by wants of physical and psychological pleasures, powers and prosperity. But what continue to haunt and damn us are anger, alienation, boredom, doubt, debt, depression, disease, despair, fear, failure, foolishness, guilt, gloom, loneliness, avoidable pain, insecurity and death.

The primary disease in America is neither coronary heart disease nor cancer.[26] It is meaninglessness, doubt of the reality of good at the heart of the universe. Today depression and suicide among our youth are pandemic, and are more a problem among the young than the old.

It is the second leading cause of death among college-aged students, students who have everything going for them. Suicide is more a problem among the white than black, the educated than the uneducated, and the rich than the poor because none of life's apparent advantages give a clue to the riddle of existence. Nearly 10,000 teenagers will commit suicide in America this year; over half a million other people will make the attempt and literally millions of American homes are haunted by this specter of the sudden, despairing, self-initiated end of life. Modern man has not only lost his way but also his address.

We always retain the freedom to choose what is meaningful. We can choose to be a master rather than a slave to our circumstances. We have the capacity to choose our own actions and reactions, our values and beliefs. We can choose to be responsible or irresponsible, positive or negative. Even when all the freedoms are taken away from us, we are still free to choose our attitude towards the oppressive conditions of life. We can either react with anger, bitterness and despair, or we can take it as a challenge to achieve spiritual growth and demonstrate the defiant human spirit. Neither biology, nor environment, but our own choices decide our character and destiny. With freedom comes responsibility. Regardless of our circumstances, we have the freedom and responsibility to do what is meaningful.

The quest for meaning is inherent in every person. The three major values essential in the discovery of meaning are creative, experiential and attitudinal values. Those who pursue success, wealth, fame and pleasure are actually seeking to discover meaning and fulfillment in a misguided way. A crisis of meaning ensues. In the quest for meaning, there are three major values essential in the discovery of meaning. Creative values are what we give to life through our work and activities, which make a difference in the world. Experiential values are what we take from life, feeling the joy of living in what we receive or experience. Finally, attitudinal values are how we view life, accepting what cannot be changed, adopting a positive attitude towards an unalterable fate.

Reflection on Addiction, Aggression and Depression

When an individual repeatedly fails to discover the meaning of his life, there is increasing danger that he will be drawn into the path of the neurotic triad of addiction, aggression and depression. When this happens, he slowly becomes engulfed in the downward draft of the mythical "Sui-circle bird" described by Sam Keen.[36] It is a downward pulling force that draws an individual inward, at ever-increasing circular velocity to an unknown destination of self-destruction. Keen describes the path of this mythical bird, as it flies in ever-tightening circles until it literally flies up its bottom and self-destructs. That self-destruction comes in the form of addictions and aggressions.

Depression is a normal reaction to a normal and reasonable reaction to a hurtful and traumatic life. It robs an individual of the *ability* to experience hope or feel joy. Nonetheless, it does not mean that an individual is hopeless. Elisabeth Kubler-Ross tells us that depression is simply a call for transformation to become the *next* possible self we can be. Holocaust survivors Viktor Frankl[20] and Joseph Fabry[16] state that life does not owe us pleasures, but always offers meaning. Frankl furthermore states that the pathway out of the neurotic triad begins by embracing attitudinal, creative and experiential values.

Depression is the wisdom within that reminds us that we need a break – to eat healthy foods, sleep, exercise, and continue to exist. It is the wisdom of our body and mind that demands we take a break. It requires that we defer major decisions, such as breaking up a relationship or marriage, quitting a stable job, or making other major, life-changing decisions until we are able to feel like our normal self once again. Depression requires that we embrace the wisdom of listening to close and trusted friends in helping us make decisions. Finally, embrace the brokenness that is depression as a temporary gift to be passed through, allowing us to become stronger emotionally and spiritually, and to once again feel hope.

Shared Meaning – Shared Creativity – Shared Brokenness:

- Imagine yourself holding your infant son, daughter or spouse while at the same time thinking how precarious life is. When you glance down at your child or spouse's sleeping face, think about how soon your child, spouse and you would die. At that moment, overwhelmed by your love for your child or spouse, aware of the very fact that your child or spouse and you have only a very short time together that makes love more than just a familial arrangement. When you fully realize that you are going to die, every moment you waste is wasted forever. Now, contemplate the life that you've had with this person and *write about the meaningful times you've shared.*

• Being human being means being creative. When creativity is in retreat, we feel arid and unmoved. The ebb and the flow in the creative process operate at various times, in varying degrees. Dry times can be disappointing, even alarming, especially if our livelihood is depending upon it. But there are many tools and techniques that help to ease those shades off. The creative spirit doesn't leave, it simply goes into retreat. And when we find the opening again, it returns in a way that feels at once familiar and new. Creative expression is in a perpetual, evolutionary stage. When it returns, we experience ourselves and our world just a bit more fully than before. Think of a creative endeavor that makes your life meaningful. *Devote at least one hour each week to what you enjoy and share it with another.*

• Ernest Hemingway says "the world breaks everyone and afterward many are strong in the broken places."[30] When you experience a flat tire on the highway, you can be depressed or give thanks that the other three tires are still inflated. Viktor Frankl "insists meaning is available in spite of—nay, even through suffering, provided . . . that the suffering is unavoidable. If it is avoidable, the meaningful thing to do is to remove its cause, for unnecessary suffering is masochistic rather than heroic. If, on the other hand, one cannot change a situation that causes his suffering, he can still choose his attitude. Long had not . . . chosen to break his neck, but he did decide not to let himself be broken by what had happened to him."[20] *You've* possibly *experienced brokenness* throughout your life, but each was undoubtedly followed by spiritually uplifting events. Take time to *note those facts.*

VIII.
Prisoner Responses to the Holocaust

We who lived in concentration camps can remember the men who walked through the huts comforting others, giving away their last piece of bread. They may have been few in number, but they offer sufficient proof that everything can be taken from a man but one thing: the last of the human freedoms — to choose one's attitude in any given set of circumstances, to choose one's own way.

- Viktor Frankl

Frankl identifies three psychological reactions experienced to one degree or another by all those fellow human beings who were incarcerated in concentration camps during the Holocaust and, presumably by prisoners of war, past, present, and future: (1) *shock* during the initial admission phase to the camp, (2) *apathy* after becoming accustomed to camp existence, in which the inmate values only that which helps him or others survive, and (3) reactions of *depersonalization, moral deformity, bitterness*, and *disillusionment* after being liberated.[20] In some ways, these are also shared by children who have been kidnapped, or recruited by gangs and war lords around the world. Frankl says that even in concentration camps, prisoners were still growing and learning whatever lessons they needed to learn.[41]

Shock

The first stage, *shock* is the initial period of being ripped from the known to the shocking unknown, admission to one of several concentration camps as an inmate. In this stage, the specific feeling that overcame the inmate was of overwhelming shock; the flight-fight response frozen in time. Everything that was happening and the brutality witnessed in the inmate's surrounding were going on so fast that it sent the typical inmate into temporary shock and disbelief. Their struggle to stay alive was overshadowed by the makeshift moral code created at the whim of a heartless and single-minded enemy determined to end their lives.

Women were forced to have abortions in the ghettos. Children were killed outright upon their arrival at the death camps. Mothers were forced to choose which child should survive and which to die in the gas chambers; others were forced to kill their babies or watch as it was killed by another. Women were stripped and paraded like animals, chosen to be sex slaves, workers or killed. Sadistic games were created on the spot. Those who chose not to play were put to death; those who played and lost were put to death.

During this initial stage in the concentration camps, inmates were stripped of all body hair, eye glasses, hearing aids, false teeth, aid devices, and everything important and meaningful; stripped of personal and family possessions; separated from family and friends; lost freedoms; and legal documents proving one's existence were destroyed.

Inmates in the concentration camps were isolated, dehumanized, mistreated, and under constant threat of death or maiming every day for seemingly pointless and illogical reasons, traumatizing witnesses to the inhumane acts as well. No longer were individual inmates referred to by their given name. The Nazis had a deliberate policy of attempting to destroy the identity of those incarcerated by stripping them, not only of their possessions and clothing, not only of their hair and dignity, but also of their name. In return they were given the cast-off, ill-fitting clothing of others already victims of the gas chamber and a number tattooed on their forearms.

Nearly every individual imprisoned in concentration camps experienced the "delusion of reprieve." Individuals held onto the hope that they would be released at the last minute, despite the realities that surrounded them. If "chosen" to be freed, logic did not tell them it would be through the gas chambers. Prisoners were arbitrarily chosen to be sent to the gas chambers for the most absurd reasons. Fellow prisoners died from malnourishment, exposure to typhoid or tuberculosis and lack of medical care; others frequently from torture. When reality began to eliminate the delusion of reprieve, suicidal ideation was the common thought of nearly everyone given the harsh circumstances.

Prisoners in the concentration camps survived on a starvation diet – part of the "experiment." Malika Oufkir states that "hunger humiliates, hunger debases. Hunger makes you betray your family, your friends and your values. Hunger turns you into a monster."[51] During the twenty years that she and her family, as young as three years old, were incarcerated they were fed rotting vegetables, spoilt meat, eggs with vile black liquid, and bread soaked with rat urine and droppings. Nonetheless, they survived by embracing attitudinal, creative and experiential values.[20] Eggs were aerated over night, whisked with sugar in the morning. Chunks of bread were soaked with this mixture and fried in oil. The "French toast" warded off their hunger.

The war in Vietnam was also a wretched, shocking experience, in some ways more inhumane than the prior wars between nations. Soldiers were isolated from their families for prolonged periods. Dehumanized and mistreated by the elements and sometimes as prisoners of war, soldiers often lived under threat of death or injury every day by ambushes and firestorms, razor sharp bamboo traps, death marches and weeks in heavy tropical jungles. Occasionally, soldiers took baths in a thimble of water, filling canteens before finding a dead body floating in the same water drawn from. Many experienced sickness from Agent Orange blanket bombardment, foot rot walking in rice paddies fertilized with animal and human waste, insects and the elements. Snipers camouflaged themselves in rice paddies, trees, extensive tunnels, and six-foot tall jungle grass. Fellow soldiers who witnessed injured, maimed and dead fellow soldiers, village women and children burned or mutilated beyond recognition by cluster bombs were traumatized. Occasionally, a soldier, weary of the war simply stood up and let the enemy kill him. Broken by war, some returned home suffering from PTSD; others, even as prisoners of war, would return home strong at the broken places.

Apathy

During the second stage, *apathy* is the period during which inmates became well entrenched in concentration camp routine. The period of time that it takes to enter this stage varied from prisoner to prisoner; for Frankl, it took a few weeks. Apathy is when everything around an inmate becomes so commonplace, the brutality, suffering and death that it tends to have no emotional effect on an individual. Apathy forces "the prisoner's life down to a primitive level" in which "all efforts and all emotions are centered on one task: preserving one's own life and that of other fellow prisoners." Sadly, efforts to preserve the life of a fellow prisoner meant that another would die.

The only thing on an inmate's mind in this stage is his survival. Therefore, the desire for food is the major primitive instinct around which mental life center. He becomes accustomed to his camp existence, in which he values only that which helps him or others survive. He conditions against making any decision and of taking any initiative whatsoever, convinced that fate is one's master. He makes no attempt to influence fate; he simply lets it take its own course. Based on the fact that independent decisions made by prisoners could result in death, maim or sadistic abuse, he resolves to let fate make choices for him, even when a decision had to be made whether or not to make an escape attempt. Death is extraordinarily commonplace. What would shock the average person before the Holocaust is no longer reacted to; emotions become numb, having lost the ability to feel any emotion.

Depersonalization

Following their liberation from the concentration camps the freed prisoners face a period of readjustment as they gradually return to the world. Initially, the liberated prisoners are so numb that they are unable to understand what freedom means, or to emotionally respond to it. Part of them believes that their freedom may be an illusion or a dream that will be taken away from them at any moment, unexpectedly like everything else that was meaningful. When the gates of freedom open, some initially confuse motion with meaning and activity with achievement, carrying on with their chaotic prison routine. In their first venture outside their former prison, they realize that they can not comprehend the simple pleasures of a sunset, blooming flowers and singing birds. All of these and the reality of the freedom they had dreamed about for years appear surreal in their *depersonalization.*

Spiritual Deformation

As the intense pressure on the mind is slowly released following nutritious meals and restful sleep, mental health becomes more and more in possible danger of *spiritual deformation.* Following the end of apartheid in South Africa, years of violence, degradation and suffering perpetrated against the majority were then dispensed against the perpetrators of abuse; worse yet was the acts of rape and violence perpetrated by the abused upon the abused. As the intense pressure on the mind is released, mental health can be endangered. Frankl uses the analogy of a diver suddenly released from his pressure chamber. He recounts the story of a decent friend who became immediately obsessed with dispensing the same violence in judgment of his abusers that they had inflicted on him, abuse that no human being has the linguistic ability adequately to represent.

Bitterness & Disillusionment

Occasionally, sadistic Nazi guards inform a random prisoner that he is free to leave the camp, that he has been liberated, given a reprieve. Acting on this belief, a recaptured prisoner is beaten or worse. This bizarre incident is witnessed by fellow inmates who are subsequently also traumatized into believing that freedom will never come. Repeatedly confronted with these traumatic camp experiences, prisoners suffer depersonalization, moral deformity, bitterness and disillusionment after being liberated. The prisoners struggle with bitterness and disillusionment upon returning home, bitterness at the lack of responsiveness of the outside world resulting in a desire to withdraw into a cave or dense forest away from all humanity. This was the case of many Vietnam veterans returning home from that war.

Frankl combines *bitterness* and *disillusionment* together in the third stage.[20] Bitterness and disillusionment are similar to Kubler-Ross' stages of *anger* and *depression*.[42] It is the "period following a prisoner's release and liberation." Frankl points out that disillusionment is the most difficult to eliminate and may take years before one is totally relieved of its symptoms. In disillusionment, the person constantly second guesses the fact that he is free and will not be harmed as he was before in the concentration camp. But, worse is the discovery that suffering does not end; that the longed-for happiness does not come; family and friends will not be there to welcome him home; jobs and careers no longer exist. Similar to the "invisible" electric fence an animal avoids following repeated experiences of electric shock, the prisoner accepts that the concentration camp is his fate; his home; his world; and does not attempt to leave, even when the gates to freedom are left open. The hope that had sustained them throughout their incarceration is now gone. As time passes, however, the prisoner's experiences in the concentration camps gradually become nothing but a nightmare.

Frankl concludes from his experience and those he observed in the camps that a prisoner's psychological reactions are not solely the result of the conditions of his life, but also from the freedom of choice he always has even in severe suffering. The inner hold a prisoner has on his spiritual self relies on having a faith in the future and that once a prisoner loses that faith, he is doomed. During the third stage, once a prisoner has been liberated from the camp, he views everything as "unreal, unlikely, as in a dream," and may feel compelled to remain in the "safe" camp.

The Truth and Reconciliation Committees set up in South Africa following the end of apartheid made it possible for that country to come to grips with the terror of its past. Shared were horrendous stories of bones of dead sons and fathers being returned to their families by their killers. Families confronted the soldiers who instigated midnight raids, taking away men, women and children, never to be seen again, and of whole villages being killed.

When asked about justice for those victimized, why their murderers should not be tried, convicted and executed, survivors of apartheid replied, "Reconciliation is always painful. So we have done away with the death penalty. To use it would be revenge. We want no more killing. We are grateful for our freedom. We want reconciliation." Wellness, wholeness, healing and health, and becoming wholly human depend on an individual being able to pursue his or meaning potential; on having gratitude for the relationships which have changed us.[20] Unfortunately, we often forget to go back and offer our gratitude to persons, events and circumstances that have changed our lives, but it is never too late.

Attitudinal, Creative & Experiential Values

Viktor Frankl's attitude towards unavoidable suffering may be one of his most valuable contributions to the art of living. He formulated attitudinal values before the Holocaust, but its validity was tested and confirmed during his incarceration in concentration camps such as Auschwitz and Theresienstadt. Men, women and children were deprived of everything that made life meaningful. It was this discovery by Frankl that confirmed that experiential and creative values are not the only sources of meaning. Even if we are facing a fate which cannot be changed, such as the loss of a leg, there is still meaning available in our lives. "When you can no longer change the situation you may change yourself, which means you may change your attitude towards your fate," states Frankl. "Changing yourself, in such cases, means rising above yourself, going beyond yourself." Jung says, "Meaning makes many things, perhaps even everything, endurable and bearable." Nietzsche says, "If you have a *why* to live for you can put up with almost any *how*."

Survivors of the Holocaust, genocides throughout history and those who may have been prisoners of war state that it may have been traumatic, but, having survived, they feel stronger physically, emotionally and spiritually. Returning to family, to an unfinished creative endeavor tended to speed their recovery in the continued search for meaning. Detachment, says Frankl, in the form of laughter, helps others survive. American soldiers used humor in the Vietnam POW camps.[20] Laughter frees the spirit to survive through even the most tragic circumstances. It helps prisoners of war shake their heads clear, get grounded with their feet back under them and restore their sense of balance. Humor is integral to our peace of mind and our ability to go beyond mere survival. Later, we will explore the similarity between Frankl's *attitudinal, creative* and *experiential values* and Kubler-Ross's latter stage of grief – *acceptance*.

Reflection Exercise on Man's Inhumanity to Mankind: Periodically re-read Viktor Frankl's *Man's Search for Meaning*. Having encountered several meaningful life experiences during our preceding *period* tend to provide a different perspective on life and, therefore, what we glean from the book's wisdom. If you have been using the Intensive Journal, it would be a good idea to re-read your writings to discover the direction your life has been taking; where you have made progress; where you have been procrastinating; where progress has been beyond your control; and where you may need to spend time in your dialogue section.

IX.
Logotherapy - Health through Meaning

For the meaning of life differs from man to man, from day to day and from hour to hour. What matters, therefore, is not the meaning of life in general but rather the specific meaning of a person's life at a given moment... Ultimately, man should not ask what the meaning of his life is, but rather he must recognize that it is he who is asked.

- Dr. Viktor Frankl

Viktor Frankl, the father of the third Viennese School of Psychotherapy, is a psychologist who studied how people develop purpose in life. His initial ideas of meaning were developed prior to World War II, but were reinforced by his experiences as a prisoner in concentration camps during the Holocaust. His experience, as a death camp survivor, is described in his first book, *Man's Search for Meaning*. Frankl and his family were deported to Theresienstadt camp in July 1942. Frankl's father died in Theresienstadt. His mother was gassed in Auschwitz. His wife, forced to have an abortion, died in Bergen-Belsen. His younger brother died in a branch camp of Auschwitz, working in a mine. Frankl's sister survived by emigrating to Australia before the deportation.

Frankl believes an individual discovers meaning "by creating a work or doing a deed," by experiencing "nature and culture," or "by experiencing another human being in his uniqueness - by loving him." Perhaps Frankl's most important contribution is his belief that individuals can find purpose even "when confronted with a hopeless situation" - what matters is how a person transforms that personal tragedy into achievement.[20]

Frankl holds that every individual has an innate desire to develop a purpose in life, which he terms the "will to meaning." "With this we designate man's striving to fulfill as much meaning in his existence as possible, and to realize as much value in his life as possible," he says. When an individual fails to experience meaning, "existential vacuum" or frustration is the result. Frankl believes that individuals who experience existential frustration compensate for their lack of meaning by engaging in risky behaviors.

Viktor Frankl refers to the "tragic triad" as those things in life which are unavoidable – death, guilt and suffering. At some point in our lives, each of us will face our own death or someone close and dear to us. The grief that follows such a loss can seem unbearable, but grief is actually a healing process. Grief is the emotional suffering we feel after a loss of some kind. The death of a loved one, loss of a limb, even intense disappointment can cause grief. During grief, it is common to have many conflicting feelings. Sorrow, anger, loneliness, sadness, shame, anxiety, and guilt often accompany serious losses. Having so many strong feelings can be very stressful. But, whatever the loss we can become stronger at the broken places.

Meeting Joe Fabry

Having read *Man's Search for Meaning* as part of my doctoral studies, and acknowledging the roll that Logotherapy could play in the rehabilitation of incarcerated individuals, I attempted to contact Viktor Frankl early in 1997. However, Frankl was in poor health and too weak to travel. He referred me to Joseph Fabry, a fellow survivor at the Logotherapy Institute in Berkeley, California. Fabry agreed to discuss Logotherapy in a round-table discussion format at Folsom State Prison in November 1997 and again in February 1998. The initial goal was to discuss the formation of Logotherapy-discussion groups for men serving life sentences. In turn, these men would share their understanding with their peers, especially those nearing parole. The following is his lecture:

"I became an admirer and even a friend of Dr. Viktor Frankl after reading his book, *Man's Search for Meaning* thirty-four years ago. I was comforted by his strong belief that life has meaning under all circumstances, even the worst ones, and that every one of us is important in our own unique way. I needed to hear that, because when Hitler overran my native Austria, I lost everything that had been meaningful to me – my family, my friends, my job, my country, my language (which was important to me because I wanted to be a writer).

In Nazi Austria I was treated like a useless insect that had to be exterminated, and this self-image remained with me for a long time although I was fortunate to escape to the United States and did not have to suffer the humiliation of an extermination camp. (In my race for survival, I had faced many moments that required a meaningful response – from ducking into a doorway from the Gestapo to writing short stories in prison. Some responses had lasting consequences: to marry, have a child, ask for a transfer to New York, quit CBS and return to Berkeley. It was not always clear until later, and sometimes never, whether my choice had actually been 'what was meant' – not taking the train to England...after Hitler's takeover, leaving my parents behind, reporting to the Brussels police instead of hiding.) Frankl's book was written by a man who had been in four extermination camps for almost three years, and had found his life had meaning even under these most meaningless conditions.

I met Dr. Frankl when he gave a lecture in San Francisco in 1963, and became his driver on his later lecture tours in California. At the end of one of his lectures, the education director of the San Quentin prison came up to him and spoke to him. One of the inmates (on death row) had read Frankl's *Man's Search for Meaning* and it changed his outlook on life, as it had done to me and many others. This inmate had heard that Frankl was in the area and wondered if he could see him.

To the consternation of all those who had worked out his tight schedule of lectures, interviews, and other obligations, Frankl immediately agreed to see the man the next morning. The meeting took place in the prison library, and the education director was so impressed by what Frankl told the prisoner that he invited Frankl to speak to all inmates on his next visit to California. This second meeting took place in the chapel and was not too well attended. After the lecture

I talked to some inmates in the chapel. One of them said: 'I never come to these speeches by psychologists because they always tell us there is no hope. It's all because of our past, our parents, our upbringing, and our early childhood. The past hangs around our necks like a millstone. And here is a man who tells us there is always hope. We still can make something of ourselves. And he is a man who was in prison himself, a prison of the worst sort, like three years on death row.

Since then, more than thirty years ago, I have absorbed the Franklian philosophy through books, personal talks with him, and the feedbacks from people in groups I developed. I have seen that his way of looking at life works, often in hopeless situations. I have seen again and again that it matters less what happens to us but how we take it. Jerry Long had a diving accident at age seventeen that left him paralyzed from the neck down. He cannot feed himself, nor go to the bathroom. He can type only with the help of a little stick in his mouth. But after his hospitalizations, he finished high school, went to college, got his Ph.D. in psychology and now has a practice helping other quadriplegics. It was his attitude that saved him. He wrote to Dr. Frankl: 'The accident broke my neck; it didn't break me.'

Frankl quoted this sentence often because it summarizes Frankl's core belief: that nothing can break us, except our own negative attitudes. He developed this core belief before the Second World War in Vienna and it was tested and confirmed in the concentration camps. As a doctor, he knew we have a body that can become weak and sick; as a psychiatrist he knew we have a psyche that can drive us to harmful actions. But he also saw that human beings are more than body and psyche, that we have something that the medical profession disregarded. This something more, which differentiates us from the other animals, is the human spirit. The spirit has always been recognized by religion, but Frankl found the human spirit in all humans, regardless of whether they are religious or not, and if they are religious, regardless of what denomination to which they belong.

The human spirit has always been a hazy concept for me. Frankl defined it clearly. The spirit, he says, is the area in us where *we* make the decisions, where *we* are in control. In the psyche, we are driven. In the spirit, *we* are the drivers. We cannot help feeling angry or sexually aroused, but we do not have to hit, kill or rape.

The human spirit is our healthy core; it cannot become sick. It can be clocked by physical or psychological sicknesses, and in these cases medication or traditional psychotherapy must be used to unblock the access to the spirit and its resources.

It is very reassuring for us to realize that we have a healthy core deep within, with resources that enable us to take a stand against the weaknesses of body and the drives of emotions, against the injustices and unfairness of life, that there is an area where we are not the victims, but are in control.

What are these resources of the human spirit? There is, first of all, our *will to meaning* – our longing to find meaning in life, goals, and purpose. Every moment offers us a meaning – often as trivial as getting up in the morning, eating at mealtime, or doing our job properly. Sometimes the meanings of the moment are more serious – to help someone, or to say 'I love you' to a child or a partner or a parent. Occasionally, the meaning of the moment has more than fleeting consequences – to decide to marry, have a child, or change careers.

We make these decisions with help of our conscience which is another resource of our spiritual dimension. The human conscience is very weakly developed. Its voice is often overpowered by physical desires, emotional needs, or social pressures. But it is there, beyond what Sigmund Freud called the 'superego,' the voices of father figures that tell us what to do. Our authentic conscience sniffs out the meaning of the moment and helps us respond in a way we decide to respond – to be able to respond, to be response-able. To strengthen our inner ear, so we can hear the voice of our authentic conscience, is one of the aims of Frankl's therapy.

Another resource of the spirit is an old acquaintance – love. It is a love that does more than gratify the physical and emotional needs important as this is for our well being. Frankl speaks of a love that goes beyond gratifying needs, a love that brings fulfillment. He often uses the term 'self-transcendence,' the reaching out beyond our self-interests to other people and even to a cause we love and consider meaningful.

One more resource of the human spirit is worth mentioning – our capacity for self-distancing, to step away from ourselves and to look at ourselves from the outside, possibly with imagination, hope, and a sense of humor – three more resources of the spirit. Frankl tells of an episode when, in the freezing mud of the concentration camp, he was forced to chop up rocks for a railroad bed, and he imagined standing some day in a warm, well-lit hall lecturing about his experiences in the camp. I had a similar experience in a Belgium prison where I was held because I had fled Germany and was in Belgium without a visa. Sitting in a single cell, hearing the footsteps of the guards on the steel corridor, being led out for exercise for half an hour each day, I saw myself writing a story about my prison life and selling it to a magazine when I would arrive in America, which at that time was only a dream.

Only human beings can dream and hope and find meanings in any situation, and we do this by making use of the resources of our inner core that remains strong when we are weak and healthy when we are sick. I have often called the human spirit the 'medicine chest' of Frankl's therapy – a medicine chest to which we always have access.

Frankl called his method 'Logotherapy,' and he translates the Greek word 'logos' with 'meaning,' so Logotherapy is therapy (or health) through meaning. He saw in the twenties and thirties what we now clearly see in the Twenty-First Century: that a life without meaning is a life without fulfillment. Many people, who have enough to live on, have nothing for which to live. Successful people can feel empty and unfulfilled, and people who are considered failures, can find fulfillment. People try to fill this inner emptiness with all sorts of things – with sex, drugs, gambling, excitement, crime, with power, material things, or prestige, but the fulfilling content is meaning.

This inner void, Frankl says, is not a sickness. On the contrary, it is proof that we are human beings who are aware that we have that inner core of the human spirit, and are frustrated when we fail to make use of its resources.

I have talked much about the necessity to find meaning, and have also talked about the meaning of the moment. Frankl believes that each moment offers us a meaning, and that this meaning changes from moment to moment, and from person to person. We are here together, sharing the moment, but the meaning is different for each of us. For me, the meaning of the moment is to explain Frankl's ideas the best I can in such a short time. The meaning of the moment for each of you is different. For some, it may be to learn something new, intellectually. To others, the meaning may be the hope that something I say may be of use in your life. To still others, it may be the hope that something I say may be of use to someone else, a child, a partner, a friend. For some, it may even be nothing more than an excuse to break the monotony of prison life.

But there is more than the meaning of the moment which changes with the situation. Is there something that could be called 'The Meaning of Life?' Something that is true and fulfilling for all of us? Frankl thinks so, and he also thinks that we all, deep inside, believe that such a *Super-meaning* exists, although we cannot prove it. It is like the horizon; we can see it in the distance, but the closer we approach (to it), the farther it recedes. We can never grasp it and hold on to it, but – in order to be healthy – we must pursue it.

The *pursuit* of meaning, not its attainment, is our goal. I have spent many years speculating what exactly this *Super-meaning*, this *Ultimate Meaning*, may be. Frankl never defined it clearly, and when I discussed it with him, he didn't disagree that my definition is okay, at least comes close to what he believed. My definition of *Ultimate Meaning* is our awareness that, in spite of all the chaos and injustice there is in life, there is order in the universe, and that you and I and everyone else are part of that order; we belong. We are part of the entire web of life, a tiny thread in the fabric of totality, and that it is important what we do or fail to do.

Some people have the intuitive feeling that they belong to some totality, and they may see it in religious or in secular terms, in terms of the ecosystem, for instance, that demands of us not to disturb the ecology of our planet, or in terms of a community of which we are a part, friends, country, hopefully the world.

Other people who do not have that feeling of belonging, may get closer to it by responding to the meanings of the moment, moment by moment, consciously or unconsciously.

Frankl's Logotherapy is based on three assumptions. They cannot be proved except by living (the assumptions), and over the years thousands of people have found them true.

The first two assumptions we have already talked about: First, that life has meaning, under all circumstances, and up to the last moment of our lives. Second, that we have a will to meaning, and that this will is the strongest motivation for our living and doing what we do, much stronger than the will to pleasure, especially sexual pleasure, as Sigmund Freud assumed, or the will to power, as Frankl's teacher, Alfred Adler, believed.

But there is a third assumption which none of the previous psychologists had considered, and that is the assumption that we have the freedom, under all circumstances, to find meaning. This is puzzling because we obviously are not always free to change the meaningless situation itself. Examples are what Frankl calls the 'tragic triad' – unavoidable suffering, inerasable guilt, and death. These we cannot change. But in those situations we cannot change, we are *always* free to change our attitude – to find a meaningful attitude in a situation which itself is meaningless and unavoidable.

Logotherapists help their clients distinguish between areas of freedom and areas of fate that have to be accepted. There is no point to run your head against unavoidable fate, so you concentrate on the areas where you still have choices.

Let me give you examples from Frankl's own practice. Where is the area of freedom in cases of unavoidable suffering? In a student demonstration he was shown an overweight woman who suffered from severe depressions. Her medical history showed that her obesity was caused by an incurable malfunction of a gland. He didn't talk to her about diets and exercises but about things she liked to do. Then he told her: 'You are *not* responsible that you are overweight. Your glands do this to you. But you *are* responsible how you live as a person whose body is forcing you to be obese. You will never be a ballet dancer. But you can do many things you say you like to do – make friends, go to concerts and theaters, and read books.' Two years later the woman told Frankl that the half hour of talk with him had helped her where years of psychoanalysis had failed.

Now, (let me give you an example of) inerasable guilt. Frankl met a woman who wore a charm bracelet, with nine children's teeth hanging on it. He asked her about it. She said: 'These are teeth of my children. This one is from Miriam, this is from Jacob,' and she named all nine. 'They all died in concentration camps.' When Frankl asked her how she could live with such a memory, she said, simply: 'I am now director of an orphanage in Israel.' I suspect that I myself have handled my own survivor guilt in a similar manner. The greatest guilt of my life has been that I was not able to save my parents from the concentration camps, although I tried my best. But it was not good enough. So, I tend to believe that I have been trying, for all these years, to apply Logotherapy and bring help to other people when I failed to help my parents.

When we feel we have done something wrong, we can repair the damage where this is possible. Where the damage cannot be repaired on the persons we have hurt, we can help others in similar situations. And true and sincere repentance will help, too. True repentance will make us new and better persons, more at peace with ourselves.

Now the third and the most unavoidable human condition: death. Many people have doubts that their life has had any meaning, because it is coming to an end. Frankl points out that the opposite is true: only because we know that life will not go on forever, are we motivated to live every moment to the fullest, as long as we can. Rather than seeing our past life as an empty stubble field where nothing will grow any more, he directs our attention to the full granaries into which we have brought the harvest of our lives – all the deeds we did, the experiences we had, the people we loved, and the tragedies we have bravely borne. Nothing can make them undone; they are stored forever (in the historical fabric of the universe).

Frankl also illustrates the same point in another way. Some people see their life as a wall calendar, from which they tear off a sheet every day as it has passed. And they get discouraged as they see the calendar gets thinner and thinner. He suggests that we write our daily experiences and achievements on the back of each sheet as we tear it off, and look with pride onto the growing pile of sheets of past days, rather than on the dwindling pile of sheets remaining.

This metaphor contains perhaps the most important message form Viktor Frankl: The past is important and we should learn from it and not take it as an excuse for our present failures. But we cannot change the past. Our past is our area of fate. But what we can change is our present and our future. In our past we have often been told what's *wrong* with us. In the present we should make a list of the things that are *right* with us.

Another thing distinguishes Logotherapy from the earlier therapies: Logotherapy pays attention not just to the causes of our troubles but rather to its solutions. Sometimes it is necessary to know why we got into difficulties and learn from past mistakes, but it is even more important to see ways of how to get *out* of them. And this is what Logotherapy is all about."

Fabry had a lasting impact on the men incarcerated at Folsom State Prison. One individual, a Vietnam War veteran serving two life sentences, developed a curriculum based on the round-table discussions and reading of Frankl's *Man' Search for Meaning*. He continues to teach other incarcerated men that they too can discover the true meaning of their lives and live responsibly.

Life as a Rite of Passage

Rites of passage are the story of life. It is about transcendence. When a plant or animal encounters an event that brings damage to the organism, it inherently attempts to repair the damage or develop strengths in other areas. When a human being loses one of its senses or physical abilities, it has the potential to develop strengths in other senses or physical areas. When he suffers from psychological or existential turmoil, he can discover or create his own meaning of life even in tough situations. If Viktor Frankl could find meaning in Auschwitz, can we not reclaim control of our lives today? Frankl's answer is: Yes, we can, but we must take his existential step of accepting choice and responsibility, and rejecting excuses.

Frankl survived one of life's most horrible rites of passage, displaying no anger or self-pity. Indeed, one of his greatest insights was that only those Auschwitz inmates who were able to find some existential meaning in their lives, even in a death camp, survived. Frankl writes about what the Auschwitz survivors learned:

"What was really needed was a fundamental change in our attitude toward life. We had to learn ourselves and, furthermore, we had to teach the despairing men, that it did not really matter what we expected from life, but rather what life expected from us. We needed to stop asking about the meaning of life, and instead to think of ourselves as those who were being questioned by life, daily and hourly. Our answer must consist, not in talk and meditation, but in right action and in right conduct. Life ultimately means taking responsibility to find the right answer to its problems and to fulfill the tasks which it constantly sets for each individual."[20]

Ernest Hemingway, in *A Farewell to Arms*, states that "the world breaks every one and afterward many are strong at the broken places. But those that will not break, it kills. It kills the very good and the very gentle and the very brave impartially. If you are none of these you can be sure that it will kill you too, but there will be no special hurry." Historically, there have been countless individuals who have been broken, but their brokenness did not prevent them from practicing, improving and becoming stronger at the broken places:

- John Milton wrote the classic *Paradise Lost* sixteen years after he had become blind.
- Ludwig van Beethoven wrote his greatest music, including five symphonies during his later years after becoming deaf.
- British fighter pilot Douglas Bader rejoined the British Royal Air Force with two artificial limbs after having lost both legs in an air crash during World War II. He was captured by the Germans three times and three times he escaped.
- Left with a paralyzed left leg at age four after contracting double pneumonia and scarlet fever, Wilma Rudolph went on win three Olympic gold medals in track and field.
- Franklin D. Roosevelt was paralyzed by polio at the age of thirty-nine. He went on to become president and was re-elected three times.
- Lance Armstrong, never having won the Tour de France, a twenty-day 2032-mile bicycle race, prior to contracting testicular cancer that spread up his spine to his lungs and brain, was given only a forty percent chance of survival. Armstrong went on to win the most grueling sport seven consecutive times before retiring.
- Henri Matisse and Auguste Renoir were two great artists, friends and frequent companions. Renoir was confined to his home during the last decade of his life, almost paralyzed by the pain of arthritis, but continued to paint in spite of his infirmities. One day

as Matisse watched the elder painter, Renoir, working in his studio, fighting tortuous pain with each brushstroke. Matisse blurted out, "Auguste, why do you continue to paint when you are in such agony?" Renoir answered simply, "The beauty remains. The pain passes." And so, almost to his dying day, Renoir put paint to canvas.

• Washington Roebling, an engineer, was severely brain-damaged, unable to talk or walk due to a tragic on-site accident. Despite his disabilities, he continued to instruct others on how to build the Brooklyn Bridge. Building the bridge took thirteen years because Washington had to tap out his instructions with one finger.

• Michael Stone set a National and International Olympics record of 17 feet 6.5 inches in the pole vault in spite of the fact that he was blind.

• Rafer Johnson, the former decathlon champion, was born with a clubfoot.

• Oscar Pistorius, a South African Paralympic runner, also known as the "Blade Runner" and "the fastest man on no legs," is the double amputee world record holder in the 100, 200 and 400 meter events. He ran a personal best of 46.25 seconds in the 400-meter race in 2008.

• Christopher Reeves, the movie actor in the Superman series, championed spinal injury research following a fall from his horse resulting in paralysis from the neck down.

• Douglas Pringle, following the loss of a leg in Vietnam, achieved several Para Olympic gold medals in downhill slalom skiing.

• Another veteran, Max Cleland, lost both legs and one arm in the Vietnam War went on to become a U. S. Senator. Max noted that "in the service of love, only broken hearts will do. Others want to hear of your suffering and how you made it back."

• Franklin Roosevelt contracted polio at age thirty-nine. Twelve years later he became president and would go on to raise money for the care of polio patients. This pursuit would become the March of Dimes.

• David Hartman is one of many blind physicians. Blind persons are doctors, nurses, therapists and chiropractors.

- Arn Chorn Pond is a survivor of the Killing Fields of Cambodia where he was forced to fight as a child soldier.
- Michael MacDonald grew up in South Boston, losing several brothers to gang and crime shootings. He transformed his anger into a non-profit organization with a mission to purchase guns from gang members as a way to end violence in his community.
- Nelson Mandela was imprisoned for twenty-seven years on Devil's Island off the coast of South Africa for his objection to apartheid. Following his release, Mandela became the president of South Africa thus ending the apartheid era.
- Aleksandr Solzhenitsyn was imprisoned in a gulag, a Russian prison, for speaking out against his country's leader, and yet, embraced the spiritual experience.
- Viktor Frankl survived living in three death camps during World War II. He lost his parents, a brother and his pregnant wife to either starvation or the gas chambers in the death camps during the Holocaust. He remembers men who walked through the huts comforting others, giving away their last piece of bread, proof that everything can be taken from a man but one thing, the last of his freedoms – to choose one's attitude in any given set of circumstances, to choose one's own way.

The same was true of each of the above individuals.

Dr. Viktor Frankl notes that "whenever one is confronted with an inescapable, unavoidable situation, whenever one has to face a fate which cannot be changed, for example, an incurable disease, such as an inoperable cancer, just then one is given a last chance to actualize the highest value, to fulfill the deepest meaning, the meaning of suffering. For what matters above all is the attitude we take toward suffering, the attitude in which we take our suffering upon ourselves."

Individuals may question the gift of unavoidable pain and suffering. Jimmy discovered the meaningful gift of two children born to a mentally ill, addicted and homicidal woman. His choices in life would ultimately lead him to his current wife, the people whom he's met along the way, and the course that his career took, events that would never have happened had he chosen a different path on the road of life.

If individuals fail to learn life's lessons, the irony is that those lessons will be repeated again and again in symbolic ways until they understand the meaning. It is when individuals begin to accept the harsh and often painful life experiences that spiritual growth, strong character development, and a greater sense of meaning and purpose result. Psychic and physical releases from constraining and painful situations then become possible. One's approach can go from "Why is this happening to me?" to "How do I transcend this situation?"

When a Rite of Passage becomes a Paradox

Initiation into a gang oftentimes includes the killing of a random stranger or an enemy gang member. By putting a bullet into the chest, back or head of the victim, a twelve-year-old can gain respect and acceptance into a gang that provides what he cannot get at home. The violent act of murder also introduces him to a continuing and ever-increasing relationship with death. Killings become easier and human life no longer has any value, whether on the streets of Los Angeles, the killing fields of Cambodia during the Vietnam War, in Bosnia, Somalia, or Rwanda.

Many of the problems that face the youth today around the world can be linked to the absence of rites of passage. If the youth are not provided this initiatory experience by elders within their community, they will unconsciously attempt to create it for themselves and their peers. We know that the youth are capable of creating experiences that are dangerous, intense, and edgy. They do this through violence, risk-taking behaviors, drug abuse, careless sexuality, bodily mutilation, and other initiatory behaviors that are counter productive to their meaning potential. What they lack is the wisdom or cosmology to initiate them in contained and meaningful ways. It is the elders' responsibility to provide this.

"The truth is," states Father Gregory Boyle, a Jesuit priest in Los Angeles, "no gang member ever seeks to join a gang. All of that talk of honor and loyalty just makes (gang membership) palatable." Most gang members join their gang because they are running form something – they are fleeing from a life that is even more painful and destructive than an existence on the streets...seeking 'security'..."

To help young people put gang culture behind them, the focus must be turned inward, allowing youth to discover and explore their own sense of dignity, self-worth, purpose and meaning. The searches for nobility and meaning help former gang members find their own personal value rather than comparing themselves with others. What Father Boyle does "is to get them to see the truth of who they really are and then guide them toward becoming that truth." Nobility is a sense of purpose and inner strength that we feel when we are clear in our goals and values. It is the recognition that our character does not change based on who is watching or whom we are trying to please. It is, to paraphrase Thomas Jefferson, the ability to "stand like a rock" on matters of principle and doing the right thing even when nobody is looking.

Living a civil life requires far more strength than living a savage one. Allowing a conflict or rivalry to escalate into violence shows a lack of control and that is a lack of strength.

Gangs are used to dealing with every confrontation aggressively. But walking away from a fight is the greatest show of strength there is. Refusing to aggressively confront shows the strength of their own commitments to their spouses and children who depend upon them to earn a living rather than winding up dead, paralyzed, in a psychiatric ward or incarcerated.

Real warriors at the dawn of the Age of Chivalry had to make the choice to use their weapons to kill and plunder for their own gain, or to be impaired by those who loved them to serve a greater good and build a brighter future.

Stepping away from the gang culture must be a choice that comes from within. "You can't scare people straight, but you can care them straight," noted Father Boyle. It is a transformative process that originates from within. To transform a person, one must first empower that person to see the world differently; to reconfigure one's way of not only relating to the world, but also fundamentally changing his or her way of perceiving that world as well.

Creating safe, caring, supportive communities is what the Code of Chivalry is all about – it is, after all, the catalyst that transformed the predatory ideals of a savage, barbaric culture by establishing the image of the honorable, noble knight.

Whether someone is a former gang member or a successful corporate CEO, living by the honorable, respectable principles of the true "way of the warrior" is not something into which he can be coerced. He must choose that path and he must guard his choice with strength and determination, because vanity, expedience and desire will challenge that choice every day. Being a knight means having the strength to walk away from those temptations rather than going "head up" – aggressive confrontations – and indulging in selfish, destructive behavior.

Rites of passage are a key part of every traditional culture. However, modern culture lacks meaningful rites of passage. The purpose of traditional cultures' rites of passage was to allow the youth to become adults. Through rites of passage, the youth discovered their gifts, their vision for their role in the community, and their own personal wisdom for dealing with the challenges that lay in front of them. Their elders facilitated these discoveries, and supported the young adults to integrate their visions, roles and paths into the fabric of the community. The rites of passage supported the transformation of the child mentality into the adult mentality. These cultures recognized that one could not possibly function as an adult without the rites of passage experience. Each culture has its own form of rites of passage, but there are common elements.

Characteristics of True Initiatory Experiences

- The youth experiencing a rite of passage need experience it only once. During the formal rite of passage needed for the journey the elders prepare the youth with the teachings and cosmology of their community.
- The youth do not know where they are, separated from their normal surroundings and brought to an initiation camp outside of their community.
- The youth, and the elders, must accept an unknown outcome. The youth would often spend long periods of time alone, forgoing normal comforts, such as food, water and sleep, and securities.

This phase is usually an awe-inspiring experience involving a degree of actual danger, challenging the initiated youth physically, emotionally and spiritually.

- The youth feel exposed, vulnerable, naked, and completely unprotected by their family or community.
- The youth are not given a choice about turning back, no matter how traumatic.
- The rite of passage often involves the body and senses (e.g., *Vision Quest & Rain Dance*).
- The youth are taught to become more accepting of the meaning of life and given tools for discovering their purpose.
- The rite of passage teaches the initiated youth to shift from their self-centeredness to a sense of community connectedness. They are welcomed back to their community not as the youth they were but as adults and helped to integrate their experiences. This is followed by community support to apply what the initiated have learned and further develop their vision.

Franklian Principles

Viktor Frankl identifies the search for meaning in life as the primary motivational force in human beings and is guided in that search for meaning and purpose by five relevant principles. First, each human being is unique. We may share many similarities, similar human nature, and be equal in value or dignity, but the odds of our uniqueness are 1 in $10^{100 \text{ trillion}}$! We are "neither expendable nor replaceable... with unique historical experiences... with special opportunities and obligations reserved for [each one of us] alone."[20]

Second, each human being is unique and unrepeatable in worth. No two human beings are the same; no double or twin are exact, no matter how perfect a duplicate.[27]

Third, "every human being is precious in worth and dignity... Each human being has a spirit... is a subject, not an object; a who, not a what; someone, not something... with unconditional value, but with no more value than any other particular person or persons... and is irreplaceable."

Fourth, we must never "use another human being, but encounter him/her in all his/her humanness; to be respected, not used... Sex is truly *human* when it is an expression of love between two persons," and not simply a drive for pleasure; not a mere means to an end or any end... On the human level, one no longer 'uses' the partner but encounters him/her... on a person-to-person basis... that is, s/he loves the partner. Encounter preserves the humanness of the partner, and love discovers his/her uniqueness as a person.

Fifth, each human being is unique and, therefore, has a unique meaning in life. "Each human being is unique... and thus neither expendable nor replaceable... with his unique personal characteristics that experience a unique historical context in a world which has special opportunities and obligations reserved for him/her alone."[22]

Ultimately, man is that same creature who invented illicit drugs, alcohol, lethal weapons and perpetrated crimes against his fellow man; but he is also that being who took responsibility for doing the right thing even when nobody was looking, chose to be a responsible spouse and parent and searched for his real meaning and purpose, and facilitated that in his family members and strangers alike. Nobody enjoys suffering but when suffering does occur it can present an existential challenge to the individual and those around him. Frankl noted that the meaning of existence is learned through unavoidable crisis and suffering. Even in the deep darkness of childhood trauma, at the peak of existential humiliation, Viktor Frankl continues to encourage us to respond to life in its entire dreadfulness as a supreme and sacred value and through that understanding rebuild ourselves out of the hell. According to Frankl, realizing the meaning of life provides spiritual strength and at the moment of truth helps man to face and cope with suffering.

A chemically dependent alcoholic has no "freedom" about the dependency but is free, after detoxification, to decide whether or not to take that first, fateful drink. The drug addict has no freedom about the dependency to increasingly addictive drugs that are decimating families, neighborhoods and communities throughout America.

A person suffering from a biologically caused depression, that comes and goes without apparent reason, has no freedom to fight the unavoidable, oncoming attack, except by taking medication to diminish the intensity of the depression. But he is freed to lead a meaningful life during periods of apparent normalcy between depressions.

Elderly people have no freedom from the unavoidable consequences of old age – loss of hearing, deterioration of sight, loss of friends who die, forced retirement, and feebleness, for example. But they are free to use their assets, including experience and wisdom to transcend.

Veterans who have experienced amputation, visual impairment, spinal cord injuries, brain trauma or other have no freedom to restore their loss but are free, given modern-day prosthetics and medicine, to pursue goals thought to be impossible, contributing greatly to research in areas such as physiology, psychology, biomechanics, performance analysis, nutrition and sports technology. Accepting the challenge, he can choose to adapt and push his body as far as he can take it.

If an individual has meaning and purpose in his life, if he has a spiritual foundation, if he has a reason for living and getting up each morning, he can withstand almost any hardship. However, when he lacks meaning and purpose, consequences do not matter, strikes do not matter, family and friends do not matter, and community and society do not matter.

Logotherapists Speak on Meaning

The following are adaptations of "meaning" affirmations by Logotherapists across America provided by Joseph Fabry, former Director of the Institute of Logotherapy.

- I know, deep within, who I am, who I want to be, and in what direction my life is moving. It is the task of the logo therapist to make these cognitions and goals conscious.
- I have the defiant power of the human spirit that enables me to take a stand against barriers and limitations.
- It is not so much what happens to me that count but the attitudes I take toward what happens to me.
- Unhealthy attitudes include reductionism (disregarding the human spirit: "I am nothing but an animal that can be trained, or a

machine that can be manipulated."); and nihilism ("Life has no meaning.")

• It is useless to ask why things happened to me; the useful approach is to ask what I can do in the situation in which I find myself.

• Life does not owe me pleasures but offers me meanings every moment. To respond to the meanings of the moment is to lead a meaningful life.

• It is not healthy to use the drawbacks of my past as excuses for present failures, but rather as a challenge to overcome them.

• If I have a task to fulfill, I can bear almost any hardship.

• Life has meaning to me last moment, even under the most miserable circumstances.

• I can find meanings by what I do (work, hobbies, leisure activities); by what I experience (nature, art, love); and by the attitude I take in situations that cannot be changed.

• I can find meaningful attitudes even in situations that in themselves are not meaningful.

• To be healthy, I must take responsibility in situations over which I have control, and not take responsibility where I have no control.

• It is healthy to feel remorse, a deep sorrow for having caused pain, and to use it to right a wrong where possible, or to learn not to repeat it where the harm cannot be repaired. It is an unhealthy burden to feel guilty without restitution or learning. To feel guilty without restitution or learning may be likened to a ten-pound weight held in my outstretched hand; eventually it appears to weigh a ton! It is healthy, on the other hand, to gain a distance between my symptoms and me. I may have had failures but I am not a failure.

• I have to find the opportunities behind my crises. This sometimes requires patience.

• It is better to have a variety of meaning areas available (work, family, creativity, leisure activities, friends, hobbles) than to put all our meaning eggs in one basket.

• I can change unwanted behavior patterns by stepping outside of myself and looking at myself with a sense of humor and exaggeration.

- My physical and emotional conditions can improve if I pay attention to the positive contents of my life, including even small events in the outside world that are pleasurable.
- My health also will improve if I pay attention to what's right with me, instead of what's wrong with me.
- Life is meaningful when I am aware that I always have choices, at least choices in my attitudes.

Several of the main tenets of Logotherapy are expressed in what Frankl termed "tragic optimism," optimism in the face of human death, guilt and suffering. Tragic optimism embraces the human potential to transform suffering into human achievement and guilt into meaningful action. The cornerstone of Frankl's philosophy is that "everything can be taken from a man but one thing; the last of the human freedoms – to choose one's attitude in any given set of circumstances, to choose one's own way."[20] Epictetus, a Stoic philosopher and former Roman slave echoed "we cannot choose our external circumstances, but we can always choose how we respond to them."

Logotherapy emphasizes a person's strengths and personal search for meaning rather than his or her symptoms. Symptom reduction is generally a byproduct of a successful meaning-based therapy. A Logotherapist employs specific techniques in persons suffering from PTSD, such as *Self-Distancing* (learning to gain distance from and observe the self), *Paradoxical intention* (wishing for or doing that which is feared), *Socratic Dialogue* (interviewing designed to elicit the patient's own wisdom), and *Dereflection* (redirecting attention from the self toward other people or meaningful goals. Logotherapeutic techniques enable an individual to transcend the self through his or her pursuit of meaning that is specific to his or her life.[20]

Frankl saw within the walls of the death camps that his fellow peers were able to "find meaning in a deed, in a work, or in love" or by the attitude that each adapted to circumstances that could not be changed.[26] Camp life was one in which there was a daily struggle for bread and for life itself. Certain prisoners were selected to act as overlords and brutalized their fellow peers even more than the SS.

Frankl says that the struggle for existence was such that "the best of us did not return." [27]

Viktor Frankl, prisoner number 119104 observed the behaviors, attitudes and emotions of both himself and others in the concentration camps as they adjusted to camp life. Everything they knew about life, and not only that but everything they knew about being decent and kind human beings was systematically challenged. He concluded from his observations that "everything can be taken from a man but the last of human freedoms – to choose one's attitude in any given set of circumstances, to choose one's own way."[27]

Frankl observed that people in concentration camps first experienced the stage of shock. Recall that *Stages of Grief* was described in Chapter VI. In the stage of shock all the distressing emotions of outrage, anger, grief, disgust, anxiety and fear, and deep, painful longing for the individual's loved ones were evident. Incarcerated individuals acted to try to deaden these feelings.

From this stage, a prisoner moved to a second stage of relative apathy similar to an emotional death.[27] Prisoners were unfairly and brutally beaten and tortured, screaming in pain but emotionally unaffected, an adapted defense against the severe conditions endured by prisoners. Human beings have show again and again throughout history that they can bear almost any physical torture. The harshest form of torture was the psychological torture that affected both the minds and spirits of the men.

Holocaust prisoners were systematically starved and yet expected to work in freezing temperature under the harshest of conditions. Under these conditions prisoners tended to focus only on those things most necessary for survival – warmth, food, staying awake for fear of dying in their sleep.

Liberated prisoners entered a third stage as they adjusted to the normal world, a world far removed from their prison experience. Returned prisoners found it hard to re-experience joy during this stage, having lost many family members and friends to starvation, a firing squad, or gas chambers. Out of these extremes of suffering Frankl observed that those men, women and children who had a meaning beyond mere survival were better able to endure the extreme deprivations of the concentration camp.

Frankl says Logotherapy provides an effective and structured paradigm for addressing the critical issues faced by those who are survivors of genocide, war, abuse, and catastrophic events, often resulting in PTSD and in so doing provides an opportunity for healing, growth and strength at the broken places created by these experiences.

Logotherapy, Intensive Journal & Rehabilitation

The basic tenets of Logotherapy and Intensive Journal are routinely presented to men incarcerated at Folsom State Prison in workshop-discussion format. Within the "safe" and confidential classroom environment most incarcerated men eventually admit to having experienced childhood trauma; some suffer as a result of their traumatic wars experiences in Vietnam, Iraq, Afghanistan and other wars. During a typical three-week program each person responds to a *Purpose-In-Life* pretest.[13] Lectures, Socratic dialogue, meaning-oriented videos, readings and written responses to the Intensive Journal process and Logotherapeutic scenarios[16] reflecting core principles of Logotherapy such as 'freedom of will,' 'personal responsibility for shaping character,' 'attitudes toward fate,' 'the will to meaning,' 'meaning fulfillment,' and 'transformation of suffering' are part of the program.[27]

At the completion of the program, participants respond to a *Purpose-In-Life* posttest. A majority of the participants reflect a significant change between the pretest and the posttest. Most choose to further their professional or academic knowledge through a union apprenticeship or enrollment in college upon paroling. Many express a desire to give back to their community through community volunteer service, thereby facilitating the daily practice of coping skills, reintegration into community life, and counteracting avoidant symptoms and institutionalization as a result of attempts to drug, divert or bury childhood existential pain. Each is able to discover meaning through service to others, through creative endeavors, and through discovering activities that offer enjoyment and personal fulfillment. Participants are strongly urged to share with others the hope of discovering meaning in spite of brokenness.

It has been my experience that the lecture, Socratic dialogue and discussion approach appear to help most participants discover a new sense of purpose in life and to attach new meaning to life experiences, whether it involved childhood or wartime trauma, or other traumatic events, circumstances and brokenness in adulthood. Each participant sees himself, perhaps for the first time as a unique human being with a meaning and purpose yet to be discovered, a survivor who could become stronger, physically, mentally and spiritually at the broken places.

Viktor Frankl in Concentration Camps of Auschwitz & Dachau

The 'Holocaust' years (1939-1945) were a concrete geographical reality spelt Auschwitz, Belsen, Treblinka, and Dachau – the death camps of Nazi Germany. Six million Jews died of starvation or were killed in gas chambers during the holocaust of World War II. Another 20 million Russians were killed by Nazi Germany. In addition, the Japanese killed as many as 30 million Filipinos, Malays, Vietnamese, Cambodians, Indonesians and Burmese, at least 23 million of them ethnic Chinese.

Except for his sister, Viktor Frankl and his other family members were incarcerated not for what they did, but for who they were. Only Viktor Frankl survived his years of incarceration in Auschwitz, Dachau and other Nazi death camps during World War II. His pregnant wife, his brother, and his mother and father, stripped of their identity, possessions and clothes, each died in prison either from a starvation diet or in the gas chambers under the most horrific set of prison conditions. Frankl's sister escaped the death camps when she traveled outside Austria.

After surviving thirty-four months in the Nazi death camps, Viktor Frankl and other incarcerated men and women were liberated. It was during this period that Frankl rewrote *The Doctor and the Soul*.[23] This book was soon followed by *Man's Search for Meaning*.[20] The reconstruction of this lost manuscript took only nine days and continues to be one of the top ten books in America. Frankl's books describe his philosophy and therapy referred to as Logotherapy. It appears that

Logotherapy, also known as "height psychology" rather than "depth psychology," is the only major theory which includes the human spirit as a prime source of healing and strength. Logotherapy recognizes the human capacity to aspire to motivational factors beyond mere instinct. According to Frankl, life is not only meaningful in the larger sense; there is meaning in each moment.

Despite the unbelievable suffering that took place in the concentration camps, Frankl held onto the belief that "life never ceases to have meaning" and the conviction that *the* "will to meaning is the strongest motivation to living and acting." Frankl remembers men who walked through the huts comforting others, giving away their last piece of bread, proof that everything can be taken from a man but one thing, the last of his freedoms – to choose one's attitude in any given set circumstances, to choose one's own way. Emphasis here is on unavoidable suffering that leads to meaning.

As a slave laborer in the Nazi Concentration Camps, Viktor Frankl was in constant danger of death in the gas chambers or from one of the epidemics of typhoid fever or diarrhea. By day he performed manual labor, digging, carting and moving dead bodies. By night he tested his newly developed therapy, Logotherapy that he had initiated prior to the war. He observed that those who found meaning in traumatic experiences of war were the most likely to survive. Frankl attributed his own survival to his determination to recreate and publish a manuscript that had been destroyed during the early stages of the war, as well as his vision of reuniting with his pregnant wife. He helped many others survive the death camps by helping them discover a reason to live.

Viktor Frankl decided that he was responsible for making use of the slightest chance of survival and ignoring the great danger around him. He states that meaning must be discovered from within, from an individual's experiences, from his worth, is courage, and his creativity. The one thing that held up American officers who had been imprisoned for up to seven years in the North Vietnamese POW camps was the vision of coming home to loved ones or knowing that they would be needed in their prior jobs; that they had unfinished creative tasks to pursue

Frankl lived by his credo that "ultimately, man should not ask what the meaning of his life is, but rather must recognize that it is he who is asked. In a word, each man is questioned by life, and he can only answer to life by answering for his own life, to life he can only respond by being responsible," especially when we've experienced brokenness in childhood. Liz Murray, Christopher Reeves, Lance Armstrong, Joni Tada, Senator Max Cleland, Nelson Mandela and countless others discovered that it was they who were being asked to offer what they had learned from life. It is my hope that the following pages will be of assistance in your discovering your meaning potential. As human beings, when we are driven by the will to meaning, we can reverse the trend toward existential frustration driven by the desire for pleasure or power. When meaning is absent the *want* for pleasure and power takes over. We then experience what Viktor Frankl referred to as an *existential vacuum* (sense of meaninglessness in life) and *frustration*. We seek pleasure and power to fill that vacuum, a vacuum that can never be filled. Thus we are less able to attain either pleasure or power. There is an inverse relationship between the development of one's meaning potential and the existential vacuum that exists; that is, the existential vacuum only begins to decrease when we make meaning a priority following our release from the war front or from a hospital trauma and physical therapy unit or from incarceration or from a dysfunctional relationship.

Who We Are

The terms "military veteran" or "ex-felon" or "hospital discharge" or "divorcee" may describe a significant emotional event, but they do not describe who an individual is. Only "human being" can describe who an individual is, *"human beings in search of their meaning potential."* The Nazis had a deliberate policy of attempting to destroy an individual's meaning potential. They fulfilled this goal by stripping him of his identity, not only of his possessions and clothing, not only of his hair and dignity, but also of his name. In return each prisoner was given the cast-off clothing of a man already a victim of the gas chamber and a number was tattooed on his arm; prisoners were identified by number, not name. To further destroy each person's self-esteem, he was given clothing that was too short, too long, too small or too big.

Each death camp prisoner would quickly learn that pain is inevitable; some would come to embrace Frankl's conviction that misery is an option. That option would be put to test in the case of Frankl when the one remaining possession that he valued above all others, the manuscript that recorded all his life's work was stripped from him along with his clothes, only to be given the rags of another who had previously gone to the gas chambers. Discovering meaning potential enables individuals to develop their capacities and endure hardships, states Frankl, while those driven by the desire for pleasure or power eventually gravitate toward the neurotic triad of addiction, aggression and depression.

The schools of Viennese psychotherapy have evolved over the past century. Sigmund Freud believed that human behavior is driven by the desire for pleasure, a desire driven by the times in which he lived. Alfred Adler, a student of Freud, believed that we are driven, not by desire for pleasure but by the desire for power in overcoming feelings of inferiority; he too founded his individual psychology based on the times in which he lived. Viktor Frankl had previously experienced the truth of Carl Jung's idea of 'synchronicity,' the theory that coincidences are not arbitrary but become meaningful when we have the courage, intuition and ability to invest it with a personal meaning.

Frankl realized that the destruction of his manuscript did not negate the meaning of his life, nor did the loss of his unborn child, his wife, mother, father or brother to starvation or the gas chambers. Repeatedly, he reminds us that the one freedom that can never be taken away from us is our freedom to choose our attitudes in the face of overwhelming events, circumstances and trauma.

Will to Meaning

We do act to find pleasure and to achieve power, states Viktor Frankl. But, "pleasure is not a primary goal. It is a by-product of having done something meaningful. Power is not an end in itself, but only a means to an end that is attained by using power in a meaningful way." Frankl says "meaning is neither a by-product nor a means to an end. Meaning is the ultimate goal." He says that "if our will to meaning is ignored or repressed, we feel empty." When we feel empty, having suffered the tragic loss of a loved one, the loss of our ability to see or hear, the loss of mobility because of paralysis or amputation, or a diagnosis of a terminal disease, our initial temptation is to vicariously fill that void with pleasure or power [or prosperity]. Meaning cannot be taught. It cannot be given. It cannot be bought. Frankl states that it must be lived by doing, observing and discovering the meaning and meaning potential of our life.

"Meaning," emphasizes Frankl, "is discovered experientially, creatively and attitudinally. Experientially we achieve meaning through unique experiences, encounters with others and in loving relationships." This is the area of life where we receive unexpected gifts that have meaningful value, regardless of our initial response. They include the natural beauty of Nature – a colorful sunset and sunrise, majestic mountains and vast oceans and seas, endless variety of plants, insects and animals - all these are bestowed on us freely to see, hear, smell and feel.

Unique and meaningful experiences are unavoidable and freely given gifts, gifts that eventually benefit us in some way. They are unique in that no single experience is encountered more than once. They sometimes appear unexpectedly as symbolic lessons.

Experientially we also achieve meaning through encounters with great teachers, painters, writers, poets and music composers who have given of themselves freely. We could not by ourselves have achieved what they have to offer. Yet it is ours for the taking. Encounters with others may involve a relationship gone badly, the death of a family member, friend, and national or international figure. It may include both living and long-deceased individuals whose wisdom we embrace. Thirdly, we achieve meaning through loving relationships that nourish us, be it maternal and paternal love. Even if we are adopted or orphaned, most of us can find periods in our childhood or adulthood at least one person in our life, who is willing to give passionate, companionate or compassionate love and affection to us.

"Creatively we achieve meaning," says Frankl, "through creative works and deeds, that is, through what we give to the world, what we do, what we contribute, what we add to life, and what we create." We achieve meaning by striving to understand as much of the universe as we can in order to make it better than it would have been if we had not been born, by creating something new of value to humanity, though it may only involve smiling at or praising another human being, or bringing a sandwich and cup of coffee to a homeless person, or returning a baby bird to the nest from which it has fallen, or simply making some difference in the world, but not the kind that bullies, family abusers or terrorists do now-a-days.

It is for each of us to decide in what way, given the powers and gifts that we possess and the situations with which we are confronted, we can add value to the world around us and in doing so, discover the meaning of our life. Creative works may simply involve making a flower arrangement for a lonely senior citizen, volunteering to change the oil on the car of a single mother, painting the home of a disabled person, creating a song of compassion, putting pen to paper a poem or short story spontaneously recited by a small child, or initiating a hobby never-before attempted. It generally involves something that we enjoy doing and gives our life meaning and purpose. Authors must write and artists must create for life to be meaningful. Whatever the vocation or avocation that is our forte, we are drawn in that direction in order for our life to be meaningful. Indeed, parenting is one of the most creative and meaningful endeavors.

Lastly, even as we face a fate which cannot be changed, there is still meaning available in our lives. Viktor Frankl says that when you can no longer change a situation, you may change your attitude towards your fate. Choosing one's attitude in any given circumstance, says Viktor Frankl, is "the last of the human freedoms."[20] In traumatic situations changing your attitude means rising above yourself, going beyond yourself. Suffering, states Frankl in itself has no meaning, but we can assume meaningful attitudes towards events that in themselves are meaningless. It's not about denying what's happening, it's about implementing a positive attitude when times are trying, taking responsibility for what's occurring in your life and the choices you make, and knowing it has a direct influence on your happiness and well being.

Attaching meaning to suffering is a wonderful and therapeutic tool for moving beyond negative events in your life. The gift is not immediately apparent. Divorce leads to a mature and loving relationship. A job layoff leads to a long-contemplated business venture. Frankl observed in the concentration camps, that those who could find some meaning and purpose to live – even in the most horrific and hopeless of circumstances – had a vastly higher survival rate than those who had understandably lost all hope or any reason to live.

Attitudinal values are all about taking the proper stance or posture towards tragedy in our own lives. It is the courage we show in facing up to the trials and tribulations of life. Some people who are visually-challenged or hearing-challenged, or handicapped in other ways cannot be very creative or cannot realize experiential values, in the sense that they cannot do memorable feats or even enjoy beautiful sights or music. How then can such people create meaning in their lives?

Disabled individuals tend to come to terms very quickly with their handicap and surmount it by achieving something in their own unique ways. People without upper limbs paint and write with their feet, visually-challenged people take up singing or active appreciation of music. Jessica Fox, born without arms achieved a college degree, two black belts in martial arts, an unrestricted drivers and airplane pilot license. Stephen Hawking (UK) suffered from a motor neuron disease at the age of twenty. He was given only a couple of years to live by the neurologists, but yet he survived. He completed a doctoral degree after getting the disease and all his unique research on Black Holes was completed years after that, when he was virtually paralyzed, confined to the wheel chair and unable to talk. Hawking's mother says that her son probably would not have achieved his success had he not become disabled. His disease disabled his body, not his mind. In 2010 he turned sixty-eight years old and continues to conduct research and publish.

Needs vs. Wants

Abraham Maslow views human needs as a pyramid or steps of a ladder. He believes that each of the basic human needs must be satisfied in order to assure a healthy and happy lifestyle. Maslow feels that the first of these needs is the need for food, water and oxygen, that is, the 'need to live and survive.' Once the physiological needs are relatively well gratified, there emerges the need to live in a secure neighborhood, having freedom from fear, anxiety and chaos, and the establishment of law and order.

A second need Maslow describes is the 'need to love, to be loved, and belongingness.' Humans hunger for relations with people in general, for a place in the group or the family. A sense of belonging may be achieved by becoming involved in a church or activity group, joining a special interest club, or networking with colleagues. This need is so important that many people will avoid loneliness and alienation at all costs even when a relationship is not good for them, i.e., codependency relationships. Babies born prematurely during the 1950's survived in incubators, but died within weeks or months following their release to their parents because of hospital policy to limit human contact.

A third need or desire is to feel important, a 'need for a stable, firmly based, usually high evaluation of ourselves, for self-respect or self-esteem,' and for the esteem of others. Maslow divides self-esteem needs into two sets. The first set includes the desire for strength, achievement, and confidence to face the world, and independence or freedom. The second set includes the desire for "reputation or prestige," which he defines as respect and esteem from other people, instead of the self. All of the above needs are known as deficit needs, according to Maslow. If we do not have enough of any of these, we have a deficit.

Once our needs have been satisfied the question must still be asked, "What then?" Suicide is the second leading cause of death among college-aged students. These are young adults who are in excellent physical health, actively engaged socially, performing well academically, and on good terms with their family groups. What they share in common is a lack of meaning.[20] Meaning crises of the young can often lead to the adoption of dangerous belief and behaviors.

Maslow believes that very few people ever reach the stage of self-actualization, the ability to achieve our full potential in a variety of ways. To be self-actualized, Maslow felt that people's needs must be entirely met. Musicians must make music, artists must paint, poets must write, if they are to be ultimately at peace with themselves, he explained. What humans can be, they must be. They must be true to their own nature. Every year thousands of fellow human beings enter prison, having suffered a traumatic past without the benefit of positive mentors. Self-actualization needs are called 'being needs,' needs that once they happen, continue to be felt and enjoyed. This is about becoming the most complete human being that one can be.

A third way to achieve meaning lays in the attitude we take toward unavoidable suffering or pain, situations in which we can do absolutely nothing, as in the case of an inoperable disease, or being stricken with blindness or losing a leg. The tragic triad that remains unavoidable includes death, guilt and suffering. It is not so much what happens to us that counts however, but the attitude we take toward what happens to us. It is useless to ask why things happened to us; the useful approach is to ask what we can do, creatively, socially, spiritually and existentially in the situation in which we find ourselves.

Spiritual Dimension

Viktor Frankl clearly understands the importance of the spiritual dimension. Even in our tragic brokenness, we are not subject to the conditions that confront us there. Rather, these conditions are subject to our decision to become strong at the broken places. The spiritual dimension is assumed to include our will to meaning, creativity, orientation towards goals, imagination, a conscience more inclusive than Freud's super-ego, faith, love (above and beyond the physical and sex), capacity for commitment, ideals, responsibility, self-transcendent potentials, and the ability to choose freely.

Aleksandr Solzhenitsyn and Russell Means both understand the wisdom of life lessons learned in our brokenness. Solzhenitsyn states, "Bless you prison. Bless you for being in my life. For there lying on the rotting prison straw, I came to realize that the object of life is not prosperity as we are made to believe, but the maturing of the soul." Russell Means likewise says that "the year he spent in prison was one of the finest of his life. On the physical side it was hard; it was hell. But on the spiritual side it was a great year."

Time and again, veterans who were prisoners of war stated that they had grown spiritually stronger. Vietnam veterans who were prisoners of war were generally older than those of World War II and the Korean War. They were college graduates as well. They were highly trained and well-educated. They had seen the world and had been exposed to a lot more knowledge. They were not physically as strong as earlier POWs, but they were mentally stronger.

While in solitary confinement, many visualized walking home to their families while physically walking the paces out in their cells. Others mentally recorded their autobiography or war experiences, an unfinished short story or novel manuscript, or poem or song. In the group cells, the POWs would encourage and support each other, and find countless things to talk about. They would use mental games to challenge themselves and each other. Meaning gave them strength to endure the hardships of war, of being a POW. At the end of the war, many discovered that they were stronger at the broken places. "People do not want to hear about your strengths and successes," states Senator Max Cleland, a triple-amputee Vietnam War veteran. "They want to know your pain and how you survived and made it back," becoming strong at your broken places.

Periodically, society suffers from a breakdown of community bonds, increasing regimentation of activities, weakening and depersonalizing of human relationships through bureaucracy, impoverishment of our means of leisure and loss of a sense of personal destiny. A lack of this sense of meaning can form the basis for apathy and frustration, and such disorders and diseases as neurosis, depression, aggression, suicidal ideation, and substance abuse. When we lack meaning and purpose, avoidable consequences do not matter and loved ones do not matter. Seeing meaning in one's life, on the other hand enables an individual to develop his capacities and endure hardships.

Summary

According to Dr. Viktor Frankl we can discover meaning in life in three different ways:
- Through what we receive from life, what we take from life, what life gives us, and what we experience (Experiential Values).

- Through what we give to the world, what we do, what we contribute, what we add to life, and what we create (Creative Values).
- Through the attitude we take when we are faced with situations in which we can do absolutely nothing, as in the case of an inoperable disease, or being stricken with blindness or losing a leg (Attitudinal Values).

"Logos" is the Greek work for "word" or "meaning." Logotherapy focuses on the meaning of human existence and man's search for meaning. According to Frankl, the striving to find meaning in one's life is the primary motivational force in man. In using the term, "man," Frankl is referring to the "Human Race" - male and female. Logotherapy forms a chain of interconnected links:

1) Freedom of will,
2) Will to meaning, and
3) Meaning of life.

Freedom of Will

Man has freedom of will which remains even when all other freedoms are gone because he can choose what attitude he will take to his limitations. Determinism is an infectious disease for many psychiatrists, educators and adherents of determinist religion who are seemingly not aware that they are thereby under-minding the very basis of their own convictions. For either man's freedom must be recognized or else psychiatry is a waste of time, religion is a delusion and education is an illusion. Freedom means freedom in the face of three things: (1) the instincts, (2) inherited disposition, (3) environment.

Will to Meaning

The basic striving of human beings is to find and fulfill meaning and purpose. People reach out to encounter meanings to fulfill. Such a view is profoundly opposed to those motivational theories which are based on the homeostasis principle. Those theories depict man as if he were a closed system. According to them, man is basically concerned with maintaining or restoring an inner equilibrium and to this end with the reduction of tensions. In the final analysis, this is also assumed to be the goal of gratification of drives and the satisfaction of needs.

Meaning of Life

Logotherapy leaves to the client the decision as to how to understand his own meaning whether along the lines of religious beliefs or agnostic convection. Logotherapy must remain available to everyone and so must hypnotherapy. The therapist can help an individual to discover his/her meaning, but it is the individual's responsibility to come to understand the meaning of his or her life.

Frankl emphasizes that we always retain the choice of our attitude towards unavoidable and unexpected life experiences. For those recovering in the hospital, returning from the war front, or incarcerated for decades this is one of the most valuable of his contributions to the art and science of living. Frankl noted that even if we are facing a fate which cannot be changed, there is still meaning available in our lives. "When you can no longer change the situation you may change yourself, which means you may change your attitude towards your fate," he says. "Changing yourself in such cases means rising above yourself, going beyond yourself."

Reflection Exercise on the Search and Discovery of Meaning through Attitudinal Values:

Read any of the following books, noting how *Attitudinal Values* enabled individuals to survive:

Man's Search for Meaning by Viktor Frankl

Stolen Lives by Malika Oufkir

Strong at the Broken Places by Senator Max Cleland

Strong at the Broken Places: Overcoming the Trauma of Childhood Abuse by Linda T. Sanford.

Once We Were Soldiers and Young by Joseph Galloway and Harold Moore, about the events that took place in Ia Drang Valley during the Vietnam War

Joni's Story by quadriplegic Joni Eareckson Tada

Intensive Journal: Participate in an Intensive Journal workshop [Refer to Chapter X.]

Reflection Exercise on Meaning through Creative Values: Most people enjoy some means of creative expression, regardless of whether they have any talent. Even without the slight talent we may gain great value is attained in venting our feelings through various creative activities, aiming to channel the effects of our creative efforts into the direction of our search for meaning potential. Through these activities we can learn new things about our own areas of motivation and interest that may be the key to the deepest and most personal meaning in our lives. With this in mind, choose one or more of the following forms of creative activities and follow up with a presentation to others:

- *Writing*: Write a short Haiku or Tanka poem, a short story, anecdote or tall tale, involving real or imagined events with imaginary characters.
- *Music*: Sing, hum, whistle or play some tune that you make up on the spur of the moment. Add nonsensical phrases to the tune.
- *Art*: Paint or draw some original picture or cartoon on a stone or driftwood. Paint or draw a prop or picture that has been placed upside down, or viewed from a mirror perspective. Draw an object from memory on a piece of paper with eyes closed.
- *Make something* out of wood, paper or cardboard. Draw an animal on a smooth rock and paint it. Write words of wisdom under the drawing.
- *If you owned the world*: Name five meaningful things you would change – in your life; your family; your community. What one thing can you realistically help to change? Describe the steps that can lead to that change.
- *Form a logos-discussion group*. Research and conduct a debate among "Freud, Adler, and Frankl" with Anne Frank as moderator.
- *Debate genocide, world starvation, or use of child soldiers*. Debate how the United States should respond to genocide, starvation or use of child soldiers in other countries.
- *The United Nations General Assembly* adopted the Convention Resolution 25 on the Rights of the Child. As of December 2008, 193 countries have ratified it, including every member of the United Nations except the United States and Somalia. Form a citizens' group; discuss the pros and cons of the United States ratifying

Resolution 25; and write a letter to the American representative to the United Nations stating the position of the group.

• *United Nations Security Council Resolutions 1612 and 1674.* Over 250,000 children continue to be exploited as child soldiers by armed forces and groups around the world. Since 2003 over fourteen million children have been forcibly displaced within and outside their home countries and between 8,000 and 10,000 are killed or maimed each year by land mines. Resolution 1674 addresses all acts of sexual exploitation, abuse and trafficking of women and children. Debate how Resolution 1612 and 1674 can be fully implemented to protect women and children during wartime.

• *Write a dialogue* that takes place between Viktor Frankl (can be a person of your choice, living or deceased) and you.

• *Write and perform a one-act play* of a memorable event in the book, Man's Search for Meaning, or on the courage of Anne Frank or Malika Oufkir, or a historical character of your choice.

• *Preventing War.* Divide a discussion group into teams, each which will create strategies for addressing wars – between nations; ethnic and religious groups; on distribution of illegal drugs; or on illiteracy, crime, obesity or child abuse.

• *Research, compare and contrast* the internment of Japanese Americans with the events leading up to and including the Holocaust in Europe and China.

• *Journal* on all that give meaning to your life using the Intensive Journal® process.

Reflection on Experiential Values: Be a volunteer in one of the following community organizations, journaling about your experiences:
Literacy Volunteers
Special Olympics
Feeding of the Poor
Mentoring of Children at Risk

X. *Intensive Journal®* Method:[1]
A Tool for Discovering Meaning

A major part of the meaning of life is contained in the very process of discovering it. It is an ongoing experience of growth that involves a deepening of contact with reality... The Meaning Dimension focuses on the fundamentals of life: values, priorities, and ultimate concerns that motivate people. We focus extensively on connecting to larger than personal aspects of society whether through symbols or experiences. When people become connected they are strengthened inside. [57]

– Dr. Ira Progoff [2]

Beginning in 1988, a synthesis of Elisabeth Kubler-Ross's stages of grief and Viktor Frankl's Logotherapy were being introduced to men incarcerated at Folsom State Prison to motivate them discover their meaning potential – something which Frankl believed all humans have the ability to do. Then, in 1992 a simple instrument, the Intensive Journal® method was added to the workshop format to further expand the men's ability to deal with their somatic and psychic dimensions and complement the noetic, or intellectual and rational, dimension of Logotherapy.

All human beings are born with meaning potential and purpose, but events, circumstances and "brokenness" may block their ability to discover the meaningful gifts of unavoidable pain and suffering. If they do not have a means of moving through these changes, they can become psychologically confused, troubled, disturbed and suffer existential frustration. Ira Progoff recognized the link between putting thoughts and feelings to paper and the creative life process during the 1960s and designed a way of helping people learn to keep their own journals of their life journey, freeing up creative energy in a purpose-driven life. In the process many experienced creative healing while discovering meaning and purpose. Progoff emphasizes, "The *Intensive Journal*® method is not journal keeping, not introspective diary keeping, and it isn't writing therapy…it is the full scale active method of personal life integration for continuous and cumulative work." [Notes on the *Intensive Journal*® Method and the Transmission of Life," FCC, July 1978, p. III-44]

The pressures of living in modern civilization have the effect of fragmenting people's lives. Lives become compartmentalized, so that individuals tend to live as partial beings rather than as whole beings. They live in terms of their physical, intellectual, or emotional selves, or in terms of a particular set of values and expectations to which their social or religious community has conditioned them. Thus they live their life seeking to fulfill the external expectations of a finite community rather than the inner and "higher" needs of development that would fulfill their integral being. The goal of the *Intensive Journal*® method is to make it possible for a person to live and unfold the potential meaning of his being in terms of the wholeness of his inner nature, rather than in terms of a partial or fragmented aspect of his life.

The *Intensive Journal*® method is a psychotherapeutic technique developed by Progoff as part of his private research and writings as a depth psychologist, therapist, and professor at Drew University.[57] He continued to refine it as a non-analytical tool to provide a way to mirror the processes by which people recreate and access meaning in their life. Joseph Campbell once called the process "one of the great inventions of our time." It consists of a series of writing exercises using loose-leaf notebook paper in a simple ring binder, divided into 21 sections to help in accessing the physical, emotional and spiritual areas of the writer's life. These include a dialogue technique designed to help deepen one's connection and relationship to various areas of life.

The original *Intensive Journal*® process contained only sixteen sections, but was later expanded to include five additional sections as part of the Progoff™ *Process Meditation* method. It has been the inspiration for many other writing therapies since then, and is used in a variety of settings, including welfare-to-work, hospitals and prisons, by private individuals as an aid to creativity or autobiography, and often as an adjunct to treatment in analytic, humanistic or cognitive therapy. One of the best ways of understanding the process is to attend one the many journal workshops held across America.[3]

Most simply, **Intensive Journal**® workshops lead individuals through a set of structured exercises that help them draw the many parts of their life together into an integrated whole. The basic exercises allow them to explore all the aspects of their life in depth — gently, privately, at their own pace. The process includes their life today, events in their history, people who matter to them, their body, their work, the society around them, their dreams and images, their emotions and beliefs. The advanced workshops go more into depth with their inner life, their dreams, and with correlation among the many parts of their life.

Many people journal intermittently rather than daily, some only during a workshop. Some choose to write more frequently at specific or critical times in their life, but that is up to them. Progoff says "we all have enough other things to feel guilty about, without feeling guilty about not journaling." He goes on to say, "The process is designed to help people tap into the underground stream of their interior lives to work out their beliefs, find answers to problems and deeper meaning in their existence." He emphasizes, "When the time is right, then it's the right time."

A certified *Intensive Journal*® workshop consultant/leader, called a "journal consultant" guides individuals step-by-step through the structure of the exercises and workshop participants supply the content. Workshops are offered nationwide and year-round (www.intensivejournal.org). Individuals can attend as many workshops as they like as well as receive CEU[4] credit. Simply being in a quiet room where other people are concentrating and writing makes it easier for workshop participants to focus and write. Over several days of writing, participants pause after each exercise and are given an opportunity to read aloud what they had written or to listen to what others had written. Reading one's writings aloud allows the reader to hear it for himself. The atmosphere of silent group support lends to group cohesiveness.

It is "intensive" in that individuals can set aside three to five days to focus on their experience and inner life, and then let the journal rest for a while. It is "intensive" in that it goes to the heart of issues without circling at the edges. However, there is no pressure to "wear down their resistance" or to uncover more than they wish. It is *not* a process where anyone picks apart what has gone before, what they are experiencing today, or what may be possible in the future. Writing in the workshop room, participants are helped through a self-balancing process that can sometimes be traumatic and frightening. Working in a safe place, at their unique speed, individuals can be honest in their privacy and move forward in their life journey.

This is *not* a workshop where a journal consultant teaches participants information, and it is not based on "sharing" feelings. There are no name tags, no circle where participants introduce themselves or tell why they came to the workshop. They do only the work they choose. Nobody intrudes, critiques or criticizes their writing. Workshop participants can remain anonymous and silent, writing quietly for the entire workshop, if that feels right to them. They can doodle, draw pictures or simply write dates that are meaningful only to them.

The *Intensive Journal*® process is neutral. It's a process to which participants bring their unique experiences and beliefs. The journal consultant has deep respect for the integrity of their life. Neither the journal consultant nor any other participant will read, judge, edit, or correct either their work or that of other individuals attending a workshop.

The ***Intensive Journal***® method blends well with most types of therapy, particularly with Logotherapy. Whereas the *Intensive Journal*® method is based on depth psychology, Viktor Frankl refers to Logotherapy as "height psychology." The *Intensive Journal*® process helps individuals to gather, sift, and focus experiences and issues. Often the journal workshop brings new energy and confidence to their work in therapy, so that more work can get done in less time. Many also continue to use journal exercises between therapy appointments, to extend and maximize the work that takes place there. Logotherapy also allows individuals to get more therapy work done in less time and may be used to supplement other therapy.

The *Intensive Journal®* method is often useful if individuals are facing life transitions or decisions, if they feel cut off from their true self by the demands of daily life, if they are recovering from a trauma or grief or if they are working a Twelve-Step program. Progoff says, ""The difficulties we encounter in our life are like logs; our inner life is like a flame. What we need is a safe way to burn the logs."... When the time is right, then it's the right time."[57]

What's different about the journal workshop experience is that it benefits unbelievers and believers alike, be they Christians, Hindus, Jews, Muslims or others. Regardless of belief no one but workshop participant goes into the "deep well" within to discover his/her meaning potential. This is done anonymously and without judgments. In the process, many experience unexpected breakthrough in their lives with minimal writing skills. Nobody reads their journal but them, and they take it with them.

The *Intensive Journal®* method was initially introduced to 105 men incarcerated at Folsom State Prison beginning in 1992 - men nearing parole; men just beginning their term of incarceration; men serving life sentences. Initially, fifty-four incarcerated men who participated in at least one of the original workshops that was a synthesis of the stages of grief, Logotherapy, and the *Intensive Journal®* method were tracked over the course of the next fifteen years; not one ever returned to prison. In these workshops the men took the time to look inward, to find the meaning that was there from the beginning, but perhaps blocked by the events, hurts and brokenness of day-to-day life. Putting their day-to-day thoughts in writing automatically forced them to become more introspective and helped them identify patterns in conscious and unconscious thinking.

Following the workshops the participants tended to be less aggressive, resulting in fewer disciplinary write-ups. The workshops appeared to generate several other benefits. Some men were able to reduce their medication for depression. Many appeared better equipped to deal with the painful aspects of their lives, rather than diverting it through inappropriate behavior. Some began to mentor others, telling their peers about the benefits of the workshops.

It is not so important what happened to them in childhood but what they did with it. Many turned to illegal drugs or alcohol. Others focused on obtaining material wealth or sensory pleasures. By putting childhood events down in writing, they are able to state "these are my roots" and "now I can deal with my present and future." The *Intensive Journal*® allowed them to acknowledge the existence of this pain for the first time in years, to diffuse their anger.

The men generally expressed appreciation for the *Intensive Journal*® workshops. Some stated that they had been renewed; that it had helped them get in touch with themselves. Others talked of exploring inner memories and searching for direction. One of the men stated, "This is my best moment in prison; I discovered that I exist." The men dealt with painful issues. One of the men stated that he was better able to "confront the skeletons in my closet and defeat them." Irish playwright George Bernard Shaw said, "If you can't get rid of the **skeleton** in your closet, you'd best teach it to **dance**." Another workshop participant said that it helped him "deal with the pain that [he has] carried for years." The men recognize that the *Intensive Journal*® method helps "defeat racism and the petty B.S." that occurs in the prison.

As individuals work in their journal, the experiences of their life - times of exaltation and despair, moments of hope and anger, crises and crossroads, failures and successes - gradually fit into place. Workshop participants discover that their lives have been going somewhere, however blind they may have been to its direction. Progoff structured the *Intensive Journal*® method to reflect the fact that our lives are continually in motion in a way that approaches self-knowledge.

Progoff recommends that individuals write in their journal when they feel the time is right, stressing the cumulative benefits from working in the method. Individuals must never *should* on themselves. Once they've established a dialogue with their journal, their inner self will tell them when there are things to be written and they'll naturally turn to their journal as a means of self-expression and discovery. Individuals need not think that they have to write something in each section of their journal each day. Some sections they'll want to write in quite frequently. Others may be saved for special occasions or significant emotional events.

Of the twenty-one sections, only the "Steppingstones" exercise will be described here. Each section the journal represents a separate aspect of an individual's life or a certain meditative way of approach wherein an individual can record certain kinds of internal life data in specific ways.

Steppingstones

A powerful journal exercise that Progoff developed is called "Steppingstones." The exercise, part of his *Intensive Journal*® program, helps uncover underlying long term patterns within an individual's life. Progoff uses the sense of "movement" in one's life to help individuals move forward on their life's journey that may include many detours. The Steppingstones exercise helps individuals look at periods and significant events in their life with the idea of carrying the thread of that movement forward. It is a good technique if an individual is in transition and looking for direction to move into the next phase or chapter of his life.

Progoff writes, "The Steppingstones are the significant points of movement along the road of an individual's life. They stand forth as indicators of the inner connectedness of each person's existence, a continuity of development that maintains itself despite the vicissitudes and the apparent shifting of directions that occur in the course of a life. The Steppingstones are indicators that enable us to recognize the deeper-than-conscious goals toward which the movement of our lives is trying to take us." [57]

The Steppingstones exercise is useful when individuals wish to understand the full context of their life, to create a vision of the significant stages of their life, and to understand who they've become and the situation in which they find themselves. Steppingstones assist in identifying times that are significantly different from others. "...In Steppingstones, we draw out of the jumbled mass of our life experiences, the thin and elusive connective threads that carry our potentials toward a fuller unfolding. ...By working with the Steppingstones, we make contact with these elusive lines of continuity that are seeking to establish themselves as patterns of meaning in our lives." [57] Steppingstones may include individuals that were important to them during a specific period; projects that they were working on; repeated dreams; or periods of death, guilt or suffering.

Progoff suggests that individuals close their eyes and sit in silence, breathing slowly, and not thinking about any specific aspect of their life, but trying to "feel the movement" of their life. He says, "Then, whatever the form in which the continuity of your life reflects itself to you now, respond to it, observe it, and let the flow continue. If images present themselves to you on the twilight level, images in any form, whether visual or not, take note of them. ...Passive receptivity is the best attitude to adopt in doing this. As you sit in silence, let the cycles, the rhythms, the tempos of your life present themselves to you. Let them be free and undirected so that they can shape themselves into whatever form truly reflects their basic qualities; let yourself be free in your quietness to perceive them as they come to you without editing or falsifying them." "[57]

Progoff suggests that individuals make a list representing significant emotional events of their life, from the beginning to the present that includes eight to ten, but no more than twelve Steppingstones, key events - ups and downs and main events - that have shaped their life. A Steppingstone is an event, image, sensation, a thought, or milestone of individual's life that comes to mind when he review his life from the beginning to the present. Individuals may write only a word, a short descriptive phrase, or a sentence that will trigger their memory when they go back to the list. They may want to use the phrase, "It was a time when..." as the beginning of the description.

Individuals select Steppingstones spontaneously, without a lot of mulling and conscious direction, but with an intuitive sense of selecting the right ones. Progoff explains that individuals need not be concerned if the events they list are not in perfect chronological order. The list includes important times in their life from childhood - school, first love, marriage, divorce, parenthood, friendship, relocation. They are periods when possibilities were opening for them, when they had alternatives, when critical decisions were made or unmade. They may even record their Steppingstones on a tape recorder to be played back later if disabled.

Individuals are told to not judge their Steppingstones. There is little validation for the assumption that later developments of their personality were caused in childhood. Individuals are warranted in making nothing more than the neutral statement that childhood is only the beginning of the human journey through life, nothing more, and that, depending upon the individual situation, it casts a larger or smaller shadow over the years of maturity and spiritual wisdom that follow it.

Participants remain *neutral* as they make the list of Steppingstones. The purpose is to make a list of significant periods or events that took place during momentous times. When individuals complete their list, they go back and read their Steppingstones. In the same neutral frame of mind they re-read the list, not thinking about whether the list is praiseworthy, disappointing, or even complete. They determine whether there is a pattern or theme; what they feel when they read the list; what things they observe about the list; what might be the thread of continuity; what they can learn from the list?

Steppingstones are like individual pieces to an ever-expanding, three-dimensional puzzle called life. Depending on an individual's point of view at the time of the writing, the Steppingstones may shift. The first time he does the exercise, he may find that he includes just the basic chronological facts of his life. Each time he repeats his Steppingstones, three days or three months later, he is viewing his life through a different lens or dimension, be it the physical, emotional, psychological, or spiritual. Identifying what the lens or dimension is may give him information about his present focus and may help him see in a new light the path he has taken, where he is today, and a redirection of his life's trajectory for the future.

Individuals can continue to work with their Steppingstones, choosing to select a Steppingstone period or event that they feel may offer insights, and explore it in depth. They can begin by asking themselves questions about the period or event to help it become more three-dimensional and tangible. They can start with general recollections - such as adjectives describing the periods, images they have, sensory recollections, and metaphors about the time period. They can go to more specific recollections, such as dreams they had, attitudes or beliefs to which they subscribed, aspirations, life philosophies, conflicts, frustrations, key relationships, feelings, and hopes. They can write dialogues between different aspects of their life during the time period, such as a dialogue with family, friends and other important relationships; a dialogue with their health; their work; their religion/spirituality; an important event; or cultural or societal norms, attitudes, or values of that period. Individuals can examine one or more of their Steppingstones in more detail in other sections of their journal as well.

Again, although journaling is important, individuals must not feel that they have to write each and every day. What's important is that they are writing...and, in doing so, learning more and more about themselves and the 'meaning of the moment.' It is important that they participate in all three levels of *Intensive Journal*® workshops at which a facilitator will guide them in the proper use of this highly effective, life-enhancing tool.

For information on journaling workshops in an individual's area and a list of relevant books and audio CDs that are available, contact Dialogue House Associates[3].

Footnote:

[1] "Intensive Journal" is a registered trademark of Jonathan Progoff.

[2] "Progoff," used as an adjective is a trademark of Jonathan Progoff.

[3] Dialogue House Associates, 2155 Ocean Avenue – Suite C, Ronkonkoma, NY 11779-6592

. Phone: 800-221-5844 or 631-471-0542. Fax: 631-471-0681. www.intensivejournal.org. Email: info@intensivejouranl.org

[4] Dialogue House Associates is authorized to offer continuing education to the therapeutic and nursing community of professionals.

XI.
Defiant Power of the Human Spirit

When we are no longer able to change a situation –
We are challenged to change ourselves.   - Viktor Frankl

Life in the Abyss

During one of the Logotherapy workshops Dan wrote, "My childhood experiences were not particularly unique. At least, those were my thoughts at the time. My aunt once told me that my father spiked my baby bottle with alcohol to sedate me whenever I began to cry. When I was about five years old I saw my father having sex with another man. Later that year I was stabbed in the leg. The following year, at age six, a fifteen-year-old female babysitter introduced me to sex. Then, in a fit of rage my mother attempted to suffocate me with a pillow. I quit school at age eleven to run in the streets twenty-four hours a day. Soon after that, I joined a local street gang[5] and learned to grow marijuana. I smoked it from time to time. It seemed to help me with my anger. At age twelve I witnessed the birth of my nephew. At age fourteen I was sentenced to the youth authority for twelve years for car-jacking with a gun. Prior to my release at age twenty I passed the GED exam. I entered college during parole and began a relationship that resulted in the birth of my first child. Faced with new responsibilities for which I was not prepared I began relying on drugs and alcohol to give me my *wants*, but my *gets* were beginning to destroy my new life once again."

Wants vs. Gets

The *wants* of addicts are more important than the *gets*. They are so important that addicts are willing to pay the price of the *gets* to get their *wants* because they don't know how else to get them. They have been willing to go through all their *gets* in order to get their *wants*. That tells us that their *wants* are the most important; not their *gets*.

Most people who counsel addicts focus on the *gets*. But addicts already know how to deal with their *gets*. When they experience their *gets*, they justify more drugs and alcohol to obtain their want to feel better, worse or just different.

Wants can become so powerful in themselves that they work for our ultimate self-destruction, the *gets*. The dysfunctional belief systems of addiction **do not believe** they are working for our self-destruction. They believe they are working for our well-being – to feel good, better, or not at all. That is where they get their power. They get their power from reinforcement. Persons who are driven by the will to pleasure take and abuse drugs or alcohol often do so to cope with immediate problems of existential vacuum or frustration. The immediate goal is to feel better right now or to eliminate pain. However, these solutions have long-term negative consequences, the *gets*.

Psychologists have shown that even when people know the drawbacks of the will to pleasure or the will to power, they still go back to the *wants* again and again and again. Even when they know the negative consequences of the *gets*, loss of family, job, freedom, and health, they still can't let go of the *wants*. It is Viktor Frankl's contention that the pleasure principle is self-defeating. The more one aims at pleasure, the more his aim is missed.

During a May 1966 speaking engagement at San Quentin State Prison, one prisoner informed Viktor Frankl that other psychologists told them that their criminal actions were a result of their childhood, a factual reality beyond their ability to change. But the men incarcerated at San Quentin did not want to hear that they have no human worth; no freedom to make choices and decisions. In contrast, Frankl told them that they are human just as he is and therefore had the same freedom to make the choices that he did. He went on to say, "You were free to commit a crime, to become guilty. Now, however, you are responsible for overcoming guilt by rising above it, by growing beyond yourselves, by changing for the better (pp. 149-150)."[20]

Members of American society need direction, instruction that life has meaning, so that individuals incarcerated in San Quentin,

Folsom, or any other prison come to realize that those whom they robbed, raped, or killed were human beings who had significance. Criminal behavior in adulthood or in youth comes from a lack of responsibility, or of meaning. When gangster youth are asked, "Why do you do these violent and criminal acts?" the typical response is, "Why not?" The absence of an answer to the question, "Why not?" can result in senseless aggression or addiction to drugs and alcohol. In other cases it results in depression and even suicide.

Viktor Frankl refers to research that shows a strong relationship between meaninglessness (as measured by "purpose in life" tests) and such behaviors as criminality and involvement with drugs. The trio of aggression, addiction, and depression is symptomatic of a contemporary world that is missing something vitally important to the nature of human existence, a perception that one's life, including one's work life, appears to be meaningless. The existential vacuum, the inner void and emptiness in American youth is reinforced by the existential vacuum the youth feel in their parents, teachers, political leaders and peers, particularly peers who belong to a gang.

As Dan discovered, there is no such thing as freedom all by itself. Freedom is always preceded by responsibility; they are connected to one another. It is a mistake to pursue freedom without the consideration of responsibility. Likewise, his pursuit of happiness was ill-fated through drug and alcohol abuse.

Dan's *wants* earned him another prison sentence of two more years. While in prison he participated in a program that was a synthesis of Viktor Frankl's Logotherapy[20], Ira Progoff's Intensive Journal® method[57], and Elisabeth Kubler-Ross's stages of grief[42]. Over time he began to realize the potential value of Logotherapeutic techniques, particularly dereflection, as well as experiential, creative, and attitudinal values. Slowly, understanding that he could overcome his guilt by rising above it, by growing beyond himself, and by changing for the better he could begin moving in the direction of his unique purpose. Dan began by redirecting his attention more and more away from himself and toward his peers, volunteering to tutor other incarcerated men illiterate in mathematics and reading. He also began and by developing meaningful goals to achieve upon being released to parole and focusing on his responsibilities as a father and husband. Throughout his parole, he continued to be involved in community volunteer activities. He has not returned to prison in over fifteen years.

Homeless and Invisible

Liz did not know any other kind of life. Her father had attended college and was very intelligent, but both he and her mother were addicted to drugs. They spent most of her mother's welfare checks on drugs. Her childhood was one of chronic, childhood hunger, family mental illness, disease and the daily struggle for survival. Child welfare services described their apartment as deplorable. Liz sometimes went for long periods without a bath, clean clothing, medical attention…or anything nutritious to eat. Happy Meals were a luxury during the first week of the month when her mother's welfare check arrived. Occasionally, her mother was carted off to a mental hospital when she had a psychotic episode. When Liz was eleven she learned that her mother had AIDS, seventeen when her father learned that he too had AIDS. There was virtually no difference between my home and the street life that she was forced to choose.

Liz recalls wandering into an elementary school classroom for the first time, ponytail matted, her face smudged with dirt and her fellow students repulsed by her body odor as she passes them. Despite her sporadic attendance, Liz does well on school exams, chalking up her performance to reading a near-complete set of encyclopedias her upstairs neighbor retrieved from the trash and library books never returned by her father. At thirteen she begins living in a group home with cruel and casually sadistic teenage girls. Six months later Liz is back living with her mother and attending school, already two years behind her classmates. Soon, Liz is back on the street, panhandling, laying her head where she can, but without any orientation toward a meaningful future.

In the Twenty-first Century America's population of homeless families has swelled from almost negligible numbers to nearly forty percent of the overall homeless population. Women and children comprise a large percentage of the homeless in the United States, which is unique among industrialized nations.

According to the National Coalition for the Homeless, 1.2 million children are homeless on any given night. Like Liz throughout most of her childhood, at least twenty percent of those do not attend school. Within a year, forty-one percent will attend two different schools; twenty-eight percent will attend three or more different schools. With each change in schools, a homeless student is set back academically by an average of four to six months. These homeless children feel like outsiders and have difficulty maintaining friendships due to frequent moves. Their lives feel out control and they often experience anxiety and depression as a result. Many lack basic school supplies and an appropriate place to do homework.

Many children of drug and alcohol addicted parents, of incarcerated parents, or military parents who are repeatedly deployed are often "invisible" because they may not be identified at the time of separation from one or both parents; because parents withhold information about their children or have no contact with them; because responsible agencies lose contact with children after services are terminated. These children often suffer from trauma syndrome or behavioral problems, including hostile responses and acting out in school, deterioration in school work, and drug and alcohol problems. Some are mislabeled; a non-relevant label such as ADHD or attention deficit hyperactive disorder often prevents appropriate family therapy.

After Liz saw her mother's coffin being lowered into a pauper's grave, her life took an improbable upward turn. She was sixteen and determined to change her life through education and started knocking on doors closed to the homeless, insisting that those doors be opened to her. She then redirected her full attention from the self toward a meaningful goal of completing her high school education. A homeless teenager who had rarely set foot in a classroom unless forced by child welfare services, she completed a four-year high school education in two years. Liz achieved all this while working to feed and clothe herself, riding on public trains and being homeless. Then, as she neared graduation from high school, Liz read about, competed in and won a full, four-year scholarship to Harvard University.

Liz's optimistic message is clear: Once broken, it is possible to become stronger and to discover meaning at the broken places. Success is not the prerogative of the rich, coddled, well-fed and connected, but a basic right of the determined. It is never too late to do something meaningful. We always have a choice of what we become and what we make of our lives, despite our family genetics or history. We are responsible to ourselves and for whatever decisions we make. Our life is a journey with many forks at which choices must be made. If we make the wrong choice, we must learn from it. We can never go back to take the other fork, but life has many other forks ahead.

Lalita's Rebellious Youth

Suffering is a universal experience, yet the search for meaning in suffering can be a lonely one, particularly for children who are neglected, or emotionally, physically, or sexually abused. Many suffer the most damaging effects in the homes of dysfunctional parents. The decisive, long-term effects lie not in the conditions in which the children lived but in their personal response to them.

Lalita, once a young rebellious teen, says that her problems appeared to begin when her parents divorced and she was sexually abused by a family acquaintance. That led to substance abuse, staying out all night, and running away.

"By the time I was eighteen, I was legally emancipated from my parents, married and had a baby son."

When her ex-husband joined the Army, Lalita was responsible for taking care of herself with only a GED and no relevant job skills. Penniless and living out of a car, she gave up her son to his father's parents. "Missing my son I would cry myself to sleep every night."

It was during the brief seven-month period of time Lalita sent her son to live with his grandparents that she could really look her demons in the eye. "I sought therapy, engaged in a tremendous amount of personal healing and growth, and kicked my substance abuse habit. My son returned home to me shortly before he turned three, and has lived with me ever since. He is now eleven."

Following intensive therapy, Lalita was able to redirect her attention from herself toward the meaningful goal of raising her autistic son as a single mother while putting herself through college and managing to keep a 4.0 G.P.A through two simultaneous undergraduate degrees. An honors student, she was accepted to Harvard University where she pursued a Master's degree in business and public policy. She financed her education through twenty scholarships totaling more than half a million dollars.

It seems harsh to say that Lalita, sexually abused by a family acquaintance was responsible for her life, but it is a fact. Each of us, no matter what our experiences, is in charge of how we live our lives simply because no one else can let go of the attitudes we have which dictate our behavior. We alone are responsible for not only our attitudes, but also our choices in life.

Jerry Long is another living testimony to 'the defiant power of the spirit.' He has been paralyzed from his neck down since a diving accident which rendered him a quadriplegic at age seventeen. He uses his mouth stick to type. He attended college courses via a special telephone. The intercom allowed him to both hear and participate in class discussions. He also occupies his time by reading, watching television and writing.

In a letter Viktor Frankl received from him, Jerry Long wrote: "I view my life as being abundant with meaning and purpose. The attitude that I adopted on that fateful day has become my personal credo for life: I broke my neck, it didn't break me. I am currently enrolled in my first psychology course in college. I believe that my handicap will only enhance my ability to help others. I know that without the suffering, the growth that I have achieved would have been impossible."

Frankl insists that "...meaning is available... even through suffering, provided... that the suffering is unavoidable. If it is avoidable, the meaningful thing to do is to remove its cause, for unnecessary suffering is masochistic rather than heroic. If, on the other hand, one cannot change a situation that causes his suffering, he can still choose his attitude (pp. 171-172).[20] Long had not... chosen to break his neck, but he did decide not to let himself be broken by what had happened to him.

Lalita had not chosen to be sexually abused as a child, but she, like Long, decided not to let herself be broken by what had happened to her. She was the only one who could see to the healing. She took responsibility and did everything she could that was therapeutic, rather than point to the abuser and say, "You are why I am broken and why I shall remain dysfunctional the rest of my life." Lalita is the only one who can choose to preserve the attitude that keeps the influence of the abuse alive. She alone is responsible for the attitudes; they are solely her own. She had a choice. The life ruined by other people has to be lived by victims; survivors do what they can to make it livable by turning a personal tragedy into a triumph. Lalita took on the responsibility for her personal life rather than lose it. Responsibility is based on the willingness to face the world as it is now and to experientially, creatively, and attitudinally make it one that is meaningful.

Viktor Frankl wrote that fulfillment comes from three possibilities: the first is through creativity and meaningful work; the second is through relationships and love; the third is when confronted with unchangeable fate, to be able to change our attitude toward that fate, thus turning suffering into human triumph.[20]

The third avenue to meaning is, perhaps, Viktor Frankl's most important one. Too often we forget that suffering is an unavoidable and ineradicable part of human life. Without it, life could not be complete. Suffering - albeit in unequal degrees - accompanies us through all our lives, eventually terminating in death. Finding meaning in suffering is not as much the ability to cope with suffering and not letting it destroy oneself, but the possibility of "rising above oneself," "growing beyond oneself," and thus "changing oneself."

Frankl writes: "Here lies a chance for a man either to make use or to forgo the opportunities of attaining the moral values that a difficult situation may afford him. And this decides whether he is worthy of his sufferings or not (p. 88)."... "When a man finds that it is his destiny to suffer, he will have to accept his suffering as his task; his single and unique task. He will have to acknowledge the fact that even in suffering he is unique and alone in the universe. No one can relieve him of his suffering or suffer in his place. His unique opportunity lies in the way in which he bears his burden (p. 99)." Frankl is living proof that a human being "may turn a personal tragedy into a triumph."[20]

Family Life on the Street

Throughout her childhood, Khadijah floated from shelters to motels to armories along the West Coast with her mother. She attended twelve schools in twelve years and lived out of garbage bags among pimps, prostitutes and drug dealers.

On the streets, she learned how to hunt for her family's next meal, plot the next bus route and help choose a secure place to sleep. She focused on her academic classes and homework, blocking out all of the sensory chatter happening around her.

Only a few mentors and university officials knew her background. She was one of the 1.2 million homeless children who remain invisible – in the classroom, libraries, bus stops, emergency rooms, and shopping centers. She never wanted other students to know her secret, not until her plane left for the East Coast hours after her high school graduation.

In her college essays, she wrote, "I have felt the anger at having to catch up in school, being bullied because they knew I was poor, different, and read too much. I knew that if I wanted to become a smart, successful scholar, I should talk to other smart people."

She was in third grade when she realized the power of test scores, placing in the 99th percentile on a state exam. Her teachers marked the nine-year-old as gifted, a special category she, even at that age, vowed to keep.

In the years that followed, her mother pulled her out of school eight more times. When shelters closed, money ran out or her mother did not feel safe, they packed what little they carried and boarded buses to find housing in six other counties, staying for months, at most, in one place.

She finished only half of fourth grade, half of fifth and skipped sixth. Seventh grade was split between two cities. Eighth grade consisted of two weeks in another city.

At every stop, she pushed to remain in each school's gifted program, redirecting her full attention toward a meaningful goal of high school graduation and beyond. She read nutrition charts, newspapers and four to five books a month, anything to transport her mind away from the chaos and smells of homeless shelters.

At school, she was the outsider. At the shelter, she was often bullied. In tenth grade, she realized that if she wanted to succeed, she couldn't do it alone. She began to reach out to organizations and mentors, teachers, counselors and college alumni networks. They helped her enroll in summer community-college classes, gave her access to computers and scholarship applications and taught her about networking.

When she enrolled in the fall of her junior year of high school, she was determined to stay put, regardless of where her mother moved. Graduation was not far off, and she needed strong college letters of recommendation from teachers who were familiar with her work.

This soon meant commuting by bus from a county armory. She awoke at 4:00 a.m. and returned at 11:00 p.m., and kept her grade-point average at just below 4.0 while participating in the Academic Decathlon, the debate team and leading the school's track and field team.

She graduated with high honors, fourth in her class. She was accepted to more than twenty universities nationwide. She chose a full scholarship to Harvard and aspires to become an education attorney.

She knows she was born in Brooklyn to a fourteen-year-old mother. She thinks her mother may have tried to attend school, but the stress of a baby proved too much. When she was a toddler, she and her mother moved to the West Coast. A few years later, her younger sister, was born.

Her mother inspired her to learn, telling her that she had a gift. When her college applications were due in December, an orthopedic doctor and a nurse invited her to their home to help her write her essays.

When they went to return her to the shelter, her mother and sister were gone. She accepted the couple's invitation to spend the rest of her school year with them. In their home, she learned a new set of lessons - table manners, money management and grooming.

Harvard University staff made plans to connect her with faculty mentors and potentially, a host family to check in with every so often. She would also attend a Harvard summer program at Cornell University to take college-prep courses.

Over the course of six months prior to her high school graduation, she saw her mother only a few times. Shortly before traveling to

Harvard University she headed to a storage facility where she, her mother and sister last stored their belongings. She found her mother sitting on a garbage bag full of clothes. She explained the details of her graduation, the bus route to get there and gave her mother a prom picture. There was no talk of coming home for Thanksgiving or Christmas. Proudly, she modeled her graduation cap and gown and practiced switching the tassel from left to right as she would during the ceremony.

"Look at you," her mother said. "You're really going to Harvard, huh?"

"Yeah," Khadijah replied, pausing. "I'm going to Harvard."

Resilience

What may crush one person may make another stronger. Often the difference is resilience. Resilience is the ability to work with life's adversity in such a way that one comes through it better for the experience. Resilience means facing life's difficulties and traumas with courage and patience, never surrendering or admitting defeat. It is the quality of character that allows a person or group of people rebound from misfortune, hardships and traumas. It is rooted in a tenacity of spirit, a determination to embrace all that makes life worth living even in the face of overwhelming odds. When we have a clear sense of identity and purpose, we are more resilient, because we can hold a vision of a brighter and better future.

In humanistic psychology, resilience refers to an individual's capacity to thrive and fulfill their meaning potential despite or perhaps even because of such stressors. Resilient individuals are more inclined to see problems as opportunities for growth. In other words, resilient individuals seem not only to cope well with unusual strains, stressors, and traumas but actually to experience such challenges as learning and development opportunities.

The most important factor in building resilience is to connect with a meaningful purpose in life larger than oneself or any one event. Some people define their purpose spiritually. Others use their life experiences to have a positive impact in the community in the pursuit of a worthwhile cause. Still others have personal goals to provide for their family, to serve a cause, to love another, or express themselves through art or action. Whatever the purpose or mission, resilient people develop goals and plans that focus beyond the present crisis.

The first coping strategy in tough situations is to find ways to be optimistic. Resilient people tend to be optimistic and make it a habit of smiling in difficult circumstances, large and small. They have the ability to bounce back from adversity and thrive in challenging conditions. Studies indicate optimists live longer, have better relationships, and achieve more success in life. Optimists are not magical thinkers, unable to see the dark side; rather, they accept reality, and put things in perspective.

Being Open to Meaning

Though they may not have realized it, Liz, Lalita, and Khadijah were being pulling in the Logotherapeutic direction with its emphasis on choice and responsibility to achieve their meaning potential. With strong egos and a noetic medicine bag, they overcame the genetic and sociological obstacles of fate. Viktor Frankl emphasized that "We are responsible for what we do, whom we love and how we suffer."[20] An individual's future is molded by conscious decisions made in the present, not the past. It is "the defiant power of the human spirit," Frankl points out, that allows man to rise above the confining restraints of his past, to resist biological, psychological, or sociological conditioning (p. 23).[17]

The defiant power of the human spirit is discovering one's meaning potential, one's life task to which one has been called. Others do not hear the call. They have not even begun the search, driven instead by the will to pleasure, power, and/or prosperity. The commitment to intellectual achievement begins with an existential commitment. Liz, Lalita, and Khadijah committed themselves to an academic goal that called upon all of their talents and abilities, a goal that oriented them outside of their own personal existence as homeless children. Each also embraced a disciplined sense of responsibility to grow beyond themselves, by changing for the better.

They continue to serve as living examples that we need not be a product of our past, but of challenges and responsibilities to find deeper meaning in life through realizing experiential, creative, and attitudinal values. Being homeless, orphaned, abused or a young, single parent need not prevent the pursuit of one's meaning potential. Others may only see the limiting conditions that surround them, but these three young women saw the creative possibilities that never cease to pull them forward.

Viktor Frankl says, "We must never be content with what has already been achieved. Life never ceases to put new questions to us, never permits us to come to rest. Only self-narcotization keeps us insensible to the eternal pricks with which life with its endless succession of demands stings our conscience. The man who stands still is passed by; the man who is smugly contented loses himself. Neither in creating nor experiencing may we rest content with achievement; every day, every hour makes deeds necessary and new experiences possible."(p. 139)[23]

Rather than asking what we want from life the question is what life wants from us. The person in crisis tends to be very self-absorbed. Logotherapists are careful not to "side with" the client against the unfairness of life in a way that would reinforce his perception of life as cruel and unjust. Instead, the therapist highlights the meaning of something that is more important to the person than the problem that is distracting him. His distress is seen in the context of the spiritual essence of the person "behind" the problem. The meaning in the situation, the therapist emphasizes, beckons the client out of the problem. The situation is seen as a challenge and an invitation to transform human suffering into a human achievement. One of the central themes of Logotherapy is that self-transcendence is the essence of human existence. Thus in dereflection we transcend our self to focus on meanings and values.

Even deeper than the capacity for self-transcendence is the fundamental principle of will to meaning – the deepest motivation to reach out towards people to love and values to fulfill. In contradistinction to homeostasis – the desire to maintain equilibrium by the reduction of tensions – Frankl believes that we are primarily motivated by the desire for purpose in our lives.[20] We have all experienced complete absorption in a task, to the extent that we forget about ourselves and our nutritional needs. We can truly be ourselves when we're not thinking about ourselves, but engaged in meaningful tasks. Our orientation as human beings is one of creativity and interest in fulfilling values. From the youngest age we are born reaching out to make contact with the world. This outward reach is essentially what it means to be human.

As human beings we have freedom of will. This is the core of self-detachment. While we are not free from conditions we are free in the attitude we take towards those conditions. Once we loosen the grip of fear, we are free us to see what confronts us as something we are called upon to do something about. We're not determined. We can take a stand. We are meant to be victors, not victims. Logotherapy empowers us to change our destiny. As Frankl says in the *Search for Ultimate Meaning*[21] "Being human is not being driven but deciding what one is going to be" and choosing to move in that direction. Logotherapy pulls us out of our existential vacuum, points towards transcendence, and effects changes in the spiritual dimension. It provokes the will to meaning, thereby allowing us to rise above, or transcend the self.

People cannot live with change if there's not a changeless core inside them. Viktor Frankl states that "When we are no longer able to change a situation – such as an incurable disease or an inoperable cancer – we are challenged to change ourselves."[20] The key to the ability to change is a changeless sense of who we are, what we are about and what we value as meaningful.[19]

With a meaningful values statement, we can flow with moment-by-moment changes. We don't need prejudgments or prejudices. We don't need to figure out everything else in life, to stereotype and categorize everything and everybody in order to accommodate the meaning of life.

Our personal meaning changes moment by moment. "These tasks," states Frankl "and therefore the meaning of life, differ from man to man, and from moment to moment."[20] For this reason it is impossible to define the meaning of life in a general way.

Questions about the meaning of life can never be answered by sweeping statements. Life does not mean something vague, but something very real and concrete, just as life's tasks are also very real and concrete. They form man's destiny, which is different and unique for each individual. "No man and no destiny can be compared with any other man or any other destiny," Frankl wrote in *Man's Search for Meaning*. "No situation repeats itself, and each situation calls for a different response. Sometimes the situation in which a man finds himself may require him to shape his own fate by action. At other times it is more advantageous for him to make use of an opportunity for contemplation and to realize assets in this way. Sometimes man may be required to simply accept fate, to bear his cross. Every situation is distinguished by its uniqueness, and there is always only one right answer to the problem posed by the situation at hand."[20] Such tasks may overwhelm some people who feel a *want* to self-medicate, unable to cope with life. They become reactive and essentially give up, hoping that the things that happen to them will be good without their participating responsibly.

But it doesn't have to be that way. In the Nazi death camps where Victor Frankl[20] learned the principle of pro-activity, he also learned the importance of purpose, of meaning in life. The essence of Logotherapy, the philosophy he later more fully developed and taught, is that many so-called mental and emotional illnesses are really symptoms of an underlying sense of meaninglessness or emptiness.[24] Logotherapy eliminates that emptiness by helping the individual to detect his unique meaning, his mission in life.[20]

Once we have that sense of mission, we have the essence of our own pro-activity. We have the vision and the values which direct our life. We have the basic direction from which we set our long- and short-term goals. We have the power of a spiritual guide based on meaningful principles, against which every decision concerning the most effective use of our time, our talents, and our energies can be effectively measured.

There are many ways of identifying a meaningful life purpose. Some of the following exercises may help. Discovering our meaningful life purpose may appear to be challenging. In fact it may be one of the most challenging tasks we face as human beings. But when we do get a sense of purpose, and then act on it, our lives begin to flow more easily, and we have a much greater feeling of fulfillment.

Reflection on the Search for Meaning at the Broken Places:

Step 1: An autobiographical sketch is one that only includes short 'chapter headings' from the beginning to the present. It includes significant emotional events, ups and downs and main events that have shaped your life. The list may begin with the event of your birth followed by objective markers in your life - entering school, graduating, changes in your family or the location of your residence, the death of close relatives or friends, major financial changes such as bankruptcy, marriage or divorce, job promotion, demotion or firing, jail or prison, or significant change in your health. The list may include both positive and negative events that are significant to you. List them as they come to you. Do not be concerned about when they occurred. These events made you who you are today. Make a list of ten of the most meaningful events or experiences of your life up to the present.

Step 2: Choose one of these events or experiences that you now believe to be tragic or traumatic.

Step 3: Now, list four to six positive life experiences or events that took place following the event listed in Step 2.

Step 4: Following the lead of Step 3, list four to six life experiences or events that may have followed if the event listed in Step 2 *did not* occur.

Step 5: What conclusion(s) can you draw from this exercise?

Reflection on Death: The Final Stage of Growth[38]:

Step 1: What unfinished meaningful tasks would you pursue if you knew that death was imminent? What broken friendships would you mend? What volunteer activities would you pursue in the hospital or community? What non-profit organizations would you donate meaningful time? To what destinations would you travel? How would you spend your time with family and friends?

Step 2: What would you regret not having done or said? Is there anything preventing you from fulfilling it now? Remember, the greatest treasures exist not in world museums but in the graveyards of regret and what might have been.

Reflection on the Defiant Power of the Human Spirit:

Step 1: At the top of a sheet of paper write: "Search for Meaning at the Broken Places"

• *Make a list of "what I would do with the rest of my life that would be meaningful in order to transcend physical, emotional, or spiritual brokenness."* Take two minutes and list quickly all meaningful goals that come to your mind.

• Then take two minutes to go over and make any changes to the list.

Step 2: At the top of the second sheet write: "How I would like to spend the next three years that would be meaningful? (If over age 40, "how would I like to spend the next five years?)"

Take two minutes to brainstorm meaningful deeds or creative works that you wish to pursue, experiences or human encounters with persons living or deceased, loves or friends, or perhaps a change of attitude toward physical, emotional, or spiritual suffering experienced in the past. Take two minutes to add to the list.

Step 3: At the top of third sheet write: "If I knew now that I would be struck dead by an incurable disease, loss of limb or cognitive ability, or an unavoidable situation, such as divorce or loss of a loved one in six months, how would I live until then?"

• Take two minutes to brainstorm and list as many meaningful pursuits as you can.

• Take another two minutes to add if you wish.

Step 4: Now go back to those three sheets starting with Step I and decide which goal you will rate most important to least.

Step 5: Next cull from these the three most important to you at this moment. This statement helps to bring your future into the present by giving you a clearer view of what the most meaningful future looks like. It is important to be pursuing only two goals at a time, but to have a follow-up goal each time one goal has been achieved.

Daily and Weekly Goals

This second part will help you plan your time on a weekly and daily basis. It has to do with meaningful activities which help you reach your goals. Example: Your goal might be to live a healthier life - exchanging unhealthy desserts for healthy ones such a fruit or vegetable; exercising three or four times per week; giving up smoking, caffeinated drinks and alcohol. Your goal might be to verbally express more often the qualities you enjoy about a loved one or friend.

Step 1: Take three sheets of paper: write down one of the goals.

• Spend three minutes making as long a list as possible of meaningful activities that could conceivably contribute toward achieving your first meaningful goal.

• Spend three minutes on each sheet.

• Then spend an additional three minutes on each sheet - adding, deleting, consolidating, refining and even brainstorming further activities. Identify as many as you can. Be as imaginative as possible. Quickly write down as many ideas as you can; like a mind map, each idea will lead to several others: speed and quantity are important. *Do not* make any attempt to *evaluate or prioritize*. Do not confuse goals with activities. The latter is something you do.

Step 2: You have now listed several meaningful activities. The next step is to set priorities.

Switch from being creative and imaginative to being practical, realistic and meaningful. Start by eliminating the least meaningful items.

One way to do this is for each activity on each list, ask: "Is my choice being driven by pleasure, power or meaning? Am I committed to spending a minimum of five minutes (or less time) on this activity in the next seven days?" If the answer is "no," draw a line through the activity. (You don't have to offer any particular reason for crossing an activity off your list. You may not feel like doing it; it may depend on someone else who cannot help you at this time; it may be too difficult, too expensive, too time consuming, etc.)

Step 3: After you have trimmed all three goal-activity lists, combine the results into one list. You will then have a dozen or so activities that are most meaningful to you. Next, set priorities and classify the most meaningful to the least. Each day provides a fresh opportunity to move closer to your meaningful goals. Select one meaningful activity to work on each day. If it seems very large, break it down into smaller, achievable parts, beginning with the easiest task. Once you've singled it out, you have given yourself a clear priority for that day. In the sixteen hours or so that you are awake each day, you can arrange a few minutes to work toward fulfilling a meaningful lifetime goal starting now.

Meaningful Values Statement

A meaningful values statement focuses on what you want to pursue. Because each individual is unique, meaningful values statements reflect the uniqueness of life, both in content and form. For example:

- Write or record an on-going autobiography.
- Seek spiritual understanding and growth of beliefs. Discuss with a trusted spiritual advisor.
- Never compromise with honesty, doing what's right even when nobody is looking.
- Contact those you care about at least once a week – by mail, phone, and email or in person.
- Listen to both sides before judging, reflecting what you hear without interpreting, judging or aggression.
- Accept that pain is inevitable, suffering is optional. Seek out opportunities to laugh often.
- Defend those who are absent or unable to defend themselves, and eliminate prejudices of any form.
- Be sincere yet decisive in commitments. Be on time and follow through on promises.
- Develop at least two new proficiencies each year – artistic, physical, mental and spiritual.
- Plan tomorrow's work and creative activities while contacting loved ones and others today.
- Be a survivor and victor in all experiences, not a victim.
- Maintain a positive attitude in all setbacks and view them as opportunities and gifts.

- Keep a sense of humor and compassion for all fellow men.
- Be orderly in person, in home and in work.
- Smile in bad times and be always optimistic.
- Do not fear mistakes or failures. Fear only the absence of creative, constructive, and corrective responses. You move toward and become your purpose by 'doing.'
- Facilitate the success of family, friends, subordinates and strangers alike by giving of yourself.
- Practice listening with compassionate understanding the unique paths others must take and endure.
- Concentrate all abilities and efforts on improving and mastering all meaningful tasks.
- Seek a balance between career, friends, family and volunteer activities. Take time to enjoy nature.
- Be a trusted friend in word and deed.
- Exercise wisdom in raising your children to love, learn, laugh, work and develop their unique talents, and to live a meaningful and responsible lives.
- Value the rights, freedoms, and responsibilities of a democratic society. Be a concerned and informed citizen, involved in the political process by presenting your views and voting in *every* election in person or in absentee voting.
- Be a self-starting individual who exercises initiative in accomplishing goals.
- Be willing always to refrain from addictive and destructive habits, no matter how small.
- Seek financial independence over time. Except for long-term home and car loans, abstain from consumer debt. Spend less than earned. Invest part of income in savings before paying bills.
- Use money and talents to make life more enjoyable for others through service and charitable giving.

Footnote:
[5] *Into the Abyss: A Personal Journey into the World of Street Gangs* . Carlie, Michael K. 2002 Website book @

http://people.missouristate.edu/MichaelCarlie/Preface/preface.htm.

XII.
Embrace the Unexpected

Embracing the unexpected represents a perfect paradox, an apparent contradiction that is nonetheless true. Life teaches us that we generally discover our potential meaning and purpose on the path we take to avoid it.

– Harvey Shrum, EdD

Solomon (Ecclesiastes 9:11-12) tells us to expect the unexpected. Jesus of Matthew's gospel (Matthew 24:36-44) also tells us to expect the unexpected. We must be ready, ready every minute of every day for the unexpected. Anticipating the unexpected, we are less likely to be overwhelmed when it occurs.

Who would expect the king of the Jews to ride on a donkey? Who would expect that his entry into Jerusalem, full of praise, song and celebration, would in a few short days end in shame, agony and an alleged criminal's execution outside the same city walls he had just processed through? Who would dare to expect some even more radically unexpected…that birth and death are not two different states, but different aspects of the same state…that there is as little reason to deplore the one as there is to be pleased over the other? Who would expect the end of the story to be the beginning of the story?

The end of the story of Jesus Christ is the beginning of hope for all. And the beginning of the hope received in Him is fulfilled when he comes again. And the fact that we do not know when or where or how that coming will be, except that it will be unexpected, is what makes it hope and not just another piece of knowledge.

"I'm a thinkaholic," paraphrasing what somebody once said. It started innocently enough. I'd think, reason, reflect, and speculate, just a little, at parties to loosen up with friends. Inevitably, though, one thought led to another. Soon, I was more than just a social thinker. I began to think alone in the silence of my id, ego, or super-ego, "To relax," I told myself, but I knew it wasn't true.

Thinking became more and more important to me. Eventually, I was thinking all the time. I would fall asleep and wake up thinking. Things began to sour at home. One evening I'd turned off the television and asked my wife about the meaning of life. She spent that night at her mother's house.

I began to think on the job. I knew that thinking and employment don't mix but I couldn't stop myself. I avoided friends at lunchtime so I could read Frankl and Fabry. I'd return to the office dizzy and confused, asking, "What is it exactly we are doing here and is it meaningful?"

One day the boss called me into his office. He said, "Listen, I like you, and it hurts me to say this: Quit thinking about the meaning of your job or find another occupation!" I went home early that day.

"Honey," I said, "I've been thinking." "I know," she said, "I want a divorce!" "But Honey," I said, "it's not that serious." "It is serious," she said. "You think more than the typical college professors and college professors don't make any money. So if you keep on thinking, we won't have any money!" "That's a faulty syllogism," I said impatiently. She exploded into tears of rage and frustration.

I was in no mood to deal with the emotional drama. "I'm going to the library," I thoughtfully stated as I stomped out the door. I was in the mood for some Nietzsche, Kierkegaard, and Heidegger.

I roared into the parking lot with NPR on the radio and ran up to the big glass doors. They didn't open! The library was closed.

To this day, I believe that a Higher Power was looking out for me that afternoon. Leaning on the unfeeling, cold glass, whimpering for more Steinbeck and Hemingway, I spotted a poster.

"Friend" it began. "Is existential thinking ruining your life?" You probably recognize that line. It's from the standard *Thinkers Anonymous* poster. That is why I am what I am today: a recovering existential thinker.

I never miss a TA meeting. At meetings we practice clearing our minds of thoughts that may lead to debate about the nature of existence, reality, the universe, space, time, death, and other existential or metaphysical issues and watch mindless videos having nothing to do with existentialism. The video playing last week was "Attack of the Tomatoes." Then we share about how we avoided thinking the previous week while watching soap operas.

I still have my old job and things are much better at home. Life just seems easier, somehow now that I've stopped thinking. I'm definitely on the road to a *complete recovery* that is promised to us on page one in the TA book. Life is good now that I'm not tempted to think!

Life teaches us to *embrace the unexpected*. Embracing the unexpected represents a *perfect paradox*, an apparent contradiction that is nonetheless true. Life teaches us that we generally discover our potential meaning and purpose on the path we take to avoid it. Embracing the unexpected occurs in looking back upon our life and seeing how all of our life experiences have prepared us or instructed us for the fullest fruition of our meaning potential and purpose, sometimes painfully. Ernest Hemingway noted that "The world eventually breaks everybody, but afterward many become stronger at the broken places."

It takes broken soil to produce a crop, broken clouds to give rain, broken grain to give bread and broken bread to give strength. Human beings are helped not through our brilliant logic or persuasive speech, but through the sharing of our struggles, failures, disappointments, and loses and how we have overcome tragedy and trauma. It may be the case of one beggar who has found bread showing other beggars where they can find bread, too or a fellow ex-felon positively mentoring another to do the right thing even when nobody is looking.

If there were an x-ray capable of giving us a picture of the human spirit, we would find that we all show evidence of emotional and psychic fractures through feelings of inadequacy, frustration, failure, or the scars of abuse, blasted hopes, unrealized dreams, and losses we cannot recapture or forget.

Hemingway talks not only of our common vulnerability to being broken; he reminds us too that we can later become strong at the broken places. Where trouble and suffering are concerned, we have the power not only to confront and endure them; we can use them constructively and creatively.

Just as pain is the gift that nobody wants, life teaches us to embrace the unexpected when we lose a loved one; when we experience a divorce; when we lose our freedom because of choices; when we lose all that we worked for during our life – a job, a home, savings and investments. Everything that happens to us, every person who comes along in our lives, every success, failure, betrayal or loyalty is meant not to debilitate us but to empower us. When tragedy strikes in our lives, it is not what we did, but about what we are called to be. Experience is not what happens to us, but what we do with that which happens to us. Likewise, it is not where we travel to but whom we take there that is meaningful.

Surviving childhood hunger, we advocate for starving children around the world. Left out, we become more conscious of including others. Neglected, we become more self-sufficient. A traumatic childhood helps us to become more compassionate toward others. Wounded by life, we become stronger at the broken places. In suffering, we discover our inner resources and feel the grief that gives us depth and character, and open our heart to compassion. We were never a mistake; we are survivors of cruelties, hardships and traumas. If things were always fair, we would have no motivation to recognize and handle the shadow in ourselves and others in creative, compassionate and positive ways.

Everyone and every event in the drama of our life is part of the metaphor of our journey. The issue from an old relationship may be how much we needed to learn. Most of us keep meeting partners who show us exactly where our work is. The wounds are openings into our missing life. Often, the only way a lost piece of ourselves or of our history comes back to us is through another person. People and events come along that help us move toward our potential meaning. The only mistake we make is hanging on to people too long or too briefly.

Sometimes an emotional wound becomes the threshold to our mission in life or to the unfolding of our talents. Sometimes it is a physical trauma or disability. Helen Keller is a moving example of this. Her own hardships and disabilities became precisely what it took for her to find her destiny of service to others. John Milton wrote the classic *Paradise Lost* 16 years after he had become blind. Beethoven wrote his greatest music, including five symphonies during his later years after becoming deaf.

Sometimes it is an educational or societal label. Most of you are aware of one of America's leading motivational speakers, Les Brown. Born in poverty, he entered school as a bored and unmotivated student. He was mistakenly declared "educable mentally retarded" (EMR) in the fourth grade. A teacher stimulated his hunger to learn and his passion for self-improvement which enabled him to rise above even those who labeled him. He became a community activist and served three terms in the Ohio State Legislature and became chairman of its Human Resources Committee. Today, Les Brown conducts seminars and motivational training for Fortune 500 companies as well as inspirational seminars for those who want to improve their lives and their relationships. Another example is Mary Groda who was labeled as a retarded, incorrigible child, and sentenced to two years in a reformatory as an adolescent. Yet she went on to achieve a GED certificate, to complete medical school and to practice medicine.

Nobody rises to low expectations. Always embrace the unexpected that resulted in not only you but all your unique experiences, encounters and loves. Always embrace the unexpected and treat others as they can and ought to be, regardless of the negative direction in which they are moving. The art of teaching others is the art of assisting them in discovering their meaning potential, not as a sage on the stage, but as a guide on their side. But the *responsibility* for discovering our meaning potential and purpose lies equally with each of us as we embrace the unexpected. It is a lifelong process of keeping abreast of change and embracing the unexpected.

The greatest of human tragedies is to be distracted from our purpose and to lose our power to activate our meaning potential because of years of addiction to drugs, alcohol or relationships that are toxic, abusive, unworkable or depleting. Our greatest potential meaning can thereby fade away, and no one will do anything to halt the dissolution.

The world will stand by as we throw away our potential meaning and purpose.

Only in letting go do we begin the journey toward gaining control. Only in letting go are we able to move on. Only in letting go are we able to achieve our meaning potential by creating a work or by doing a deed; by experiencing something or encountering someone; and most importantly in facing a fate we cannot change, rising above ourselves, growing beyond ourselves, and by so doing changing ourselves, thus turning a personal tragedy into a triumph. To let go means to embrace experimental, creative and attitudinal values, and in the process, to achieve goals once thought unthinkable and unachievable. Being human means pursuing a lifetime of learning and embracing the unexpected.

Isaiah [11:6-8] fills our minds with images of the unexpected – a wolf dwells with a lamb; a leopard lies with a goat; a calf and lion lie together; a cow and a bear graze together; a lion eats straw like an ox; a baby plays over the hole of a cobra. Isaiah has a vision of a different world – a little child shall lead, making peace in all creation. A child leader; what a paradox! The Bible reveals that God is always working in mysterious, unanticipated ways – a young boy, David slays the gigantic Goliath [1 Samuel 17:51] with a rock from a sling shot; Joseph [Genesis 41], sold into slavery by his own brothers, becomes Pharaoh's main assistant and ends up providing relief for the very same brothers, now starving and dependent on Joseph. Who could have seen this unexpected twist of fate? The apostle Paul, once the leading persecutor of Christians, becomes the most articulate spokesperson for the gospel of Jesus Christ.

Trees are drawn forth out of stumps; babies are made leaders; sense is made out of rubble; life is drawn out of death, creating a new world. As Isaiah informs us, God's thoughts are not our thoughts and his ways are not our ways. He rarely answers prayers as I – or anyone else – expect Him to answer them. I need to keep my eyes on God and my feet firmly on the gospel. And I should never forget that with God I should expect the unexpected.

When we open ourselves to God's work in our world and in our hearts miracles happen, and the unexpected takes place. Viktor Frankl experienced the truth of Carl Jung's idea of 'Synchronicity," the theory that coincidences, the unexpected, are not arbitrary but are meaningful.

However, they only become personally meaningful when the person to whom the coincidences occur has the courage, the intuition and the ability to invest it with a personal meaning. God lures from the darkest situations and the darkest corners of our hearts the most wonderful and unexpected things. God draws out from the root of Jesse a child, the Christ, one who is both the one unexpected and the one for whom we wait with longing. God brings hope out of tragedy and life out of death. What a paradox. What a blessing to be graced with the task of an *Unfinished Masterpiece.*

XIII.
Life – The Unfinished Masterpiece

We are all paintbrushes in the hand of God on the
canvas of a yet unfinished masterpiece called Life.
- Harvey Shrum

Leo Tolstoy states that "from the child of five to myself is but a step. But from the new-born baby to the child of five is an appalling distance." A newborn child is an unfinished masterpiece that will experience an infinite number of experiential, attitudinal and creative brushstrokes from birth to age five. The newborn apprentice will study various art forms of the masters that surround her everyday life – realism, surrealism, impressionism, cubism, pointillism, post-impressionism, and others.

An individual needs only to look at the child to see that she is beauty in motion. She is in perpetual motion, always in the act of doing and experiencing meanings of the moment at an exponential rate. The child must not only study her first mentors (a mother, a father and siblings), she must be involved in the act of discovering the meaning of enumerable brushstrokes applied daily to her own canvas. She is given tools, rather than an answer that enable her to discover the meaning of her world. It is the art of living. Born with only a voice (cry) not understood for millennia, she has no 'rules' to go by. She sleeps; she nurses; she mirrors the mentors in her immediate world.

The initial brushstrokes appear to be random and imperfect to her inexperienced eyes and ears. In time, she becomes more graceful in her actions and loses her original awkwardness, perhaps even begins to develop her own unique style. Her art of living becomes natural to her. Day by day, she imitates the brushstrokes of the mentors, elders and masters until they become second nature. But there will be days of unavoidable pain, suffering and brokenness. Helen Keller states that "the marvelous richness of human experience would lose something of rewarding joy if there were not limitations to overcome. The hilltop hour would not be half so wonderful if there were no dark valleys to traverse."

Eventually, this child will be broken, physically, mentally and emotionally, but always able to depend on the medicine chest that is her spiritual dimension. The human spirit is a specifically human dimension and contains abilities other creatures do not have. Every human is spiritual; in fact, spirit is the essence of being human. You have a body that may become ill; you have a mind that may become psychically challenged. But the spirit is what you are. It is your healthy core. It is the medicine chest.[17; 20]

The mentors, elders and masters pass on not only the meaning of the experiential brushstrokes that bring pleasure and empowerment, but also beautiful, spiritually nourishing and meaning-discovering driven tools, like Logotherapy and the Intensive Journal. The child gradually begins to learn, moment by moment, to embrace the paradoxes of her life and comes to learn what is essential to physical, mental and spiritual health and growth in both her conscious and unconscious world.

'Meaning' generally comes early to indigenous youth who experience elder-guided formal rites of passage. The spiritual journey of rites of passage both broadens and enriches the developing masterpiece with each unique brushstroke, each one never to be repeated. As the layers of brushstrokes blend with one another and spread here and there with apparent randomness, brushstroke by brushstroke, new meaning is gradually added. Each brushstroke is almost like poetry, capturing and communicating the meaningful life experiences of a child, an infinitesimal glimpse toying with us just on the horizon.

The unfinished masterpiece has to be pursued; it must be discovered, one brushstroke at a time. But it has to say something more than simply that a three-dimensional painting works. It brings the world as the child lives it into her unique art, and as meaningful as her unique work is, experiencing it is like experiencing life in an intense, revelatory moment. It is unique. No one else has experienced that which she experienced; no one else can manage and discover those moments in the same meaningful way; and no one can ever remove them from her life story.

Viktor Frankl states that "life is not a Rorschach test; a meaningless blotch into which we can read our own meanings. Rather it is like a 'hidden picture puzzle,' with lines showing clouds, trees, flowers, and people, and a caption that challenges viewers 'to find the bicycle in this picture.' The viewers are asked to twist and turn the picture this way and that way, until they discover the bicycle in the jumble of lines (and brushstrokes). In the same way we have to view our lives from all sides until we detect its meaning in its dimensions."[18]

During most of our life, experiential brushstrokes upon the multi-dimensional canvas appear random, chaotic and without any apparent meaning. But with the passage of time, knowledge and wisdom we somehow manage to get small glimpses of movement – a word, a postage-stamp picture of 'something' on the future horizon. It is what it is, not as we wish or expect or pray for.

Frankl contrasts man, on the one hand as *Homo sapiens*, the man who knows how to be a success, with what he called *homo patiens*, the man who knows how to suffer, how to mold even his sufferings into a human achievement on the ever-evolving canvas of human history. Each is a different dimension of man, the latter being the superior or higher dimension of man. Frankl notes that when we can no longer change our fate we can change ourselves by rising above and growing beyond ourselves in fulfilling the potential meaning of our life.[20]

Even on the battle front of war, in a prison cell or in a hospital recovery room "we are not subject to the conditions that confront us there; rather, these conditions are subject to our decision," states Frankl. [20] Aleksandr Solzhenitsyn realized this spiritual gift from the straw-covered floor of his cell in a Siberian gulag[62] as did Nelson Mandela, prisoner 466/64, who affirmed from his cold prison cell on Robben

Island, "I detest racialism, because I regard it as a barbaric thing, whether it comes from a black man or a white man."[50]

Russell Means, too, understood the wisdom of life's lessons, noting that the year he spent in prison was one of the finest of his life. On the physical side it was hard; it was hell. But on the spiritual side it was a great year.

Veterans often return from the traumatic events of war stronger at the broken places. Doug Pringle, a Vietnam War veteran, states that the loss of his leg in that war was one of the best things to happen to him. Following that war he achieved several gold medals for downhill slalom skiing in the Paralympics and committed his life to help fellow veterans broken by war to discover the meaning of their life.

Senator Max Cleland, a triple amputee of the Vietnam War, emphasizes that "people do not want to hear about your strengths, prosperity or worldly successes. They want to hear about your weaknesses and brokenness, and how you were able to survive."

Every human being has experienced, is experiencing or will experience unavoidable pain and suffering. Each must decide whether he will face up to the need to change, to improve or give in, whether or not he will succumb to the pressures of life and let himself be determined by his unique set of conditions. No one person or thing caused those choices in his past or present. He is responsible for choices he makes in relationships, careers, and parenting.

"Being human means being confronted continuously with (unavoidable) situations (that) …challenge (us) to fulfill its meaning. Each situation is a call, first to listen, and then to respond."[26] … Viktor Frankl says that "A man who becomes conscious of the responsibility he bears toward a human being who affectionately waits for him, or to an unfinished work, will never be able to throw away his life (to addictions, aggressions, and depressions). He knows the *why* for his existence, and will be able to bear almost any *how*."[20] There can be no greater pursuit than that which leads to the *ultimate masterpiece* otherwise described as one's autobiography. It is all the more remarkable, perhaps, that it is pursued at the broken places to become another *David*, a masterpiece created out of brokenness.

During most of a child's life, the apparent random chaotic brushstrokes on the multi-dimensional canvas of her life may initially make little or no sense. However, with the passage of time, discovered knowledge, wisdom and, eventually discovered meaning begin to make sense page by page, chapter by chapter, short story by short story, and brushstroke by brushstroke, on an ever-evolving and transcending, yet incomplete masterpiece.

Reflection Exercise on the Unfinished Masterpiece: We can name numerous writers, musicians and artists who took their last breath, leaving behind unfinished masterpieces. Wars and genocides account for the deaths of over 150 million citizens worldwide during the past century. Each victim of war, genocide, starvation or lack of proper health and medicine left behind unfinished masterpieces. Procrastination results in many more left unfinished. We are not in charge of the final brushstroke, the final word in the final chapter of our autobiographical masterpiece, but we are in charge of *today*; the present.

1. Finish the thought: "It came as an unexpected..." Make sure to keep on writing. Before true learning and wisdom can advance, questioning must take place. Wisdom is not driven by answers but by questions. Every thought stays alive only to the extent that fresh questions are generated and taken seriously as the driving force in the process of thinking through the meaning of the moment.

2. What is the most unexpected thing that happened to you in your life? What about something unexpected that happened to you recently? What about something that others had not expected of you? Write about those experiences.

3. Write a poem, story or essay that uses the word 'Unexpected'. Then, write a short story, poem or song using only *six* words.

4. What can you write using any one of these titles: The Unexpected Hero, Unexpected Moments, Unexpected Joy, The Unexpected Gift, An Unexpected Guest, An Unexpected Traveler, or An Unexpected Life?

5. Write about a déjà vu experience.

6. Write about an experience that resulted in an unexpected gift.

7. Read or write a children's short story. Now, add the "Unexpected Ending"

8. Write a musical score; then, play it in reverse or mixing of the lines, for example, cut and paste.

9. Cut a picture from an old magazine. Position it upside down and draw what you see.

10. Print an unusual word on the center of a blank sheet of paper. Create a family tree, lines radiating out from this word and write whatever this word brings to mind. With each word that comes to mind, do the same – what does the new word bring to mind?

11. With eyes closed, scribble some lines on a sheet of paper. Now, with eyes open create something out of these meaningless lines. Then, color it.

12. Write about a repeated dream that appears to keep drawing you back to discover its meaning.

13. Your missing pet cat suddenly reappears after a year. Write a short story of its adventures, going from first to third person or vice versa; in rhyme; as a comic book, another time period in history, for example.

14. Invent an imaginary character. Have her or him fill out an application with physical stats and biographical information, home planet, family and pets, likes, dislikes, obsessions, life changing moments, friends, customary breakfast.

15. Keep a journal of dreams over a period of several months. Write a short story or screen play with elements of the dreams.

16. Make a list of unfinished masterpieces you will commit to begin working on today; not only literary, musical, artistic endeavors, but relationships with self and others as well.

XIV.
The Journey Continues

We all like to find out the truth about ourselves, make choices, and feel unique. But freedom of making choices will not lead to a meaningful life if it is not lived responsibly and lived only for one's own sake. Responsibility presupposes a demand quality in life to which we have to respond and which requires transcending our self-centeredness.   - Joseph Fabry

Frankl says that no man has the freedom to undo what he may have done, but he does have the freedom to choose the right attitude to guilt. Any man who has failed by a deed cannot change what happened. Any misdeed cannot be fully traced back to biological, psychological, and/or sociological factors. Man cannot change what happened but by repentance and transformation he can change himself. Totally explaining one's crime would be tantamount to explaining away his or her **guilt** and to seeing in him or her not a free and responsible human being but a machine to be repaired. Criminals, abhor be treated as they are and prefer to be held responsible for their deeds.[20]

Criminal behavior comes from a lack of responsibility, from a loss of meaning and values passed down from generation to generation. When an individual suffers from an "evil parent complex," he has shifted the responsibility for his behavior onto his parents. You see, it is a prerogative of mankind to realize guilt. It is also his responsibility to overcome guilt by pursuing his meaning potential and purpose in life and not perpetuate criminal values through his children.

There is no such thing as freedom all by itself. Freedom is always preceded by responsibility; they are connected to one another. To be human is to be responsible. It is a mistake to pursue freedom without consideration of responsibility. Responsibleness refers to a meaning for whose fulfillment we are responsible, and also to a being, family and community before whom we are responsible. As for the pursuit of happiness, the more we make it a target, the more widely we miss it. Happiness is, and will always remain, the unintended effect of meaningful activity. Thus, liberty + responsibility = freedom.

Responsibleness cannot be addressed without involving freedom, since only free human beings can be supposed to be responsible. Dr. Viktor Frankl suggested to President Clinton that a statue of *Responsibleness* be erected on the Western coast as a counterpart of the *Statue of Freedom*[6] on the Eastern coast. He held that even as a person broken by the trauma of war, incarceration, illness or death of a loved one you could maintain your inner freedom. You can be enslaved and even killed but still remain a free human being, since there is an inner freedom of which nobody can bereave you, unless you accept to be bereaved. The inner freedom is one of will. Freedom of will, noted Frankl is one of the three pillars on which Logotherapy's concept of man is based; the two remaining being the will to meaning and the meaning of life.

There is more to healthy human motivation than the pleasure principle, more than the striving for superiority. These are only degenerated, neurotic forms of existence. However, in the healthy human, there is a will to meaning and it is this that sets man apart from the animals. Meaning in life, emphasizes Frankl cannot be given but must be discovered by each person individually in situations in which we discover a truth about us, by experiencing our uniqueness, in situations in which we exercise the power of choice, in circumstances that require responsibility, or in transcending our self-centeredness and reaching beyond the self towards causes to serve or people to love.[20]

Life is not easy. It comes with so much unavoidable pain, the gift that nobody wants. Jimmy lost a sibling, a child and a grandchild. His first wife was mentally ill, addicted to prescription drugs and homicidal, both threatening and attempting to kill both him and his infant children, yet was still able to discover his life had meaning and purpose. Millions of children continue to lose their parents to epidemics and genocidal wars.

Recall that Ernest Hemingway saying that the world eventually breaks everybody, but many become strong at the broken places. In the most painful moments, a breaking takes place that drives us even further in our search for the meaning. Those who have suffered much in life can transform their pain, creatively, socially, spiritually and existentially, and deeply touch those around them. It is not so much by the words that are spoken but rather whom they become in spite of their brokenness. In the end, people do not wish to hear of our successes; they want to hear about our brokenness, our survival and our becoming stronger at the broken places in meaningful ways.

To be human is to strive for something outside of oneself. Self-transcendence describes this quality behind the will to meaning, the grasping for something or someone outside of oneself. We are made to turn outward, toward another human being to whom we can love and give ourselves. Only in such a way do Homo sapiens demonstrate themselves to be truly human. Only when in service of another does a person truly know his or her humanity.[20]

Remember every unavoidable life experience, loving relationships and encounters with others, particularly those that involve pain, grief and suffering become gifts to us in some unique way. If we choose not to learn the unique lessons intended for us, we can expect that the symbolic lessons to be repeated again and again with all of its possible physical, emotional, psychological and spiritual consequences. The consequences can be endless and lifelong: repeated addictions, divorce, and separation from family and children, disease, jail and prison, bankruptcy, and underemployment.

In the final analysis, failure to gain insight and wisdom from the life lesson(s) presented to us and failure to consciously make the choices to change in responsible and meaningful ways have consequences. Individuals may have experienced a series of traumatic events, many of which may appear difficult to face and insurmountable. However, answers do not lie in self-medicating, or in diverting anger and pain, or in burying the anguish with powerful and self-centered people or with an expensive lifestyle.

Individuals must consciously choose to take part in determining their meaning potential; to become responsible, no matter what the odds; to believe in their own survival; to internalize their goals, visualizing only positive end results; to restore strained relationships with their family; to achieve peace of mind and expand their life on all fronts; and to choose to love and give, instead of to hate, take, and use. Life is about loving people and using things, not loving things and using people.

An elder or mentor can help in the process. A child can be lead to discover that what happened to create unavoidable pain and suffering was not her/his fault, that experience is not what happened to her/him but what s/he does with that which happened to her/him. What is going on today is based on making responsible choices. And a meaningful life is discovered when he/she pursues it experientially, creatively, and at-titudinally.[20]

We have potentials that can be fulfilled to our last breath, be they positive or nega-tive. And there are but three pathways to finding meaning through responsibility according to Frankl and Fabry:

• *By responding to the meanings of the moment through what we receive from life, what we take from life, what life gives us, and what we experience (Experiential Values);*

• *By making responsible choices where choice exists through what we give to the word, what we do, what we contribute, what we add to life, and what we create (Creative Values);*

• *And, by not feeling responsible when there is no choice through the attitude we take when we are faced with situations in which we can do absolutely nothing, as in the case of an inoperable disease, or being stricken with blindness or losing an arm, leg, or power of speech.*[20]

Viktor Frankl emphasizes that Logotherapy is not a panacea, but then, neither is any other form of psychotherapy. Human beings are complex organisms. Becoming stronger at the broken places – in body, mind and spirit – depend on the strengths and resources of the client as well as random, chance happenings. It also depends on the quality of the relationship between the therapist and the client. No two therapists have the same empathy, respect and genuineness. The client must be ready for change, have goals for therapy, and have a positive view of the quality of the relationship. At this point, the specific therapeutic technique can then be objectively assessed. Lastly, some combination of hope and the placebo effect account for some of the change in the client.[47]

Healing comes from the sufferer's ability and willingness to find the words with which to speak of his tragedy and the eventual ability to put meaning and sense to it. Meaning is discovered, but without the tools it becomes overwhelming. Without the appropriate tools, the sufferer often chooses to drug, divert or bury the pain.

Frankl believes in the potential of human beings. He believes in the power of love to heal. He believes in the ability of the client to heal himself, given the appropriate therapeutic tools and guidance. In Logotherapy, Frankl creates a sacred space within which a client experiences shared acceptance, patience, and willingness to enter the darkness of tragedy and suffering together with the therapist.

To discover meaning in indescribable suffering is not a simple task for the sufferer. Yet, without meaning, there can be no healing and growth in the broken places. Healing and growth involves going beyond the self; giving oneself to a cause to serve, or another person to love in all his or her uniqueness.

The *Search for Meaning at the Broken Places* is a culmination of having entered the darkness with a long list of men and women who survived being broken and lived to tell their story: *Cleland, Fabry, Frankl, Gandhi, Hemingway, Jesus, Kubler-Ross, Mandela, Oufkir, Progoff, Solzhenitsyn, Wiesel* and countless others. The discovery of meaning involves changing ourselves when we are no longer able to change a situation; finding meaning in what we do, and what we experience; and taking a stand when we are faced with a situation of unchangeable suffering. "…in every thing give thanks (1 Thessalonians 5:17-18)," we are told. By remaining aware of the life of God within and around us, we can affirm our lives by creatively accepting, embracing and living through the tragic triad of death, guilt and suffering in order to become what we are not – an unfinished *masterpiece*, a creation of God. The art of living, after all, is the most creative art of all, full of paradoxes; of unexpected gifts.

Footnote:

[6] www.sorfoundation.org is the official website dedicated to the building and erecting of the *Statue of Responsibility* on the West Coast of America. This monument will enshrine the idea that the core principles of liberty, responsibility, and freedom go hand in hand, an idea put forward by Dr. Viktor Frankl over forty years ago.

Appendix A
Dream Journals

With few exceptions, everyone dreams. Dreams can be curious, scary, uplifting, empowering, and many other things. Without interpretation or analysis and with neutrality as objective as is possible, an individual should write down any dream upon wakening. But, before an individual opens her eyes she should attempt to "replay" the dream in her head several times. She need not be concerned if she cannot recall everything. She simply writes anything that she does recall – scenes, words spoken, characters and images, colors and other sensory images, feelings of sad, mad, glad or fear. The symbolic language of dreams often appears as one-act plays, or multiple chapters of several dreams, or significant repeated dreams or 'off-the-wall' dreams with symbolic meaning to be discovered.

An abbreviated manuscript on "Tending Your Dreams," by Stephen Aizenstat, Ph.D. was provided at a workshop I attended nearly twenty years ago. It purported to provide a unique method of recording and discovering the meaning of dreams. Over the next twenty years Aizenstat's work with dreams led him to develop a way of relating to dreams that he calls "tending," which is based upon certain beliefs about the nature of dreams. In 2009 he published his completed manuscript, *Dream Tending*, available in hardback and audio book format.

The following is a summary of that original, brief manuscript. One of Aizenstat's beliefs about *dreams*, presented in the original manuscript, is that they *are alive*, that is, the images in dreams have lives and bodies of their own. A second belief is that the human psyche is inherently multi-dimensional and that a given dream may emphasize one level more than others. He felt that these levels, as well as "what" and "who" live between them, needed to be explored.

Aizenstat offers a sequence of methods for dream tending presented in four phases. Individuals listen to the dream in phase one as it presents itself, without the temptation of integrating personal feelings and associations. Dreams are written in the present tense, noting the 'where, what, and how' of the dream landscape. He suggests that individuals identify the 'plot, characters, and creatures' of the dream, that they look for 'repetitions, contrasts, and/or similarities," and that they watch for poetic puns and metaphors.

During phase two, individuals associate themselves to the actual dream, exploring associations and connections with a particular period of their personal, outer life history. Staying with and becoming curious about the dream, individuals explore mythological and literary themes that present themselves in the dream, being open to the unexpected associations and connections.

In phase three individuals interact with the dream images in a playful way; touching and smelling, looking at and listening to the dream images. This includes moving, feeling, and dancing rhythmically with the dream images. They can give artistic expression to their dream images, be it to draw, paint, or sculpt.

In the final phase individuals experience the living quality of the dream. They designate a particular place to reflect in silence, to talk with the dream figures, or to develop a dialog relationship with the inner life of their dreams. They present life issues to dream figures, and interact with other dreams and dreamers in an ongoing dream group, sharing but not imposing their feelings and intuitions. In this phase they ask for guidance and listen to the teachings of the dream figure or location.

Aizenstat concludes that, as individuals work with their dreams more and more, they become individuals' friends, their guides, and their mentors. And they become a caring witness to their activities, listening to what they have to say, watching what they do. In tending their dreams, individuals must wait for and trust their own experience of insight. Other persons with whom they share their dream may have interesting and useful intuitions or suggestions, but the dream is their experience. They are the 'final authority' on what their dream is for them based on their unique life experiences. They must not be intimidated by fears of being off-base or of going down blind alleys. They must enjoy the 'detours,' aware that there may be many forks to explore that, over time, provide additional clues to the meaning of their dreams. Dreams may lead them through new and significant territory. They must stay curious and attend to the images. They must tend them.

Aizenstat goes on to say that "Dream Tending is an art in which there are *no* 'wrongs' – only possibilities." The same could be said of experiential brushstrokes upon the canvas of life. Each is unique, never to be duplicated. After the first brushstroke the canvas takes on a life of its own. Each brushstroke has its own personal meaning. A painting never ends; it simply pauses in meaningful places.

References

*If we could read the secret history of our enemies,
we should find in each man's life sorrow and suffering enough to disarm all hostility.*   - Longfellow

1. Achterberg, J. 91985). "Imagery in Healing." New Science Library, Boston.
2. American Psychiatric Association - Diagnostic and Statistical Manual of Mental Disorders. Washington, DC, 1952
3. American Psychiatric Association - Diagnostic and Statistical Manual of Mental Disorders. (2nd Edition.) Washington, DC, 1968.
4. American Psychiatric Association - Diagnostic and Statistical Manual of Mental Disorders (3rd Edition.) Washington, DC, 1980.
5. American Psychiatric Association - Diagnostic and Statistical Manual of Mental Disorders (4th Edition.) Washington, DC, 1994.
6. Beal, Lisa S. (1997). "Post-Traumatic Stress Disorder: A Bibliographic Essay." A version of an article published in CHOICE, 1997. 34(6). 917-930.
7. Becker, E. (1973). *The Denial of Death.* NY: The Free Press.
8. Brand, P. (1993). *Pain: The Gift Nobody Wants.* Canada: HarperCollins.
9. Castaneda, Carlos (1998). *The Teachings of Don Juan: A Yaqui Way of Knowledge.* Berkeley: University of California Pacific.
10. Cleland, M. (2000). *Strong at the Broken Places.* Atlanta: Longstreet Press, Inc.
11. Cohen, Barry M. ***Managing Traumatic Stress through Art: Drawing from the Center.*** Sidran Foundation, 1995.
12. Colodzin, Benjamin. ***Trauma and Survival: A Self Help Learning Guide.*** Ghost Rocks Press, 1990.
13. Crumbaugh, J., & Maholic, L. (1976). *Purpose in Life Test.* Abilene, TX: Viktor Frankl Institute of Logotherapy.
14. Eareckson Tada, J. (1992) *Joni's Story.* Grand Rapids, Michigan: Zondervan Publishing Company
15. Elsevier (2009, March 17). "New Strategy to Weaken Traumatic Memories." ScienceDaily.

16. Fabry, J. (1988). *Guideposts to Meaning - Discovering What Really Matters.* Oakland: New Harbinger Publications.
17. Fabry, J. (1994). *The Pursuit of Meaning.* Berkeley, CA: Institute of Logotherapy Press.
18. Fabry, J. (2000). *Making Sense: The Meaning of Life.* Boston, MA: Skinner House.
19. Flannery, Raymond B., Jr. **Post-Traumatic Stress Disorder: The Victim's Guide to Healing and Recovery.** Crossroad, 1992.
20. Frankl, V. E. (1959, 1984). *Man's Search for Meaning.* NY: Simon & Schuster.
21. Frankl, V. E. (1997). *Man's Search for Ultimate Meaning.* NY: Perseus Publishing Books.
22. Frankl, V. E. *Psychotherapy and Existentialism: Selected Papers on Logotherapy.* New York: Washington Square Press, 1967.
23. Frankl, V. E. (1973). *The Doctor and the Soul: From Psychotherapy to Logotherapy.*
    New York: Vintage Books.
24. Frankl, V. E. (2004). *On the Theory and Therapy of Mental Disorders.* New York: Brunner-Routledge.
25. Frankl, V. E. (1975). *The Unconscious God: Psychotherapy and Theology.* New York: Simon and Schuster.
26. Frankl, V. E. (1978). *The Unheard Cry for Meaning.* NY: Simon & Schuster.
27. Frankl, V. E. (1988). *The Will to Meaning.* NY: Penguin Books.
28. Galloway, J., & Moore, H. (1992). *Once We Were Soldiers and Young.* NY: HarperCollins Publishers.
29. Harper, J.L. "Anatomy of a Habit: America's Unnecessary Wars," *Survival,* Summer 2005, pp. 59, 63, 69, 73, 76.
30. Hemingway, E. (1984). *A Farewell to Arms.* NY: Barron's Educational Services, Inc.
31. Hoge CW, Castro CA, Messer SC, McGurk D, Cotting DI, Koffman RL. "Combat Duty in Iraq and Afghanistan - Mental Health Problems, and Barriers to Care." New England Journal of Medicine. 2004; 351(1): 13-22.
32. Hoge CW, Auchterlonie JL, Milliken CS: "Mental Health Problems, Use of Mental Health Services, and Attrition from Military Service after Returning from Deployment to Iraq or Afghanistan." JAMA 2006; 295:1023-32.
33. Hoge CW, Terhakopian A, Castro CA, Messer SC, Engel CC: Association of Post-traumatic Stress Disorder with Somatic

Symptoms, Health Care Visits, and Absenteeism among Iraq War Veterans." American Journal of Psychiatry. 2007 Jan; 164(1):150-3.

34. Hollerman, Jeffrey R., and Wolfram Schultz (1998) Dopamine neurons report an error in the temporal prediction of reward during learning, *Nature Neuroscience*, **1(4):** 304-309

35. John-Roger & McWilliams, P. (1986). *You Can't Afford the Luxury of a Negative Thought*. Los Angles, CA: Prelude Press.

36. Keen, S. (1991). *Fire in the Belly: On Being a Man*. NY: Bantam Books.

37. King DW, King LA, Foy DW, Gudanowski DM. "Pre-war Factors in Combat-related Post-traumatic Stress Disorder: Structural Equation Modeling with a National Sample of Female and Male Vietnam Veterans." Journal of Consulting Clinical Psychologists. 1996; 64: 520-531.

38. Kipnis, A. (2004). *Knights without Armor*. Santa Barbara: Indigo Phoenix Books.

39. Kroenke, K., MD. *Caring for Patients: A Critique of the Medical Model*. 1 April 1996 | Volume 124 Issue 7

40. Kubler-Ross, E. (1975). *Death: The Final Stage of Growth*. Englewood Cliffs, New Jersey: Prentice-Hall, Inc.

41. Kubler-Ross, E. & Kessler, D. (2000). *Life Lessons*. NY: Touchtone.

42. Kubler-Ross, E. (1979). *On Death and Dying*. NY: Macmillan Publishing Co., Inc.

43. Kubler-Ross, E. (1997). *The Wheel of Life*. NY: Scribner.

44. Lambert, M.J. (1992). Implications of outcome research for psychotherapy integration. In J.C. Norcross and M.R. Goldfriend (Eds.), *Handbook of Psychotherapy Integration*. New York: Basic.

45. Lewis, C.S. (2001). *The Screwtape Letters*. NY: HarperCollins Publishers.

46. Lukas, E. (1984). *Meaningful Living*. NY: Grove Press.

47. Lukas, E. (1986). *Meaning in Suffering*. Berkeley, CA: Institute of Logotherapy Press.

48. MacNair RM. "Perpetration-inducted Traumatic Stress in combat Veterans - Peace and Conflict." Journal of Peace Psychology. 2002; 8: 63-72.

49. Mandela, Nelson (1994). *Long Walk to Freedom*: The Autobiography of Nelson Mandela. Boston & New York: Little Brown.

50. Millman, D. (2000). *The Way of the Peaceful Warrior*. Tiburon, CA: HJ Kramer Inc.

51. Oufkir, M. (2000). *Stolen Lives*. NY: Miramax Books.

52. Peck, S. (1978). *The Road Less Traveled*. NY: Simon & Schuster Inc.

53. Peniston, E. (1986). "EMG Biofeedback-Assisted Desensitization Treatment for Vietnam Combat Veterans Post-Traumatic Stress Disorder." Clinical Biofeedback and Health. 9, (1). 35-41.

54. Peniston, E.G. & Kulkosky, P.J. (1989). Alpha-theta brainwave training and beta endorphin levels in alcoholics. Alcoholism: Clinical and Experimental Results, 13(2), 271-279.

55. Peniston, E.G. & Kulkosky, P.J. (1990). Alcoholic personality and alpha-theta brainwave training. Medical Psychotherapy: An International Journal, 3, 37-55.

56. Peniston, E.G. & Kulkosky, P.J. (1991). Alpha-theta brainwave neurofeedback therapy for Vietnam veterans with combat-related posttraumatic stress disorder. Medical Psychotherapy: An International Journal, 4, 47-60.

57. Progoff, I. (1992). *At a Journal Workshop: Writing to Access the Power of the Unconscious and Evoke Creative Ability.* NY: Penguin Putnam.

58. Rosenheck R, Fontana A. "Changing Patterns of Care for War-related Post-traumatic Stress Disorder at Department of Veterans Affairs Medical Centers: The Use of Performance Data to Guide Program Development." Military Medicine. 1999 Nov; 164(11):795-802.

59. Sanford, L. T. (1990). *Strong at the Broken Places – Overcoming Trauma of Childhood Abuse.* NY: Random House.

60. Seal KH, Bertenthal D, Miner CR, Sen S, & Marmar C. (2007). "Bringing the War Back Home: Mental Health Disorders among 103,788 US Veterans Returning from Iraq and Afghanistan Seen at Department of Veterans Affairs Facilities." Archives of Internal Medicine. 2007; 167, 476-82.

61.   Solzhenitsyn, Aleksandr (1985). *The Gulag Archipelago*: 1918-1956, Volume 2. NY: Harper & Row Publishers, Inc.

62. Tedeschi, Richard G. and Lawrence G. Calhoun. ***Trauma and Transformation: Growing in the Aftermath of Suffering***. Sage Publications, 1995.

63. "The Practice Parameters for the Assessment and Treatment of Children and Adolescents with Posttraumatic Stress Disorder." Journal of the American Academy of Child and Adolescent Psychiatry, 37:10 Supplement, October 1998.

64. Van Devanter, L. & Furey, J. A. (1991). *Visions of War, Dreams of Peace - Writings of Women in the Vietnam War.* NY: Warner Books, Inc.

Recommended DVDs

It is natural for the lower self to resent pain and suffering, but when you can surrender to God, so that your heart overflows with love and acceptance of the wisdom of God's plan, then you can make real progress, and you are filled with a deep peace which is beyond the power of the world to give.   - White Eagle

Groundhog Day [Theme: *Stages & Values*]
Columbia Pictures

Homeless to Harvard [Theme: *Brokenness & Meaning*]
Lifetime Entertainment Services, Inc.

Peaceful Warrior [Theme: *Brokenness & Meaning*]
Universal Studios

Strong at the Broken Places: Turning Trauma into Recovery
Cambridge Documentary Films

The Ultimate Gift [Theme: *Brokenness & Meaning*]
20th Century

ABOUT THE AUTHOR

Harvey Shrum is the first of seven children, whose parents came of age during the deprivation of the Great Depression. His father went on to fight in World War II as a B-24 ball turret gunner out of England while his mother stayed on the home front making decisive material contribution to the war effort and giving birth to their first child. Shrum's mid-grade school education was not particularly productive or enjoyable. Observing his teachers apply physical punishment and bullying almost on a daily basis did little to motivate him to learn. He was one of many who were mislabeled in the sixth grade, but this did not deter his devoted father, an engineer who tutored him and ignited a spark of excitement for learning.

After high school Shrum entered college and supported himself by working on gas and oil rigs during the summer months. Following two years of college he entered the United States Air Force for foreign linguistic training. He initially ranked in the top twenty on the Chinese language placement exam, but later received orders to attend Syracuse University to study in the Slavic Language Program. This was followed by two years in Turkey as a translator on the coast of the Black Sea. He traveled throughout Turkey, but spent most of his off-duty time in a rented home on Buyukada, the Grand Island in the Bosporus Sea, walking the streets of Istanbul to view its mosques, museums and the shops of the Grand Bazaar, and touring the ancient biblical sites of Ephesus.

After completing a B.A. in Secondary and Special Education at California State University – Chico, Shrum worked as the director of the emotionally and educationally handicapped department at Napa State Hospital. He then worked five years as the mathematics and science department head in a Northern California high school. He returned to the California State University – Chico to complete his M.A. degree in special education. He then completed an EdD at the University of Nevada – Reno focusing on education as it pertains to incarcerated individuals.

Shrum worked for the California Department of Corrections and Rehabilitation from 1977 to 2010. Beginning in the 1980s, he became particularly interested in the work of Viktor Frankl (*Man's Search for Meaning)*, Ira Progoff (*Intensive Journal*), and Elisabeth Kubler-Ross (*On Death and Dying*). It was during this time that he developed a treatment approach to correctional rehabilitation that involved a synthesis of Logotherapy, the Intensive Journal, and the stages of grief. He then contacted Viktor Frankl requesting that he present a workshop on Logotherapy to men incarcerated at Folsom State Prison. Frankl was too weak at the time, so he referred Joseph Fabry, Frankl's friend and fellow Holocaust survivor to present the workshop. Fabry conducted two workshops. Following the workshops Shrum presented Fabry with a copy of the first draft of his manuscript, *Search for Meaning at the Broken Places*. Fabry made some editorial suggestions and motivated Shrum to continue refining it while furthering his studies through the Viktor Frankl Institute of Logotherapy.

Shrum is a published author of "A Compilation of the Educational, Psychological and Medical Research on Learning Disabilities due to Minimal Brain Dysfunctions," and "Modified Instructional Strategy for the Accelerative and Mastery Learning," and "No Longer Theory: Correctional Education that Works." He is a workshop presenter, researcher, and consultant. He is a speaker at local, national and international conferences, as well as on radio and television. He is married to Dee, his best friend and partner of twenty years. Together they have three children and seven grandchildren. His devotes his time with family, friends and his three dogs. He may be contacted at docshrum@gmail.com.

Made in the USA
Las Vegas, NV
26 April 2024